OPEN ROAD

AXEL MADSEN

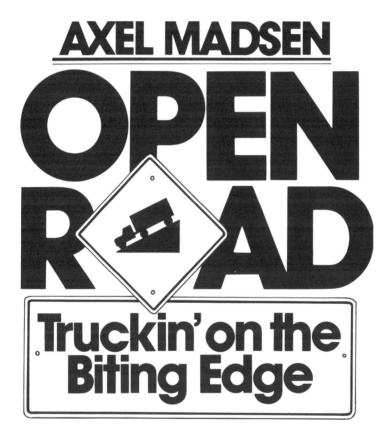

OPEN ROAD

Truckin' on the Biting Edge

HARCOURT BRACE JOVANOVICH, PUBLISHERS
San Diego   New York   London

Library of Congress Cataloging in Publication Data

Madsen, Axel.
Open road.

1. Trucking—United States. I. Title.
HE5623.M255 1982   338.3′24′0973   82-47666
ISBN 0-15-170029-X

Printed in the United States of America

First edition

B C D E

OPEN ROAD

1
BLACK ICE

She didn't see it. She just felt herself skid, all 42 tons of her. She geared down fast and gave a thrust of power to pull out, but kept spinning. She flicked on the headlights to check the roadway. All she saw was tire marks and wet rock on the side. Half a mile back at the summit, the signs had warned that the downgrade was 7% for the next 12 miles. Then she felt the load begin to push her.

God, no!

She applied the air brakes, ever so gently. The thing to do, they said, was to keep an eye out for spray thrown up by other rigs. As long as you saw the other guys' splash you knew the road hadn't frozen over. The trouble was she had the road to herself as far as she could see, and that was pretty far despite the growing darkness. Straight ahead of her the interstate ran down into a crevasse, a huge east-west rift in the towering mountains. She saw the repeat signs—big yellow diamonds depicting a nose-diving black tractor-trailer on a black incline, and indicating the distance to the beginning of the incline. The two halves of the highway were separated by a long gully already plunged in darkness.

TRUCKS USE LOW GEAR. The sign went by so fast she looked down on the instrument panel and saw the needle edge past 55. But she was out of the skid and let it run. The westbound traffic, laboring uphill, was lost behind clumps of pine and aspen, but on the side of the road the snow was no longer the even blanket it had been at the summit, only splotches of white between the trees.

The road really began to plunge and to curve left over

several short bridges. Her palms were clammy, but she didn't dare take her hands off the wheel and rub them dry on her jeans. EXIT 195. LEADVILLE, COPPER MOUNTAIN, 1 MILE. She came out of the curve and saw a car's taillights ahead of her when she felt the tractor begin to swerve behind her.

She geared up, ready to outrun a jackknife. She was doing 65, but the swerve stopped. While she had time, she swung out in the fast lane so she could pass the slow four-wheeler. She saw houses all of a sudden on the right—condominiums, townhouses, alpine lodges. The structures were the same as the winter resort condos at Vail an hour ago, oversized Swiss chalets that looked silly in the snowless crevasse she was racing through.

There was no spray as she passed the car. She flicked to high beam and back to low, but couldn't see any ice. Besides, it wasn't raining. LEADVILLE, COPPER MOUNTAIN, NEXT RIGHT. The highway curved left again and she saw the straight exit, a short uphill ramp ending with a stop sign at the road crossing the freeway. She'd never be able to stop there.

After the exit, she came out of the curve. The straightaway was her best chance. She put the clutch to the floor, shifted into neutral, came down one gear and eased up on the clutch again. There was the sudden sharp increase in rpm. Then she hit ice.

"Junior!" Her voice was scared. She geared up. She wanted to tell him to jump into a snowbank. It was the only thing she could think of, even if there wasn't any snow here.

"Yeah!" he shouted. He sounded wide-awake and she either heard him hit the sink or the sound of the Port-a-Potty slamming down.

"Junior, I'm hitting ice!" In her mind she saw the trailer swerve and keel over, pulling the tractor with it. But the wheels must have hit a stretch free of ice because the rig remained upright, going 70.

"Try the brakes, gently!"

She touched the brakes and felt the wheels lock and skid under her. She took a quick look in the rearview mirror on her door side to see where the trailer was.

"Where are we?" Junior asked.

4

"Five, six miles east of Vail Pass, but I can't *see* any ice."

"Coming off a mountain in curves and hitting black ice is the worst." There was nothing he could do except get into his boots. She didn't turn to look, just kept her eyes on the road and the curve coming up. The westbound lanes snaked behind tall pines and reappeared in a graceful arc farther down.

"I'm doing 70," she announced hoarsely.

"And dropping fast. Betcha there's no ice farther down."

It was his rig, his investment; she couldn't blame him. She tried the brakes, felt the beginning of a skid and eased off.

He slipped into the jump seat, rubbing his eyes. He mumbled that the black ice was newly formed, fresh ice so goddamn clear you could see through to the roadway. It was so slippery you couldn't walk on it, only crawl on hands and knees. Temperatures had to drop very quickly, like in mountains after sunset.

"I won't make it!" She said matter-of-factly. She was on an icy incline 10,000 feet up—okay, 9,000 feet and dropping—but with a right-hand curve coming up. And if she made that one, how about the next curve, and the one after that? By the time she was below the freezing level, she might be doing 100 miles an hour.

"Try to downshift once more," Junior shouted over the racing engine.

She glanced at him for a second and saw him lean forward, staring at the curve coming at them.

She geared down and when she came up on the clutch, felt the load behind her begin to lurch. She gasped, afraid of blowing her concentration. "I can't!" she cried.

They were thundering down into a widening canyon. Ahead of them a mountain face rose, massive and snow-covered from halfway up. She gave herself both lanes, knowing that if there was a car around the curve she'd send it flying and that if a truck was slowly clawing its way down, it would be the end. FRISCO, BRECKENRIDGE, 1 MILE. She flew past repeat warning signs—the black tractor-trailer tilting on the yellow diamond. She had never seen this traffic sign before, but then again, she had never crossed the Rockies before. The road seemed to level off a bit. Could they be at the valley floor? The road plunged on. She felt the speed and in the middle of the curve saw she was doing 80. Centrifugal force thrust her out to the left lane after that. Just in time. As she came out of the bend she saw a flatbed in the slow lane. Junior grabbed the air horn, gave a distress hoot and got on the CB. She never saw the exit.

"Mayday, Mayday!" Junior shouted into the mike. "Where's the escape ramp?"

"The what?" she asked, hanging on to the steering wheel.

A male voice came over the static. "That you shooting past me, good buddy?"

"Sure is. Where's the escape ramp? Over."

She wasn't sure what Junior meant, but this was no time to ask.

"Be damned if I know," the guy came back. "Ask smokey. The way you're flyin', one of them ramps better come up fast."

She saw the next curve was left.

Suddenly a highway patrol override came over the radio, and a trooper's slow voice asked for position of eastbound runaway truck.

"Runaway here," Junior shouted happily. "I don't know my position. Last sign was something like Frisco-and-something exit."

They listened to the static for an unbearable eternity as they hurtled toward the curve around the rock face.

"Mile 201, Frisco and Breckenridge. Estimate yourself to be less than two miles from escape ramp," the trooper came back.

"What do I look for?" she asked.

Junior repeated her question into the mike and was told, in the same deliberate drawl, that the escape ramp was adequately marked and came after a long right curve. "We will try to escort you into it."

She tried the brakes. Nothing swerved.

The trooper was back. "This ramp is very *inviting*, built so dumb truckers don't even have to turn the steering wheel to get into it. You come around the curve, see our flashing lights, go over the shoulder at the designated spot, and drive right *up* the mountain."

She kept her foot on the brakes, just easy. On the radio, the trooper warned eastbound traffic of a runaway tractor-trailer. She applied more pressure and gave Junior a wild grin. Not that you could roll off a grade like this and expect the brakes to do all the slowing. At this speed and with this weight, the brakes would overheat and fade within a few miles. It happened so fast. The trailer began to rock, the tractor wheels locked. She had to outrun the trailer and geared up again, ready to hit the throttle, when she felt the tires bite.

"Maybe only patches down here," Junior shouted. He was half-standing, half-crouched on the jump seat on the other side of the wraparound instrument panel. Ready to throw himself out if she went totally out of control? He rolled down the window on his side and they both strained to hear tires on wet surface. All they got was a blast of arctic air.

"State patrol to eastbound runaway," the CB crackled. "State patrol to runaway. Come in, please."

"The handle is Class Act, officer," Junior corrected coolly.

She kept braking while the slow-talking smokey told Junior the state patrol cruiser was in place, *across* from the escape ramp. "We are stationary on the left shoulder and you run off to the right, repeat, to the right. Confirm, please."

"Class Act here and confirming we run off right."

She started the long curve on the extreme right shoulder and allowed herself to drift toward the center and the sloping left median. She was doing 80 again and had no more gears to go up into. She had never heard an engine revving this high. She was on the lip of the left shoulder in the middle of the curve, just *guessing* it was frozen, not mushy, since she had 10 tons on the steering axle at this speed, which meant there were over 5 tons on the left front tire.

The westbound lanes had dropped out of sight and her roadway plunged into a narrowing crevasse again. She realized she wasn't steering anymore. The tachometer needle was hovering near 90—as far as it could go. She had to come off this shoulder since the cops were sitting on it.

The road did it for her, straightening out and tumbling across a spectacular gorge. She eased off the brakes, certain there was ice on the bridge. RUNAWAY TRUCK RAMP, RIGHT, ¾ MILE. More of the warning signs. STEEP GRADE NEXT 3 MILES. The road took a dive through a cleft blasted through the rock. The engine roar echoing between the rock faces was deafening and she thought she could smell the brakes. As the road curved again she saw the reflection of pulsating red light on the rock.

"Class Act to highway patrol," Junior shouted into the mike. "We see ya!"

RUNAWAY TRUCK RAMP, RIGHT, 2000 FEET. The bend was long and the outward thrust forced her toward the right shoulder. In the left mirror the broken line ran away from her. The mountain fell away on both sides and there was the cruiser, red roof light blazing. NO STOPPING OR STANDING. RUNAWAY VEHICLES ONLY. A second later she understood. The road curved on, but between markers across from where the cops sat, something went straight.

She thundered off the highway, totally out of control. For a long second she was weightless, out of the seat, her knuckles white on the steering wheel, then all 18 wheels hit dirt. *Dirt!* She heard a crack under her and Junior's body slam against something. Crazily, she plowed forward into pea gravel and an inch of old snow. The gravel machine-gunned the mudguards and pelted the chassis, but in the headlights she saw the dirt track *rise* in front of her. She let out a shriek, a wild, savage scream. Things flew around in the cab; the dangling CB mike hit the windshield. Her heart went wild with terror and joy. The 84,000 pounds of wayward truck sank back in the uphill gravel. Slowly, the fury was spent. The oil pressure and the manifold gauges dropped, the air-cleaner restriction gauge shot up and the air hissed as she let off the brakes totally and just let it spend itself. She looked for a sec at Junior's grimacing face and saw his temple.

"You're bleeding!" she shouted.

They bounced and kicked up gravel for another couple of hundred feet before they came to an aching halt. She set the emergency brake, cut the engine, but left the parking lights on before she opened her door. She just had to feel solid ground under her feet.

It was only when she was down that she realized she was trembling. She let herself slump down on the step next to the fuel tank and held on to the steel bar. She thought of Tim and Melissa for the first time, closed her eyes and felt her head throbbing, her muscles aching. She breathed deeply and smelled the pines around her. When she opened her eyes, she adjusted to the stillness. Only the Thermo King refrigeration unit up on the front of the trailer was humming, indifferently, reassuringly. She saw everything was bathed in soft moonlight.

She looked back and saw the ramp had been bulldozed up through a stand of pines like a firebreak. The solitude was absolute.

"I'm sorry." She sighed.

"Hey, listen." He stirred in the cab above her.

She had wanted so much to impress him with her professionalism. Now, she didn't want to screw up by not knowing how to handle herself in an accident. Hard as it was for most drivers to swallow, when a truck got wrecked it was usually their fault. Everybody knew that. The driver went too fast, he braked too late, he braked too hard. She stood up, smelled the pine, put her hands on her hips and stretched to get the stiffness and the pain out of her back. She felt the cold and wanted to climb back up and get her parka. Then she saw the flashing lights wobble up toward them.

"Smokey's coming to see if we're alive," she said.

His response came with the sour-mash grin she had liked from the beginning. "More likely to give us a ticket for getting off the road too fast."

She asked him to throw down her jacket. It was behind the driver's seat. She heard him rummage around in the cab, open the door on his side and climb down. He came around from the front, holding a couple of Kleenexes against his temple. In the other hand he had her parka and a flashlight.

"You didn't hire me to go careening around the country breaking the law," she said, relieving him of the jacket and slipping into it. "Let me see your boo-boo for a second."

"Stopped bleedin' already." He handed her the flashlight.

She beamed it on the side of his head and had him lift off the Kleenexes. Blood had trickled down his chin into his goatee and coagulated in a long streak. The gash was superficial, but men were like kids when they got hurt—especially if it was your fault. She shined the light into his blue eyes and told him it sure looked dramatic. He squinted and grimaced, as if to say it wasn't the first bruise in his life.

She heard the highway patrol cruiser climb up toward them.

When she handed him the flashlight again, he began to survey the scene. He let the beam run along the undercarriage of the trailer. He peered at the interlock and the trailer coupling pin, walked to the very back to see how deep the rear wheels were in the gravel. "We'll need a wrecker to get back down," he announced.

"I just hate myself," she said, biting her lip.

"No you don't."

She wanted so much to be a pro. "How does it look?"

"Okay, but I heard somethin' crack when we flew off."

"Me too." She stamped her feet to shake off the mountain chill and decided that she felt pretty good, all things told.

2
MIDNIGHT SOAK

Chuck Carlton, Jr., stretched in the hot water and day-dreamed about his *next* power unit. The Peterbilt was less than two years old, but on the next tractor, he might go for one of those Florida Livelab sleeper jobs with bath and shower, queen-sized bed, microwave, refrigerator, and raised roofline so you could stand up in the sleeper compartment to get your clothes on. Home on wheels, they were called. Or he could go for a Double Eagle walk-in unit from Shipshewana, Indiana. He had talked to sleeper teams who had them. The construction was lightweight welded tubular framing, fiber-glass insulated, and padded with Naugahyde. You had fluorescent interior lights, a 12-volt built-in refrigerator, digital alarm clock, and flush-mounted doors with recessed chrome latches. Anytime you were running through Indiana, you could have the sleeper installed, painted and trimmed to match in one day.

Junior could see himself in a Livelab sleeper, soaking in the tub like this while some honeycup codriver was at the wheel. You'd probably pay for the damn thing by saving on downtime like this here Ramada Inn. He flipped the ash from his Tiparillo in the soap dish and began to feel pleasantly sleepy. The garage had the injector in stock, but it would take all day anyway. He'd call Atlanta in the morning when he'd had a good look at the load. The bath was Karen's idea. That's what she said she'd do when she got to her room, she had told him after the wrecker dropped them off up here. He closed his eyes and tried to imagine her in the tub across the hall.

He had run a lot of sleeper teams and he knew trust had to be earned, had to be developed. As lady truckers went, Karen Long had handled herself more than okay up there, even if she had scared him shitless. There was no such thing as crawling back in the sleeper with total trust in your codriver, male or female. If *he* had been at the wheel and she in the bunk, he'd have scared her to death. To trust each other took a long time, a lot of riding together.

He liked female codrivers, and not just for the obvious reason. Like himself, most lady truck drivers firmly believed a clean truck ran better. Also, LTDs had an easier time accepting help when they needed it. Men already knew the answers without even knowing any of the questions. Gail Aplin and other women truckers he had worked with appreciated their jobs, and not only because they could do what was expected of them. As far as he was concerned, women had as much right on the road, driving a sleep team, as anyone else. A lot of people—a lot of wives—hadn't accepted it yet. Gail said that if she could avoid it, she stayed away from running sleep teams with married guys.

He sucked on the slender cigar. He was a shower person, but this *was* good, he had to admit. It was their second night out of Seattle, their second 24 hours as a sleeper team. Forecasts of a spring storm in Montana had made him decide against crossing on I-90. West of Butte, he had turned south on I-15, and by the time they entered Ogden, he had thought I-80 wouldn't be much better—the summit there between Laramie and Cheyenne was always a bitch. He had continued south to Provo and turned east on U.S. 6. When he crawled into the sleeper to let her drive her first full stint, he had told her to cross on I-70, figuring that the 12,000 feet of the Vail and Loveland passes would be no worse than the mean elevation of near 8,000 feet clear across rolling Wyoming. And now they were in goddamn Silverthorne, Colorado (elevation 7,000 feet) for a whole day of repairs!

Getting out of their cruiser, the troopers had turned out to be a mean, old smokey and a tall skinny fellow who did the legal talking. They had already radioed the wrecker. "He comes from Silverthorne," said the tall one, shining his flashlight into their faces. "So it'll take awhile, but he's got a 50-ton Atlas hydraulic that can yank just about anybody out of anything."

After Karen said she had been at the wheel, they wanted to see her Class A. They wanted to see Junior's Form D, his logbook, waybill, Colorado fuel permit, and the rest of the papers. They filled out a whole questionnaire. What kind of brakes, were the brakes working, what was the estimated speed upon entering the ramp, the distance traveled in ramp before stopping, and the distance from ramp when driver became aware of problem. There, Karen said, "Gosh, I began skidding a mile after the Vail Pass summit."

"You mean you ran wild for 12 miles, ma'am?"

She guessed she had, and the skinny officer then wanted to know if her mountain driving experience was none, less than one year, or more, and how many trips she had made this year over this route. She answered she was from Yakima, Washington, and that she knew the Snoqualmie Pass on I-90, but that this was her first time on I-70 here. They didn't give her a ticket in the end, but told her they had clocked her doing 90 just before she flew off the highway. "Last week we had a truck run up the Slick Rock ramp," the chubby one said, while the rawboned officer inspected the papers. "The driver went into the ramp at close to 90 and came to a stop almost at the end of the ramp, like you. It's my understanding there was no damage. Maybe you aren't so lucky." With that, he walked to the front of the truck and the three of them followed. He squatted to shine his flashlight under the truck. Something dripped and smelled of diesel. Then the trooper went to the side, bent down, sniffed the wheels and said he was looking for loose lug nuts.

"We'll have to inspect the brakes, you realize." He went on with his flashlight inspection while talking about the cost to the state of Colorado of building these escape ramps and how 16% of all trucks inspected by the state patrol had defective brakes. The first runaway ramp was built on Rabbits Ears Pass over by Steamboat Springs, on an 8% grade running downhill for 12 miles. "I don't know if you've been on Slick Rock Hill, but it's a mean one. It winds a lot and it has the most accidents for the amount of traffic of any downhill in Colorado. Last spring we had a Baptist school bus from California lose its brakes due to overheating. The bus was going 70 when it went into the ramp. It came to a stop in two feet of snow and loose gravel 200 feet in, and all 33 people walked away."

The skinny one gave Junior a ticket ordering him to have his brakes inspected at the Silverthorne state patrol station, any weekday between eight and four. When the troopers left, Junior had Karen start the engine while he crawled underneath to see where the leak came from. After that, they stamped around, keeping warm. The wrecker appeared an hour later and began backing up toward them. It was a huge mother, owned by a guy with a sense of humor. On the side it said ADVANCED RECOVERY UNIT #1.

He imagined her in the tub across the hall, her boobs half out of the soapy water. He had answered her letter to the WIT (Women in Trucking) column in *Road King*. She was honest, sincere, and just needed some help finding a company or an owner-operator who'd give a woman a fair chance. Her over-the-road experience was two years in 13-speed Peterbilt and International cabovers, plus other minor experience on Kenworth 10-speed and Macks. Her P.O. box was in Yakima, Washington, and he wrote her he was an O and O (owner-operator) running sleeper team coast-to-coast and that he had a load of frozen food from Seattle at the middle of the month if she'd call his broker's toll-free number in Los Angeles and leave a message. She had done that, and when he called her from the Alameda truckstop in downtown L.A. Thursday to ask if she was still interested and ready, she said yes. He told her he'd come to Yakima Saturday evening.

It wasn't just that he was a nice guy and that Yakima wasn't that much out of the way if you ran up U.S. 97 from Weed, California, instead of I-5 through Portland. It was also because he wanted to see where she lived, wanted to make sure he didn't walk in on domestic troubles.

Her little house was on the edge of town, out toward Fruitvale, beyond the new Red Oak Shopping Center, Dunkin' Donuts and Whataburger, and a Sizzler Family

Steakhouse on the right. When he roared up and hissed the air brakes, she came to the door, taller and prettier than he had expected somehow, with a small boy at her side and a smaller kid on the arm. "Hi, I'm Karen Long. You must be Charlie Carlton." "Call me Junior," he told her. She squinted into the sun behind him as he walked up. "This is Tim and this here is little Melissa. Come on in."

She made coffee, and once Tim had had enough of gawking at the man mom might be working for, they talked. She was used to pitching in and seeing things done. Marianne Adams, her girlfriend, who lived across the road, had two children of her own. Marianne would take Tim and Melissa, hopefully for no more than two weeks at a time. Less than that, he explained. The way he liked to run was to take no more than three days coast-to-coast, each of them driving six hours at a stretch, around the clock, stopping only for fuel, food, and the occasional shower at a truckstop. So, counting no more than two and a half days to find a backload—and he had good brokers in Rahway, New Jersey and Atlanta—she would be gone just over a week at a time.

With the little girl sitting on her mother's knee and sucking her thumb, he explained that to make any sense and any money, they'd have to be "dephased," one getting into the habit of sleeping while the other drove, and so on. In fact, there was nothing more stupid than one driver starting out driving and the codriver sittin' and sippin' coffee and watchin' the landscape for the next five, six hours. Real sharp sleeper teams dephased before they even hit the road, one getting used to staying up nights, the other hitting the sack after the evening news. "It'll take a real effort to become dephased for the running," he said, "but when you get accustomed to a set amount of time to work and to sleep, you find sleep coming easier. When it's your turn to sleep, you might try new eating habits. Some people like to put away a full meal before hitting the sleeper. They say it keeps the belly from bouncing."

It got dark and little Melissa got cranky. Bouncing the girl on her lap, Karen told him she carried a thermos bottle on long hauls, to save downtime at truckstops, and asked him about the rig and about himself. He listed the specifications and told how he was thinking of replacing at least the driver's Cush-N-Air highback with a Koch pulsating seat for passive exercise, which really meant you had airflow rippling through the seat's cushion, pushing blood upward, relieving pressure on thighs, and allowing the blood to circulate better. As for himself, he said he wasn't married. "Put my furniture in storage in 1979 and been livin' on the road since," he said, leaving it at that.

She put an extra hamburger on, and after they had eaten and she put the kids to bed, she brought out a couple of Coors. John, Tim and Melissa's father, had walked out on them two years ago, came back for a while, and dropped out of sight again. "He just can't handle responsibility," she said, adding that when he worked, he was a mechanic. Actually, it was John who had taught her to drive a truck, the first time for fun when they were going together and she was working as a waitress. She had had the last money order from him at Christmas, and as far as she knew, he lived in Portland. She didn't care to dwell on all that, she said, and switched to her professional experience. As she had said in her letter to *Road King*, she had had two years on a flatbed and the last six months solo driving on a reefer (refrigerated truck). "I mean, I know refrigeration and the driver's role in maintaining transit temperature." Her run was between San Fran and Vancouver, B.C., "fresh perishables up, frozen tuna back." Funny she should mention tuna; he grinned. His first reefer run was San Diego–Chicago, he told her, and until he heard a Los Angeles disk jockey use the name, his CB handle had been Charlie Tuna.

"Why Junior then?" she asked.

"My dad was a trucker, and so's my brother. And my brother-in-law drives for Yellow Freight Lines. If you gonna drive for a carrier, Yellow Freight is the best. They've got a waiting list yea long."

She wanted to know where he came from and he told her he grew up in Conroe, a little town in Montgomery County, Texas, off I-45 going north from Houston toward Dallas. Both his parents were dead, but trucking was in the blood. He was 17 when he first drove his dad's Mack and couldn't wait to be one of 'em. He was back in Conroe recently, passing through with a load, and all the people he had gone to Montgomery High with had left. The old story. The girls left first, then the boys, for construction jobs in Houston. He had tried offshore drilling work for a while, to get enough money for a down payment on his first rig. "What I like about truckin' is that even if you drive for someone else, there ain't anybody standing over you when you're out there on the highway."

She took a swig of beer and told him the instructor at the trucking school she had gone to in Seattle was also from Texas, a lady instructor called Pat, who was just great. "She called drivers with low job seniority 'woodchucks' and novice truckers 'boll weevils.' " Karen had found out soon enough what it meant to be the woodchuck. She had been laid off because the haul was seasonal—Canadians didn't import as much California produce in the summer—and since she was the last hired, the woodchuck. Of course she realized this would be her first cross-country experience, her first sleeper team, too.

He didn't want to pry, he said, but how about her boyfriend? She gave him a look that told him she wasn't too eager to discuss her bruises. Instead, she repeated that with the kids, the rent, and the payments on her 1980 Mustang, she needed a good job, "as badly as any man out there." He took that to mean that if she had someone, the guy obviously didn't contribute to the groceries.

He had a feeling that she was running on empty, emotionally, but that she was still in touch with the more tender aspects of man-woman relationships. Then, before they shook hands on the deal and he went out to sleep in the truck, she made sure he understood what she thought of men who had to be sneaky about it. Last month, she said, while he lit a Tiparillo and had a last beer, she had realized the reefer haul to Vancouver wasn't going to last. So one afternoon she dropped Tim and Melissa off at Marianne Adams' house and tooled up to the big truckstop on I-90 in Ellensburg in her Mustang to post a lady-trucker-needs-job notice on the bulletin board. While she was tacking up her ad, she got to talking to a trucker and his buddy. They were Rick and Frank, they told her, running tandem out of Seattle, mostly to Billings. Over coffee, she told them about her experience and they seemed interested, talking it over and offering her a position with them, starting right then and there.

She was ecstatic and phoned Marianne to ask her if she could keep Tim and Melissa for two days. Half an hour later she had locked her Mustang at the far end of the parking lot and, with $20 in her purse and the clothes on her back, was in Rick's Kenworth 12-speed, with Frank tailgating them in his GMC, heading for Billings. Rick waited until they got to Montana before confessing that he and Frank weren't just turning around in Billings, as they had said, but were actually going to Minneapolis. They also had something besides driving on their minds. It was night, they were somewhere east of Bozeman. She decided to stay with them long enough to get back. After all, they hadn't tried to hurt her; they just didn't have the decency to be honest.

"Just inside North Dakota, the quiet woke me up in the sleeper," she continued. "It was morning and cold and I realized both trucks were stopped at a truckstop. Both guys were in the café and I went inside to let them know I was going to the shower room. When I came back ten minutes later, both trucks were gone."

He looked at her across the glow of his Tiparillo. Then he asked how she got back to the Mustang. Seven hours later, she told him, a westbound trucker gave her a lift. "Don't get me wrong," she said, finishing her story. "I enjoy intimacy as much as any other trucker, but I object to being misled."

He squashed out the cigarillo, thinking they both had a lot of emotional mileage on them. For every troubled woman there's a troubled man, right? He rose, stretched and realized how tired he really was. "When do you think we can get going tomorrow?"

She got up. "Early, if you want."

"As long as we're in Seattle to load up Monday morning."

He reached for her hand. "Okay, it's a deal," he said. Her handshake was firm and promising.

She turned and picked up the ashtray and their empty glasses from the table.

18

He crossed to the door, turned and grinned. "And thanks for the hamburger and the beer."

She looked up and smiled. "Sleep tight. And don't worry about us getting dephased. I'm too excited to get to bed anytime soon. I think I'll clean the house a bit before we leave."

3
HURTING

The easiest and most popular way of making some money trucking is to own a tractor, know how to drive it, and have a couple of thousand dollars in operating capital. Half the truckers in the United States are "hired hands," salaried drivers, a lot of them belonging to the International Brotherhood of Teamsters, who get a paycheck every Friday. The other half are the independents, who work for themselves by riding the interstates in search of freight and "backloads." They own a hunk of their rigs—the finance company always seems to own more. The part that is theirs is the tractor, which can pull a variety of trailers consigned to them. In the case of refrigerated rigs, the independents own both tractor and trailer. These owner-operators, or O.O.'s, are America's last cowboys, celebrated in country-and-western lore and in movies and TV shows as a bunch of lovable fools—all play and no work.

Except for years of recession, the tonnage hauled by road is always increasing—as is the notion that independent trucking is a glamorous way of getting rich on your own terms. Getting rich is part of the fiction, but to call yourself one of the last of the breed of small entrepreneurs, earning a living by the seat of your pants, is pretty accurate.

The independents don't belong to the Teamsters. They think of the Teamsters and the American Trucking Associations (ATA) as part of the enemy force. "I used to belong to the Teamsters, and if your drove a truck and you didn't belong, you were a prick, and I'd be the first to tell ya!" is the way Al Terry puts it. "Now, truckers are a minority of the

Teamsters' membership. Besides, we can't *afford* to belong. We can't pay ourselves $16 an hour, park our rigs Saturdays and Sundays, and stop after eight hours." Terry is a steel hauler from Fontana, California. He shakes his head, rubs his calloused hands, and wonders what America has come to.

Trucking companies are called carriers and the ATA represents all the big names in regulated trucking. The ATA has its five-story headquarters on P Street in fashionable northwest Washington, but out on the highways, the working stiffs' perception of the carriers' trade organization is that it is against everything and for very little. On deregulation, the ATA came out swinging in all directions, and when the dust settled it had won a few skirmishes and lost the war.

The independents are on the road over 300 days a year on the average and have no real voice in Washington. They work for themselves, concentrating on the more than 600 billion ton-miles of long-distance freight that is hauled by truck every year. Half the intercity haulage in the country is in the hands of these self-employed truckers who, to make ends meet, work harder than the hired hands, most of them averaging 130,000 miles annually on the road. Just over a thousand of them are killed in traffic accidents every year.

Like ranchers and cowhands, the independent truckers have shaped their lives after myths—after the dream of rugged individualism and roaming freedom. Thousands of them dress, walk, and talk like images, and some of them go broke doing it. "Southern fried truckin' " is not just a job or occupation, it's a way of life that sometimes makes the business part of it confusing and contradictory.

The numbers aren't encouraging. Soaring fuel prices, creeping deregulation, the 55-miles-per-hour speed limit, and the anarchy of state weight and length standards that even Congress finds bewildering are widening the gap between the reality and the "keep on truckin' " bravado. Charles ("Junior") Carlton's Peterbilt cost $98,000 when he bought it with a 25% down payment (most of it raised by selling the 1976 Kenworth W 900) and a four-year loan carrying a 16% interest rate. That means fixed monthly costs of $3,800, even before Junior buys fuel. In the mid-1960s, a gallon of diesel fuel was 17 cents;

today it hovers around a dollar. "Last month my truck grossed $7,100. The fuel came to $4,400, codriver's salary and food to stay alive on the road came to $1,490, my California operating plates and insurance cost $410 and repairs $568. You total that up and you'll see I managed to make $230 last month."

Independents are operating below realistic profit margins, and to stay afloat they drive harder, pop more stay-awake pills and run sleeper teams. When they get desperate, they vent their anger with violence that draws attention all right, but not the kind that elicits public sympathy. But when you're highballing down a stretch of superslab, you can't always think of cost itemizing, cents-per-mile costs, and verified estimates. You've gotta think about true grit and the original dream of being your own goddamned boss. Trucking is a very exacting profession, but it's also a way of living on the biting edge of contemporary America.

So let's suppose you've got a roadworthy tractor, you know how to drive it, and you have the start-up capital. To get work, you hire out the tractor and yourself to a carrier—a middleman who lines up customers for you and handles the paperwork. For doing that the carrier takes 25% off the top, or if you put it the other way, the carrier is willing to let you have 75% of the money it earns being in the hauling business if you'll provide the services of owning, maintaining, and driving the rig. If you "lease on" for a long period with one carrier, you must paint your tractor in the company color scheme, like independents in furniture and household moving ("bedbug haulers" in their vernacular) must do, and fly the colors of Mayflower, North American, United Van Lines, and so on. A new tractor costs almost a hundred grand and a lot of older power units are sold and resold. It is common for a tractor to undergo total overhauls and refittings with new or rebuilt engines and run a million miles. That may sound impressive until you figure that at the 130,000 miles annually that most owner-operators put on their rig, that's just over seven years.

Practically everything we eat comes to us in owner-operated trucks. Food is the "exempt" commodity anyone can haul. For this reason, carriers use produce as their backhaul.

Traveling outbound, they ship the commodity for which they hold "authority"; for the return leg they look for a produce haul. The market arrangements that bring food from diverse sources to the tables of all Americans are highly complex. In the Northeast, more than 80% of the food consumed comes from elsewhere (New York State imports nearly 85%).

The demand for owner-operators with late-model equipment and good driving records is always high because independents are a carrier's quickest way to profits. It doesn't cost a carrier much to expand when O.O.'s act as subcontractors, carrying out the assignment work with their own money, equipment, and time. Before deregulation in 1980, you had to have "authority" (the official right or franchise) to haul most commodities on most routes. Such authority was prohibitively expensive, and could be obtained only by buying the rights from someone going out of business or by petitioning the Interstate Commerce Commission (ICC)—the longtime bureaucratic mother hen of trucking—to grant new authority. A guy with one truck almost never had ICC rights. If someone had rights, he most likely had terminals and salaried drivers as well as owner-operators under lease, and his business was probably worth hundreds of millions of dollars. The Big Five are household names to anyone driving the interstates with any regularity—RLC Corporation, Leaseway, Roadway Express, Yellow Freight System, and Consolidated Freightways.

Predictably, the carriers—and the Teamsters—were against deregulation and independents were, generally, for it. What the carriers and their salaried drivers feared, of course, was that deregulation would bring rate-cutting and unlimited competition on profitable routes, but given the relative size and strength of the trucking companies, that's not what has happened.

Nothing divides truckers more than lease-purchasing. Since few would-be independents have the front money to get started, and since banks are reluctant to loan money for a first rig, some carriers have simplified everybody's problem by offering lease-purchases. Here, the trucker comes in with some cash—much less than he would have to put up if he went to a truck dealer for financing—and the carrier sells him the tractor on time and leases it back from him. There are those who think lease-purchasing is simply a modern form of indentured servitude, and they call it sharecropping. Because of the high failure rate among owner-operators, there are enough marginal trucking firms who will take advantage of the situation to hire one dreamer after the other, "greenies," who will haul for less than full compensatory rates. Periodically, horror stories surface. In 1981, 25 independents sued Bray Lines, Inc., of Cushing, Oklahoma, for kickbacks, overcharges, freight rate skimmings, and fraud. Young truckers, several of them married couples who started out after going to Bray's Trucking School for a week, hauled poor-paying loads that never quite paid the lease-purchase. After they gave up in disgust, usually within a year, the tractor was repossessed and sold to another couple, drawn by newspaper ads headlined: "Truckers, $500 will put you in business."

To others, however, lease-purchasing has its advantages. If the owner-operator stays with a carrier for about five years, the tractor is his, but should independent trucking prove not to be his cup of rum before then, he can take the tractor back to the leaseholder and walk away free. If he had bought the rig on time through a truck dealership, he would, to put it mildly, have a hard time disposing of the equipment. "I couldn't afford a truck unless I did it this way," says Ron Costa of Winslow, Arkansas, a young trucker happily trucking for Willis Shaw Express in a company tractor-purchase program. "They've been a real good company for me. At the end of four years I'll have a used truck to show for my efforts instead of a bunch of paycheck stubs." The shakedown seems to happen in the first year. According to Dun and Bradstreet, most new owner-operators fail in their first year, mainly because they didn't know what they were doing.

But the grapevine works fast. Communications on the highway are like conversation at a crowded cocktail party. Strangers drift into range, converse on their CBs, and everyone listening feels free to join in. The mood is either jovial or businesslike, and an astonishing amount of information floats constantly up and down the interstates, to be amplified in truckstop coffee shops and lounges. It doesn't take long for a young trucker to be told, "Don't be bamboozled by gross percentage figures, boy. A carrier will tell ya: 'Come with us. We pay 75% of the gross freight bill while carrier Z only pays 64%.' The real question is 75% of *what?*" The road positively buzzes with information on who allows you to refuse loads, especially low-paying or unprofitable runs, who handles backhauls for you and at what rate, how long it takes to get paid after making a delivery, how much advance you get paid, and if there is a charge for this advance. An eagerly asked question is, What guarantee is there that you'll be able to make enough money to pay off the tractor? Veterans will tell you that if you make a $3,000 "down payment" and six or eight monthly payments of $800, but still don't have a piece of the tractor, the carrier may be in a position to make more money if you fail—that is, if you can't meet your payments. If the carrier controls what loads you haul and when you haul 'em, it decides whether you make enough money to pay for the tractor. And, wink the wise guys, there are carriers who will intentionally "slowload" you to bring about this situation.

Self-deprecating voices compete with the knowing drawl of the once-burned. "Hell, due to our 'expertise' in trucking," says a wife, "we bought a discontinued model. Our truck literally fell apart due to the 'fantastic' service we got from the repair shop that fixed the rig. They used Elmer's Glue. I kid you not!" She gets a laugh. And other beefy voices tell other stories. There are truckers who think that truckers goddamn *talk* too much. On television and in movies, truckers are shown plowing their rigs through herds of police cars with never a scratch on the truck when they're done. In reality, truckers just talk too much when they're doing "downtime." Their only social contacts are with other truckers at truckstops, pit stops, and warehouse terminals. News travels, and although veterans will warn you not to believe everything you hear on the CB, this is a wonderful world of free-flowing information.

The rap on the highways today is about making a living, about fuel economy and fiscal fitness. It's about the mess of regulations that have the appeal and consistency of week-old spaghetti. There is a persistent feeling among truckers that they are being picked on by federal and state regulators because they *are* independents, because they seldom speak with one voice and therefore carry little political clout.

To make ends meet, more truckers than ever have put their furniture in storage and taken to living in sleepers carried piggyback on their tractors. A lot of them are now husband-and-wife teams, and some of the sleepers are big-ticket customized jobs that can cost as much as a conventional home. Driving sleeper team beats the long separations, the wife watching TV while the man is on the road burning diesel. Sometimes, preschool kids go along, too. You see them at truckstops, tots carried on their fathers' arms, in sleepwear brushing their teeth in the rest room. The successful sleeper teams concentrate on getting good leases, carrying out their business as intelligently as possible, and staying on the road for months on end. At the same time the CB explosion—now mercifully on the wane among the general public—has helped truckers develop a sense of themselves, expressed in a language of their own that is another wall to keep strangers out. Who could guess that "ten-four" means "yes, okay," or "three by three" means "good luck"? It has given them a place in pop culture, and more important, it has given them a very real sense of safety. Nobody is alone out there. All a guy has to do is grab the mike and give his "handle," and human contact starts pouring into the cab. Says Junior Carlton, "I've never met a trucker who wouldn't tell you the CB radio is the greatest thing since air brakes."

But it's tough. Owner-operators live in what they call "a hostile environment." To start with the first problem—buying a tractor—carriers or fleet owners can purchase trucks in quantity and get them up to 20% cheaper then the independents. Until the passage of the 55-miles-per-hour speed limit in 1974, the independents could compete because they traveled faster. "When they lost that edge, they lost the edge in their ability to survive and their numbers aren't growing," says Forrest Baker, president of the Salt Lake City–based Transportation Research and Marketing Group. "The hostile environment is turning the independent into a bandito. He has to run over 10 hours a day and lie in his logbook, and he has to run faster than 55 mph. Many of them have a whole stack of driver's licenses. And the irony is that they are the ones who believe in the system, in the American way! The American way has turned them into criminals."

Run long distances they do. All independents exceed the 500 miles per day the Department of Transportation in Washington would like to enforce. Tough guys run 1000 miles in an 18-hour day and sleeper teams keep trucking around the clock.

When the American Trucking Associations ran out of arguments against "dereg," as road people contemptuously call the government's attempt to lessen the swollen regulatory burden, the carriers' lobby hit upon the outlaw image. Ignoring the fact that independents take more pride in their rigs, drive more carefully, and have lower accident rates, the ATA claimed deregulation would play havoc with highway safety. In the words of one ICC bureaucrat, "the ATA uses the argument that the independents are a bunch of cowboys and need looking after."

Under prodding from the Carter White House, the ICC became something of a champion of deregulation, and a rule allowing owner-operators to lease their rigs and themselves directly to shippers was proposed. Ronald Reagan's Republican victory in 1980 upset the apple cart again. The Reagan administration had to pay off its political debt to the Teamsters and began putting the brakes on dereg. During the first year of dereg-spawned competition, the Teamsters lost over 10% of its trucker membership and was now openly opposed to the whole idea. In 1981, the ATA and the Teamsters threatened to take the ICC to court, alleging the agency lacked the authority to even make such changes, and newly elected Teamster boss Roy L. Williams hinted he could lobby Congress to reregulate trucking. In the meantime, it was humble pie for Williams. As the Reagan administration's economic policies failed to pull the country out of what looked like the worst economic mess since the Great Depression, he signed a very modest 1982–85 labor contract which, he hoped, would help put some 50,000 laid-off teamster drivers back behind unionized wheels. The chances were slim. Carriers could no longer pass along the teamster wage increases to shippers in the form of higher freight rates and some of the big boys changed their tune and blamed the teamsters and not dereg. Said Arthur E. Imperatore, president of the A.P.A. Transport Corporation of North Bergen, New Jersey, "The biggest enemy of our industry has been the teamsters union, which ostensibly protected job security for its members but essentially destroyed it. The union has priced us out of many markets."

Independents weren't doing very well either as the recession hit. During the harsh 1981–82 winter, a lot of them holed up at Sunbelt truckstops, laying over for weeks on end, while produce freight rates slipped to unheard-of minimums before moving back up again, as independents refused to move loads at a loss. The hard winter and the hard times reinforced the comradeship and the sense of alienation.

Long-distance independents almost never meet any of the other inhabitants of the country. The separation started back in the 1950s when cars would refuel at regular gas stations, but trucks had to go to stations selling diesel fuel. These stations stopped selling gas to cater exclusively to their truck customers and de facto car-truck segregation was born. When John Steinbeck roamed the highways at the end of his life and wrote *Travels with Charley* (1962), he noticed truckers didn't really belong anywhere, that their wandering ways made them brothers in solitude, ready to help each other at every turn, but aloof from local affairs. In a leaner America 20 years later, it's even truer that truckers live a life apart from the retrenched and less generous mainstream.

4
ROCKY MOUNTAIN HIGH

Karen Long walked through the motel lobby, past a Hispanic maid struggling with an industrial vacuum cleaner, and into the breakfast room. It was nearly as empty as the lobby—a couple at a table and a guy eating and reading his newspaper at the counter. No Junior. Before the waitress could intercept her with her oversized menu, Karen walked out again. She'd have loved a cup of brew, but she wanted to find Junior first. He'd have to be over at the garage. The wrecker had dropped them off up here at the motel, but if she remembered correctly, the garage was just below on the state highway.

She slipped into her parka and walked outside. God, it was gorgeous. The sun drenched the valley in beauty and made the snow halfway up the mountains glisten. She wished she had her sunglasses, but they were in the cab. To the left, the interstate snaked lazily from one mountain range—the one she had come off last night—to the other. It had nothing of the terror of last night. The state highway ran under it and up on the other side toward the huge dam that contained Dillon Lake and—she had read in the brochure on the nightstand—all of Denver's water. Between the freeway and the earth dam was a shopping center, with McDonald's yellow arches beckoning behind Exxon's turning red-white-and-blue rectangle. Two Safeway rigs chugged westbound on the interstate. Everything was so bright and peaceful. She breathed deeply and noticed the ground cover wasn't really green yet. Spring came late this high up.

She walked down the hotel driveway toward the combined state highway–main street. Junior wanted to get going as soon as possible. Atlanta was 36 hours away, nonstop, and that was cutting it close, he had told her last night when they got their keys. Like any owner-operator, he would want to get empty and loaded up again before Friday afternoon so they could spend Saturday and Sunday running up to Rahway, New Jersey. To get to Atlanta too late Friday and have to lay over until Monday morning was to cut by a third the truck's weekly earning power.

Like other new western towns, Silverthorne was a scattered sprawl on both sides of the freeway. But she spotted the auto parts sign of the night before on the right across the state highway. Behind the garage were other small-town businesses and on the rising slope behind, new winter resort condos were going up. The collective name was Wildernest, spelled out on a billboard facing the freeway.

The parka was too warm in the sun, but she felt good. She had slept like a log finally, and felt perked up and ready to push on. She was happy that he hadn't tried anything last night when they got rooms across from each other. Nothing seemed to rattle him. She hadn't quite figured out yet whether he was playing it straight or whether he was some manner of clever rube. He sure seemed to know what a woman liked. She liked that. And she liked him. That is, she smiled to herself, as long as he hadn't taken off and left her in a lurch here, like the two bozos in Montana.

She crossed the main street–highway and walked past Elaine's Beauty Parlor, occupying two combined mobile homes, past an imitation log-cabin bar with small pickups in front, and saw the trailer parked on the curb next to the garage. She walked a little faster. She was glad she had a job. Marianne's boyfriend had sneered when she went to truck school, but here she was, away from soiled diapers and tuna casseroles for a while.

When she got to the trailer she heard the reassuring hum of the Thermo King. The load was a mixed consignment of processed food and convenience items. A reefer driver's big responsibility was to make sure the load was frozen when loaded and that it stayed that way.

The tractor was on the garage lot, the cab tilted up, and

Junior and a pair of mechanics were busy underneath. She crossed to them.

"Hi, there," she called.

They turned and squinted up at her.

"This is Karen, my codriver who wrecked the baby." Junior winked and introduced her to the two mechanics, whose oval name patches on their shirts identified them as Bob and Steve.

"Hear smokey clocked you doing 90." Bob grinned.

She played along. "Ever hear the one about the lady trucker arrested for speeding, whose excuse was that she had just had the rig washed and was trying to dry it off? Well, that's me."

Bob liked that. "Reminds me of the one about the woman driver who was arrested for speeding and told the trooper that President Reagan had raised the speed limit, but that, due to the budget cuts, the signs hadn't been changed yet."

Steve was the serious type. "Understand they had a pair of real wrecks, westbound, last night, on this side of the Eisenhower Tunnel."

She turned to Junior. "When can we leave?"

"This afternoon, Steve here tells me." Junior got up and told her that besides the injector problem, they had found a busted fuel jumper line, which explained the dumping of raw diesel last night.

She thought he was cute like that, with his blue eyes that looked at you with directness and authority, his rakish goatee, crooked lips, and Band-Aid on his right temple. If the fuel jumper line was left like that, he explained, it could contaminate the lube system, since diesel fuel mixing with oil would leak out like water.

"Had breakfast yet?" she interrupted. She wanted to sit down alone with him and really make sure last night was behind them.

"Ever heard a trucker say no to *two* fried eggs?"

Five minutes later, while Steve began dismantling the jumper line and Bob checked the Dahl filter-separator, the two of them left the garage. They headed up toward the underpass and the shopping center. According to Steve, the Golden Cup up there was the only breakfast place besides the Ramada Inn within walking distance.

"How did you sleep?" she asked as they passed Elaine's Beauty Parlor.

"Took a while to wind down. And you?"

"Same thing." She kept up with his stride. "I wanted to call my kids, then I realized how late it was. I called this morning, though—on my own. I mean, I'll pay my own long distance. Also to tell Marianne I might be a couple of days late. I mean I guess I will."

"Maybe you'll get home a couple of days early. That is, if you wanna continue."

She stopped cold. "What are you trying to say?"

He turned, stopped and looked at her.

"Are you trying to fire me?" she asked.

"Just wanna make sure you want to go on."

"I take this job seriously, Chuck." She couldn't call him Junior all of a sudden. "When we shook hands at my place, I meant it and I assumed you did, too."

He began to walk.

But she wasn't through, and as they passed under the freeway, she said, "I don't know what kind of a person you think I am. An icy road is damn scary, but it isn't going to make me chicken out, if that's what you mean. Nor will the fact that I might be a couple of days late. I told you I need this job, and somewhere in Utah yesterday you told me you thought we'd make an okay team."

"I did?" The grin was back.

As they entered the shopping-center parking lot and headed up toward the Golden Cup, it occurred to her that if he wanted to make sure *she* hadn't changed her mind, his asking her if she wanted to continue wasn't that crazy. Maybe she was overreacting. But she couldn't take another failure, another going back and telling Marianne there had been another screw-up. On the other hand, to come across as a neurotic female was the last thing she wanted.

"How's the load?" she asked as he held the door for her.

They took a booth by the window and he explained that

things wern't so bad after all. He had inspected the load. It was okay, and he had phoned the receiver in Atlanta and his broker up in Rahway, New Jersey. There was a possibility the load would be redirected to Houston. He'd find out when he called back this afternoon.

Yesterday, he had told her he was blessed with good brokers on both coasts. A broker's only function, as far as she was concerned, was to secure loads for a trucker, but he had told her the subtleties of the trade. You judged a broker by the number of truckers who regularly came to him or her, by how many regulars a broker had. A good broker went out and dug up shipper contacts in order to get loads. A lot of it was done through the Blue Book or the Red Book, which listed the brokers, but still more loads were obtained by word of mouth. The transportation industry made the wire services look like slackers when it came to making news travel fast.

"If we can pick up a backload in Houston, we'll turn around there," he said. "Houston's good for loads to the West Coast."

She bit her lip. The first thing a broker did when a load was going to be late was to see if the shipper had another place it could go. "If we leave this afternoon, can't we make it to Atlanta Friday morning?" she asked.

"That's gonna be tight."

"We can try."

The waitress was back, pouring them coffee.

"Houston is a good 12 hours closer," Junior said.

Not going to Atlanta and on up to the New York City region was a letdown, a bad omen for her debut as a coast-to-coast driver, for the two of them as a coast-to-coast sleeper team. But she didn't want to sound upset or disappointed, so instead of saying anything she had her first sip of coffee.

5
ACCIDENTS—CAUSES—
HUMAN ELEMENT

The hood had been rolled up into a dense mass and part of it had gone through the windshield. Body panels were distorted around the car's engine, the carburetor was sheared off. Brake lines were broken and the steering column (the energy-absorbing type) was forced downward with the instrument panel, shearing the joints at the brackets, but not producing collapse of the web jacket. The front seat had slid forward on its tracks and the left door seemed to have been forced open on impact.

It was Chuck Carlton's worst accident. Skid marks measured by New York State Police showed the car was driving on the right edge of the right lane. The marks showed the driver had realized he was about to ram into the rear of a truck, but only in the last minute, because the 34-feet-long straight skid marks terminated at impact. The two pairs of wheels on each side of Junior's rear axle left skid marks showing the rear-end impact was forceful enough to throw the whole rig three feet forward. The 1980 Chevy sedan came to rest against the axle, which was displaced about 18 inches forward. The driver, who was alone in the car, received the impact in position, the coroner's report said. His neck was crushed; his larynx apparently took a large impact and was severely distorted and smashed. Cervical spine fractures and a blow to the front of the neck which sheared the spinal cord were found. The forensic report from the Newburgh coroner's office said this may have been the result of restraint of the neck by the steering wheel when the head snapped forward at impact.

There was a large area of blood on the windshield, which was associated with the victim's facial injuries. There was also subdural hemorrhage and rupture of the left common carotid artery, rupture of the liver, together with fractures of lower jaw, right humerus, and feet. Toxicological examination showed 0.04% blood alcohol and 0.3% barbiturates (a driver is only considered impaired at 0.1% blood alcohol level).

One place to begin looking into highway accidents is the huge second-floor library at the Department of Transportation, which sprawls over a block area between D and E and Sixth and Seventh streets, a short walk from Independence Avenue in Washington. Under "accidents–traffic–causes–human element," you can go from *Accident or Suicide, Destruction by Automobile,* to Zylman, Richard, *Accident and Alcohol and Single-Cause Explanations.* The bookshelves, which stretch for nearly a quarter of a mile back from the E Street entrance and circulation desk, contain papers written on such subjects as Social Roadblocks in Utilizing Highway Safety and Research (we really don't wanna know) and Behavioral Approaches to Accident Research (so what else is new?). But "accidents–causes" does yield information that is both hypnotic and terribly obvious:

—Driver fatigue is the major factor in accidents involving commercial vehicles.

—Weather and machinery have little to do with highway deaths. Over 70% of all accidents occur in clear weather, over half in broad daylight. Only 13% of trucks-at-fault accidents are the result of mechanical defects.

—Four-wheelers do it to each other, mostly. Trucks are involved in less than 7% of all traffic deaths.

Almost half of the driver-caused accidents are single-vehicle accidents and are traceable to sleepiness, dozing, inattention, or momentary distraction. Every other trucker fatality is a driver who fell asleep at the wheel and ran off the road.

The Bureau of Motor Carrier Safety is a division of the

federal Department of Transportation—universally called DOT in the trucking industry. All fatal accidents involving trucks or buses must be reported to the Bureau. The acronym is FARS, for Fatal Accident Reporting System. Not everybody is happy with FARS. Its critics say it dodges responsibility (and possible lawsuits) by concentrating on cargo, vehicle configurations, date, time, etc., instead of asking questions that relate to fault of causation, but over the years the system has collected an awful lot of data. The Bureau's *Study of the Relationships Among Fatigue, Hours of Service and Safety of Operations of Truck and Bus Drivers* is famous. It comes to the not unsuspected conclusion that "the highest potential for truck-accident reduction is in restricting drivers who are overly fatigued from operating trucks."

Long-distance truckers prefer to drive late at night when four-wheelers don't clutter up the interstates and smokey is on skeleton graveyard shifts. Not surprising, the Bureau of Motor Carrier Safety study has found that truckers' lowest level of alertness is between 2:00 and 7:00 A.M. Nearly 80% of the truckers who ran off the road had been driving 7 hours, but curiously, of those who ended in a ditch, only 2% had been at the wheel over 10 hours, leading the statisticians to suspect that if a driver keeps going beyond the 7-hour "fatigue trough," his level of alertness picks up slightly again. When truckers were asked to rate themselves in such driving errors as lane drifting, they agreed they have the tendency to begin weaving all over the road after some 4 hours at the wheel, but that there is indeed an "end-spurt" increase in their alertness. The survey distinguished between tandem relay teams, who relay each other for 16 hours, then pull into a motel to sleep for 8 hours, and sleeper teams who keep going around the clock, one sleeping in the bunk while the other drives. Not surprisingly, the sleep you get in a sleeper while your codriver keeps trucking isn't as good as the sleep you get in a motel bed. After about 6.5 hours, from the start of their run, relay drivers show a higher than expected accident frequency. For sleeper teams, the critical time comes much earlier, after about 4 or 5 hours.

Junior was running solo, Boston–St. Louis, when drowsiness—and prudence—led him to park partly off the right lane of four-lane N.Y. 17 connecting the New York Thruway with I-84. The time was 3:45 A.M. The driver of the Chevy was either pinned in the right lane by traffic or failed to see the rear of the rig partly in his path. New York State Police estimated the impact speed at 60 mph. The car passed under the rear, striking the rear axle, and the windshield hit the trailer body, moving the whole rig forward three feet and jolting Junior awake.

When smokey arrived, Chuck had rubbed saliva in the corners of his eyes and stood holding his fire extinguisher over the pool of gasoline leaking from the car's tank. For fear that the cops would really scrutinize his logbook, he didn't say he had pulled over to obey an irresistible urge to snooze for half an hour. Instead, he told them he had stopped to consult his map and have a slurp of coffee from his thermos. The victim, it turned out, was a 51-year-old short-order cook returning home from work. His widow supplied little information about him, but medical records submitted at the inquest in Newburgh the next morning showed he had been under treatment for cerebellar ataxia and was taking barbiturates for this loss-of-muscular-coordination condition. Also, he had recently undergone bilateral cataract surgery. A pair of glasses was found folded on the smashed-in dash and the police report said that "as nearly as can be determined, he was not wearing glasses at the time of the accident." The judge at the inquest, a big, serenely paternal black man, didn't like the autopsy review, especially the toxicology report. "This man shouldn't have been in possession of a driver's license," he said. Minimum standards for physical condition, vision, and ability to react should exist, he commented, if society was serious in its efforts to reduce auto fatalities. Clearly, the judge didn't think society was serious. Junior was fined for illegal parking.

Millions of dollars are spent trying to find the answer to drowsy long-haul truckers. Remedies range from pneumatic lumbar-support seats and dressing drivers in special panty hoses to help blood circulation, to stricter enforcement of hours-of-service rules. In any discussion of promoting driver safety, the 5 hours of nondriving loading and unloading that are tagged onto the 10 hours at the wheel have to be considered. Reduction of those 5 hours would appear to be among the first logical steps toward improving safety. How many employees in other industries are called upon to perform 15-hour workdays? In 1981, DOT finally acted and made it illegal, punishable by fines up to $10,000 and two years imprisonment, to coerce any interstate for-hire trucker to load or unload any part of a shipment.

Trucking is a high-volume, low-profit-margin industry. Most long-haul fleet owners structure their routes for top productivity, and most carriers require their drivers to spend 70 full hours behind the wheel. Owner-operators work even harder to make ends meet. As for enforcement, federal road patrols to monitor drivers' hours are considered too costly, although the DOT does perform some road inspections. Hours-of-service enforcement remains tricky, even for fleet owners. Out there on the highways, very little management "eyes-on" supervision is possible.

Drugs are a heavier killer than sleepiness, but drugs are merely the flip side of the same coin, since truckers pop pills not to get high, but to stay awake. Sleeper teams run over a thousand miles a day and the use of "stay awake" drugs is on the increase. An estimated 10% of long-haul drivers use amphetamines "regularly," and nearly a third of them use multiple logbooks to get around the hours-of-service hassles. Lieutenant Norris Deville of the Louisiana State Police says illegal drugs can be found at many truckstops, that CB listeners can hear truckers call in their orders before arriving, and that at least one truckstop near New Orleans will charge both drugs and prostitutes on the bill as "fuel" and "repairs." To stay awake for 18 or 20 hours when he is running solo, Junior uses Dexedrine and Methedrine—commonly known as "L.A. turnarounds," "cartwheels," and "copilots."

Louisiana State Police use two different kinds of tests on drivers involved in accidents when there is a question of chemical influence. They use either blood alcohol or blood drug analysis to determine whether a person has a "controlled substance" in his system. Deville has also taught his troopers to use their eyes. Heavy users of amphetamines sweat a lot and smell heavily of perspiration. So if a cruiser pulls up to an accident scene and the troopers see a trucker dabbing heavy doses of shaving lotion on himself, they order a blood drug test. "If in addition, he is confused, unable to think clearly, lacks coordination and his speech is lethargic and thick, you know what you're dealing with," says Deville.

6
OFF AGAIN

Junior's wallet was the only thing that weighed less when he and Karen pulled out of Silverthorne shortly before sunset and headed up toward the Eisenhower Tunnel and the Continental Divide. The bill had come to $338, labor included. Since neither of them was tired, he had offered to toss a coin, but she had told him to drive first, "to see what $300 worth of new fuel jumper line feels like."

Crawling up the on-ramp, Chuck saw the Colorado State Police citation under the sun visor and pulled it down. Before leaving Summit County, it said, he had to have the brakes inspected at the local CSP station. Any weekday between eight and four.

Karen watched him. "You don't think they've got that one on you in their computer?"

He crumpled the ticket. "Maybe we can sneak out of Colorado without finding out."

She swiveled her highback toward him, but didn't say anything. Instead, she wedged her towel-wrapped thermos, filled at the Golden Cup, between her seat and the emergency brake panel.

"Anyway, I checked the brakes." He had to stay in the creeper gear. GEORGETOWN 21, IDAHO SPRINGS 33, DENVER 67.

"How far's the Kansas state line?" she asked.

With 67 miles to Denver, he calculated another 100 to Burlington, Colorado. "A hundred and thirty, I'd say, and pretty flat *after* Denver."

"Yeah, I saw that."

"You like maps, don't you?"

"I like to know where I am."

He saw a couple of rigs, westbound, coming down, flat out. "If you travel 100,000 miles a year, you know, it all tends to be the same thing, geography."

"I don't agree. When you've been someplace it's no longer just a name on the map. Salt Lake City, for instance, nestled there between the foothills and the desert . . . once you've seen it coming from Wyoming on I-80, that long sharp downgrade, you don't forget it. At night, the sharp clear mountain air makes the lights sparkle."

The climb was slow. He had a feeling the Houston turn-around was a disappointment for her, that she'd have liked to run through to Atlanta and up to Rahway, to have a peek at the Staue of Liberty and the Manhattan skyline across the Hudson before turning west on I-76.

They were above the dam now and he could see the lake, on the right behind her. On his side, the snow-covered sugar-top caught the rays of the sinking sun. He looked at her. She had gotten a tan sitting outside the garage half the afternoon, studying tourist brochures and maps and reading off names: Snake River and Dillon Reservoir, Copper Mountain, and after the tunnel, the Loveland Basin and Valley. She told him the Eisenhower Memorial Tunnel was 11,000 feet above sea level, that it was nearly two miles long and higher than any other underground tunnel in the world, that it had cost $267 million to build it.

He smiled. "You know that the tires experience a tiny wheel slippage on a long grade like this, that they turn just a tiny bit faster than the forward speed of the truck?"

She didn't, and he told her the proof was that if you stopped just as you flattened out at the crest, got out and rubbed your hand over the tires of the drive wheels, tiny balls of rubber would dust off. "Excessive tire wear."

They were doing 25, climbing, and he explained that besides saving fuel, the major benefit of not powering the grade was that you prevented engine lugging. She knew about excessive combustion-chamber pressures on steep grades. It had happened to her on Stage Road Pass on I-5 in Oregon and their conversation drifted to Jubitz's in North Portland, which they agreed was the best truckstop on I-5, excepting the 76 stop in Redding, California, maybe.

"You get in there after driving 300 miles and you feel at home," he said. "Makes you forget the bears and the potholes."

She liked Jubitz's off-highway location because it discouraged tourists, and he remembered the telephone room—not just a hallway with a row of pay phones, but a room where you could call your broker or dispatcher in relative peace. She liked the laundromat and the clean ladies' showers.

He kidded her about the influence LTDs had on truckstops. Yes, she said, some places now had hair driers in the women's shower section, but from what she'd heard, the guys also liked the cleaner showers and rest rooms and the better chow that lady truckers seemed to be responsible for.

"Even the hookers like the clean ladies' rest room." He laughed, to see what she'd say. "A lady tourist told me she couldn't get inside the women's rest room at the Ontario 76 truckstop in I-10 east of Los Angeles because six hookers were camping there. Two of the girls were soaking their feet in the washbasin, maybe sore from doing too much canvassing in the parking area. If a guy wants action, a quick blink of the headlights and a girl comes and climbs in." He didn't quite know how to tell her he didn't mess with them.

He also didn't tell her he'd gotten all excited lying in his sleeper one night listening to the CB conversations. One girl used the handle Eager Beaver, and she and her prospective client used language so lewd that a trucker got in on the talk and began enumerating all the dirty words that were illegal on the airwaves. It was funny and crazy. Another guy came on the air to say Eager Beaver couldn't talk now because her mouth was full.

Mile 211. The climb was slightly steeper. SNOWPLOWS TURNING ON HIGHWAY. The mountain range rose ahead of them.

She said trucking didn't lend itself to much normal socializing, which explained the growing number of husband-and-wife teams, couples who preferred companionship on the road. "The majority of lady truckers are driving with their husbands or boyfriends."

He thought that he sure wouldn't mind pulling over to

climb into the sleeper and become her lover. "I know." He grinned wistfully. "But you're not."

She gave him a glance and he asked her how she handled enterprising guys when she ran solo.

She smiled. "I try to be polite and nice, but if the person doesn't get it, I tell him off—firmly. And if he says, 'Why not, LTDs are supposed to be like the guys,' I say, 'Exactly, *you* don't try to mess with the guys.' "

He could see her say that. "No situation you couldn't handle?"

"Not so far." John, her husband, had been on a rifle team in school and knew how to use a gun, she explained. He had taught her and at home she had a .38. On the road, however, all she carried was a piece of pipe up her sleeve. "I like to think I'm different from other lady truckers."

"Yeah, in what way?" The mountain face came down to the highway on the left. On the right, it plunged thousands of feet. SNOWSLIDE AREA. He came up one gear as the grade began to flatten out in one enormous curve.

"I like men to open doors for me, to respect a woman. If only they knew the difference it makes."

He concentrated on the driving. Runoff water crossed the roadway in thin streams, and the snow was down to the median and the ditches on the right. TUNNEL AHEAD. The highway climbed again and he fell back to the creeper gear, doing 10 mph. VEHICLES CARRYING HAZARDOUS MATERIAL MUST EXIT NEXT RIGHT. The interstate was built on one long right curve, a terrace carved out of rock. SPEED 50 MPH. ELEVATION 11,000 FT. It looked as if the highway was going to run smack into the snow-covered rock face. Then he saw powerful lights on tall standards, bleak against the snow, and spotted the eastbound tunnel entrance. Between it and the westbound bore was a concrete bunkerlike building with huge aeration turbines on top. PARKING AREA. Wet snow covered the roadway and he heard the slosh of the tires.

"What made you get into this line of work, anyway?" he shouted.

They thundered into the tunnel, and he rolled his window up to hear her say she had tried to be a secretary.

"And?"

"And it just wasn't for me."

The walls reverberated with the roar of the full throttle 2,000 rpms, but the tunnel evened out and he came up four gears. Ahead, a house trailer, or something odd-shaped, had its emergency blinkers on. He crossed to the fast lane. "A secretary doesn't have to replace fuel filters," he said.

"Nor does she have to chase down the guy carting off her chains at three in the morning."

He smiled. "That happened to you?"

"I had the chains laid out in front of the drive wheels and was heading for the coffee shop to warm up first."

He tried to imagine her running after the guy across the snowy parking lot. "If only you had driven onto the chains before going for coffee."

"Sure. But I have the impression that these kinds of things happen only to truckers who are female and 26."

It was the first time she'd told him her age.

She swiveled toward him in the jump seat. "Listen, I change my own flat tires when the nearest station is 30 miles away. I argue with state troopers and scalemen. And on top of that I try to keep my end of the deal by acting like a lady."

She was cute when she was angry. "Looking like one, also." He grinned.

She gave him a glance in the neon running light. The tunnel slanted downhill and he passed the van pulling the housetrailer. No one was immune to the increase in cargo and equipment theft.

Just before they came out of the tunnel and he began to pick up speed, a neon sign advised that there was a 7.5% grade for the next seven miles and that trucks should stay in low gear.

"Reminds me of last night," she shouted as they shot out of the tunnel.

The roadway was bone-dry, but he said, "I can imagine."

The roofs of the highway department building on the right were covered with snow. WEST LOVELAND PASS 1 MILE. It was almost dark.

"You just don't *see* black ice," she said.

44

"Normally, as long as you see spray you know the road isn't frozen."

"Trouble was there wasn't anybody's spray I could watch last night. Like now."

It was true. They were alone. He wanted to lean over the side console and hug her—for all lady truckers. It wasn't easy for them. They had to work hard to gain respect from the guys. She had nothing of the loudmouthed, one-of-the-boys bluster so many LTDs affected. Maybe that was what she meant this afternoon when she had told the kidding Bob that lady truckers had come a long way. He let his mind play with becoming her lover. He looked forward to it and he didn't mind prolonging the sweet agony. He had to keep his cool, he knew that. She wasn't someone to yield to a fast grope in the dark. She wanted to see it coming, to have a say in when and where. She wanted to want him, too. He felt a warm swell of excitement at the bottom of his spine.

They were curving right among the pines and the snow, the white splotches between the evergreens making a strange mosaic at the speed they were running. It was almost dark, but he could see they were coming down toward a swath of a valley. He imagined her back at the Vail Summit Pass last night, with him snoring in the back. He was doing 60 without effort, and if he hit ice now, he too would be in trouble. He kicked the gear up and laid on air to see if the brakes were there. A wild creek followed them on the right.

For the next hour they talked about couples they knew as they waltzed sturdily down past Silver Plume, Georgetown, Lawson, and Idaho Springs. She told him about Mike and Kathy, who had trucked together on the Alaska pipeline for two years. They were from Yakima also, and in a Seattle newspaper had seen a 1972 Kenworth, with a lease to haul Seattle to Fairbanks, for sale. Mike's workmen's compensation was running out and they both wanted something that could change their lives. The ad sure brought them that. They knew the Kenworth was a pile of junk and on the first trip up, the turbocharger conked out in Yukon. Somebody finally took pity on them and pulled them back to Edmonton. A year later, they were hauling pipe from Valdez to Prudhoe Bay. Survival trucking, they called it, with grades as steep as 20%, no guard-rails, no shoulders, and nothing but desolation for 798 miles. They wrecked two tractors, but made a pile and were now in antiques in Seattle.

He knew a lot of sleeper teams, but no one really good. He remembered an Indiana couple. The husband always wore a 4X Stetson, the same hat Burt Reynolds wore in *Smokey and the Bandit*. If they helped you on the road, you had to pray with them. Then he remembered Ray and Hazel Wadleigh and their handsome Model-F Mack leased to Bekins. A lot of movers were husband-and-wife teams, maybe because they never got home regularly. Most freight haulers got home once a week, but the average trip for bedbug haulers was at least a month, with two months pretty common. There were always stories about long-lease Bekins, North American, and May-flower owner-operators being gone for "years." He had con-voyed with Ray and Hazel.

"They have the neatest Double Eagle sleeper with cup-boards, clothes closets, tan-colored ceiling, and mahogany on the sides, Jensen 20-watt stereo system, and all the comforts of home, including Felicia."

"Felicia?"

"Pretty lady." He winked. "Seal-point coat and piercing blue eyes."

"I got it, a Siamese cat."

"A clever Siamese cat. When she wants a drink of water, she puts one paw on the shoulder of whoever is at the wheel and taps their face with the other paw. They pull immediately over and Felicia gets her water. When they're stopped, she's on a leash, and if startled, she leaps atop the drive wheel, snug there between the tire and the trailer bottom."

She knew about truckers who had German shepherds with them to prevent crime. From pets, Junior and Karen got to talking about kids on the road, toddlers living in sleepers and truckstops, usually with one of their divorced parents. "Usually, they belong to bitter fathers who still don't know what hit 'em," he said.

"If the kids are cared for, maybe it's not the worst that can happen to them."

46

He gave her a glance and wondered if he had touched a sensitive nerve. To find out, he asked, "You miss yours?"

Her smile was wistful. "I'll promise never to ask you to take them along. How's that?"

"Maybe I should ask if you think they miss you."

"Tim at bedtime like this, yes."

"And your little girl had to be held the other night."

"You noticed?"

He knew that was meant to be a compliment and told her about a little boy in his pajamas dutifully brushing his teeth in the men's room at the Redding truckstop the other day. "He was beginning to lose his baby teeth and had a front tooth missing. His father was waiting outside with the kid sister already asleep on his arm. He was a young guy, with a beard and a front tooth missing, like his kid. 'Where are ya heading?' I asked. He said back to Georgia. He was running a 32-ton arctic. He warned me about a crackdown at the Arizona port-of-entry and I told him I was heading north, to Yakima, to pick up my new codriver. The boy came out and showed his dad the row of pearls with the gap in the middle. I asked if the kids were on the road with him a lot and he said this sure wasn't the first time."

"Maybe their mother was sick, or something," Karen suggested.

"I don't think so." He looked at her. "He looked abandoned and unloved. Like me." She caught his grin. "Lost and looking for meaning in life."

"You!" She laughed.

He sighed with mock sincerity. "Looking for a bosom to lay our weary heads on."

"You've got a lady friend in every terminal, I bet."

"We're so misunderstood."

"Yeah, sure."

He kidded around some more and told her to put on some music. She went through his collection, asking him what he was in the mood for. He wanted her to choose, and when she slipped a cassette into the player, he heard Tanya Tucker's twangy flat voice sing about lovin' and learnin' and the time after the thrill was gone. He highballed through a pair of short tunnels, and after a curve they were out in a valley. The road went uphill a bit again, and when it crested and began running down again, he saw the twinkle of White Ridge and the other western suburbs of Denver. He felt great. The woman next to him was somebody. She hadn't gotten them killed last night; she hadn't smashed up the rig. They had a load to Houston. He was up on the payments. The engine hummed under them and he let the moment and the music invade him. "You're not quite lovers and you're not quite friends, after the thrill is gone," Tanya sang. For him the thrill was still to come.

He pressed himself back into the seat and put his neck on the headrest. "What can you do when the dreams come true?" Vibrating guitars overwhelmed the girlish voice on the stereo. He fingertipped the wheel ever so lightly to follow the last gentle downhill curves. He was doing 65, in top gear, his best gear, humming along at 1,800 rpms. The next tune was "Don't Believe My Heart Can Stand Another You." If he had been running solo, he might have stopped in one of the country-and-western saloons. They were in the southeast part of Denver, where singles apartments and condos were concentrated. Sleepy La Beef or Dodge City. He liked the sagebrush saloons because people were not all plastic, like in the discos. He liked the laidback buddydom, couples whirling through the cotton-eye Joe, the Texas two-step. He liked the long bars, the live bands, the urban cowgirls. Besides, everybody looked good in a cowboy hat. The cactus cabarets were all over now. In Detroit, truckers had helped make the Urban Cowboy Club a hit by touting its charms on the CBs.

"Care for some coffee?" Karen asked. She had the tall thermos bottle between her knees and was putting the plastic cup on the side console between them.

"Sure." He nodded.

Next came the Tanya Tucker tune he liked best. "Here We Are." "Here we are in lovin' arms so tight." To make sense of it all, you had to place yourself in the fantasy of things, he thought. There was no other way. Like so many other indepdendents, he was riding hard and fast to stay ahead of all the questions.

48

7
THE HOSTILE ENVIRONMENT

The only public hearing Chuck Carlton ever attended had to
do with harmonizing state regulations. He was in Dallas, waiting for a load west, and on a truckstop TV monitor saw the
meeting advertised. He sat on the sidelines in the Holiday Inn
conference room with a Styrofoam cup of free coffee and heard
Omar Ellerby, representing R. A. Corbet Transportation, say,
"If anyone wants to find out what the word 'united' means, he
sure won't find out by driving a truck across the United
States."

The Yoonited States, Omar jeered.

The Federal Highway Administration, the Department of
Transportation, and the Interstate Commerce Commission all
had bureaucrats at the meeting, one of eight regional gather-
ings held in 1981 to get input for a report mandated to be laid
before Congress the following year. Regulatory people from
the Texas, Arkansas, Oklahoma, and Louisiana state govern-
ments were there. Trucking-company types, with neckties and
briefcases, were there and, sitting in a clump, a dozen truckers
chewing on toothpicks and sipping lukewarm coffee. "On behalf of Texas," said R. W. Townsley, director of the state
Motor Vehicles Division, "it's our suggestion that the secretary
of transportation and the ICC report back to Congress that it
should do no more than enourage the states to participate in
state-sponsored reciprocity." Martin Zell, the guy from the
ICC, said his regulatory commission certainly had every right
to study the aspects of state economic regulations that concern
interstate commerce. To which Ed Hicks of the Arkansas Department of Revenues responded that the states could work

out this problem without federal involvement. And on and on. Chuck shifted in his seat.

Virtually no two states do anything alike when it comes to trucks, and virtually no state bureaucracy leaves alone the regulations it does promote. There is no yearbook in which a trucker can look up things because the regulations change so fast the reference book would be obsolete before it reached the printer. *Owner-Operator* magazine prints constantly updated "Guide to Legal Trucking" charts, and in *Overdrive*, Joe Fitzgerald runs a monthly column called "Keep on Truckin' Legally—If Possible." *Owner-Operator* publishes color charts on reciprocity, toll-road size and weight limits, and vehicle size and weight limits twice a year. Fitzgerald is considered the most knowledgeable person on truck licensing, permit prorating, and reciprocity. He sits in Altoona, Iowa, with a P.O. box that is always overstuffed, since he is on regulatory-agency mailing lists from California to Nova Scotia, Alaska to Florida.

"I awaken in a cold sweat, wondering if some poor trucker has read a back issue of *Overdrive*, relying on information I included in an article a year ago," he says. A typical Joe Fitzgerald column will advise that Indiana is doing its bit to make it more difficult for the trucker to make ends meet, increasing registration fees by 25%, that enforcement of the Pennsylvania inspection law is comparable to a yo-yo, that Ontario grants reciprocity for trailers pulled by a tractor registered in Ontario and has reciprocity with 23 states. Kentucky has eliminated the nine-cents-per-gallon tax in favor of a tax of 9% of the wholesale price, and the fuel tax in Vermont is now figured at 7% of the sales price, federal tax included.

If you're a trucker hauling beef from Nebraska to the Chicago stockyards, chances are you're loading up in Omaha. Maybe you realize your two 100-gallon tanks are close to empty before you get to Omaha and fill up in Council Bluffs, on the Iowa side of the Missouri River. From there you drive across on I-80 to Omaha, swing south on Kennedy Expressway to the livestock market and load up. Heading east to Chicago again, you cross the bridge to Council Bluffs. And now you're a criminal. Iowa state law says you can only "import" 30 gallons. So you now pay the state of Iowa fuel tax on the extra

170 gallons you just bought in Iowa. And don't think it helps if you show the receipt or you say you've got 10 witnesses ready to swear you bought the goddamn diesel fuel in Iowa a couple of hours ago. You pay your tax on the 170 gallons in the tanks and you buy yourself a $12 Iowa fuel permit. It's only good for 72 hours and you can't use it to reenter the state.

Allan A. Nichols is an owner-operator from South Carolina who can tell you all about it. Allan and his wife are a reefer team, and on Friday evening, July 18, 1980, they were heading east on I-80 and dutifully pulled in at the scales east of Des Moines with their $80,000 cargo of meat they had just picked up in Omaha. The Iowa DOT inspector on duty was D. R. Page and he looked at the papers. Nichols had bought the $16 Iowa fuel permit *going*. Now, he was halfway back across Iowa and the permit was no longer valid since he had dipped eight miles into Nebraska to get to the livestock market. Next, Page discovered that the company the 56-year-old Nichols was pulling the meat for hadn't given the owner-operator the proper ICC authority. On the spot, Page fined Nichols $106 for the missing ICC paper and $16 for a new 72-hour Iowa fuel permit.

Nichols told Page he'd have to contact someone, as he didn't have $122 on him, and that it might take a while, this being Friday evening. Page said Nichols was under arrest. The way the Iowa DOT describes what happened next is that Page accompanied Nichols to his truck and informed his wife of the arrest. Nichols told the officer his cooling unit was low on fuel, and Page told the wife she could purchase the $16 fuel permit and drive the rig to a nearby truckstop for service. She became upset and insisted on being arrested and jailed as well. When the incident blew sky-high and Iowa Governor Robert D. Ray had to respond to the national outcry from truckers, his DOT told him, "Mrs. Nichols was informed that no charges were filed on her and that no arrest would occur. She was again informed of her right to purchase a fuel permit and move the truck. Since Mrs. Nichols was capable of driving and could move the truck with a proper permit, she was not offered a ride."

At the county jail, Nichols was stripped and thrown into

a filthy, oven-hot cell. (DOT to Governor Ray: "It is impossible for us to comment on the conditions of the Polk County Jail or their procedures.") At 9:00 A.M., Nichols saw the judge, who arbitrarily decided to raise the cash bond from $106 to $150 and the fuel permit from $16 to $35, and told him he could make his phone call. In the meantime, Mrs. Nichols was sitting in the truck back at the weigh station, not knowing when he'd be back or what to do. According to Iowa DOT Director Raymond L. Kassel, the scalemen asked her if she wished to be taken to breakfast: "While it may appear that the Iowa DOT was not responsive to a woman in need, the facts remain that she was a truck driver and was no doubt acquainted with spending time in a truck at rest areas and weigh scales."

Eventually the Nicholses paid their $185 and drove out of Iowa. Three months later, when *Overdrive* published a letter from Nichols and added its own open letter to Governor Ray, Kassel defended his department's action by wondering why the owner-operator of equipment worth between $100,000 and $200,000, and hauling a cargo worth $80,000, didn't have the operating capital to purchase permits and pay fees and fines. In reporting the Nicholses' story, *Overdrive* editor Mike Parkhurst stood the Iowa DOT argument on its head and asked whether holding an $80,000 load of fresh meat ransom for more than 24 hours in order to settle a $185 fine was the best possible advertisement for the fuel permits.

Highway departments are broke and money has to come from somewhere. Trucks pay a combination of state road-use taxes, fuel permits, registration and license fees, gross weight receipts, and gross ton-mile taxes. Happily, there is only one federal government and it has only two levies: a four-cents-a-gallon tax that truckers, like everybody else, pay at the pump, and a federal highway–users tax, administered by the Internal Revenue Service, and proportioned to the weight and number of axles on each truck. Where it gets to be confusing is on the state level. There are 50 of them (and 10 Canadian provinces, if you run north of the border, too) and each levies a bewildering array of taxes on the transportation business originating or terminating there, or merely rumbling through.

The rules, regulations, and laws can be boiled down to three vast categories: 1) registration fees, 2) operating authority fees, and 3) fuel or road-use taxes.

One. When a four-wheeler buys license plates for his car, he pays a fee to his state treasurer that allows him to drive that car in every state, Canada, Mexico, and in most other parts of the world. When the owner of a truck buys a set of license plates, he pays several thousand dollars for them, but they really aren't worth much in any other state. Since the greediest of state legislatures realizes the national economy would come to a screeching halt if each truck had to pay $100,000 a year in license plates (50 plates at about $2,000 a throw), they have invented "reciprocity." I'll recognize yours if you'll honor mine.

Two. Suppose you're an Arizona-based trucker running coast-to-coast five times a year—Los Angeles to Jacksonville, Florida, say. On each 4,700-mile round trip, you're in Texas for 1,660 miles and in Alabama for less than 200 miles. You obviously use up more of Texas's roads than Alabama's. The states have therefore invented prorated fees, meaning that the money from the license fees is divided up among the participating states on a use basis. Whichever state has the highest road use by a truck receives the largest part of the license fee. A fair enough system, but so complicated that the northeastern states don't even bother to try to divide these fees; they simply honor each other's plates much like the passenger-car plates.

To show you're okay, you have a "prorate" plate next to your license plate. The prorate plate is divided into little squares where you display the various state decal stamps or stickers, showing that you or your carrier has paid the state fees, and incidentally, that you have liability insurance. With the prorate sticker comes a colorful 8½-by-11-inch Form D, or "bingo card." If you truck "all over," you'll have a handsome, expensive document to flash at the scalemen. When an owner-operator leases on with a carrier, the first question is who pays the prorate fees. A large carrier will apportion its annual fleet mileage to the various states in which it does business and will pay the state for its whole fleet at one time. Some carriers specify that their owner-operators absorb the prorate cost, but most demand only that their lessors supply the base plate.

The bureaucrats have tried to simplify all this by coming up with the International Registration Plan (IRP). Devised in 1973, the IRP is now in effect in almost 35 American and Canadian jurisdictions. It provides for one single home registration plate with the word "apportioned" embossed across the top. Each year the overall registration fees of the member jurisdictions are divided on the basis of the mileage history or the anticipated mileage of each long-distance truck.

Three. A fill-up of Diesel Number 2 comes to over $200; the 7% tax that some states charge could mean $15 in their coffers. No wonder no state wants a trucker to fill up in the previous state, run clear through, and fill up again in the next state. Of course it isn't easy to calculate it right on the nose so that you enter the state with only the amount you're allowed to import. Hence the fuel permit, usually a distinctively colored decal stuck on the truck door.

You're supposed to contact the state fuel-tax agency before you get there. If you don't and roll in without the sticker on the door, you're fined. Some states don't have such provisions and let you purchase fuel in an amount equal to that consumed on the state's highways. Wisconsin, for example, is such a state, but neighboring Minnesota has a fuel-reporting law. Minnesota even provides for refunds on overpurchases, but there's a catch to this. Minnesota and Wisconsin have a bilateral reciprocal agreement which calls for any over- or under-purchases in one state to first be offset by any over- or under-purchases in the other state.

Oregon, Ohio, and other states have a road-tax system based on a mileage fee charged against the truck, whether fuel is purchased or not. A "ton-mile" tax is based on how much weight you carry over how many miles.

The administrative cost of complying with this morass of licensing, taxation, and registration rules is prohibitive. For a company with 300 tractors and 1,000 trailers—some owned, others on long-term lease—operating over irregular routes in all 49 states (nobody trucks to Hawaii), the yearly compliance cost exceeds $200,000. A carrier like Overnite, of Richmond,

Virginia, uses four full-time employees plus data processing to fulfill fuel-tax and registration-reporting requirements at a cost of $400,000 annually.

But how will smokey have time out there on the interstates to check decals on cab doors and prorate stickers as he pulls ahead of you? The answer is that he doesn't. That's mostly left to the scalemen.

Four-wheelers rarely notice the scales. When we tool down the interstates in the family Ford, all we see is the welcoming signs greeting us on the state lines: big handsome portents of pleasures to come, sometimes with the state flower or state flag, sometimes with the governor's likeness and name in the right corner (New Jersey and Pennsylvania like that). The color of the median markings and the roadway surface may change too. New signs remind us of the speed limits, and in some states tell us what the fines are for going too fast. However, the same red-white-and blue interstate crest is used in each state, as is the numbering system—even on east-west, uneven on north-south superslabs, and three digits on beltways and loops around cities. Even the now wordless international traffic signs are the same, although many states continue to subtitle them as if they were a strange foreign movie.

A few miles after we pass the state line, a sign says TRUCK SCALES NEXT RIGHT. We zoom by a kind of siding with what looks like a maintenance shed, where all the big mothers who tailgated us for the last 50 miles are now meekly queuing up. Makes us feel better.

Virtually every state has a port of entry, although no building is ever labeled that. The inspectors working here are state DOT employees, and they are more hated than any cop. They are there with their truck scales to control weight—to protect highways from wear and tear—but their purpose is also to insure that trucks have all the required papers—the trip sheet, the prorate and the fuel-tax permits, the bingo card and the ton-mile or the gross-receipt-weight sticker. The scalehouses are all truckers' nightmares and the major source of corruption.

The worst are in the South, although truckers have lately singled out Arizona and Oregon as pretty bad too. The scalehouses of the Mississippi Tax Commission are the most infamous, and the worst of *them* is the one at Kewanee on the Mississippi-Alabama line, where I-20 and I-59 run together for 137 miles between Meridian, Mississippi, and Birmingham, Alabama. Mississippi is the poorest state in the union and this is a nice stretch of highway to make some money. I-20 carries all Dallas-to-Atlanta traffic and I-59 is the most direct route between New Orleans and the Northeast. The fused interstates bypass the abandoned hamlet of Kewanee, which sits astride the old, two-laned U.S. 80, but to be sure no map-reading trucker slips off at the Kewanee exit and tries to run into Alabama on U.S. 80, the State Tax Commission maintains a scalehouse on the old road and keeps it open 24 hours a day, year-round except the Fourth of July and Christmas Eve. Go into the aggressively air-conditioned scalehouse and ask the crisply uniformed officer why Mississippi weighs trucks going *out* of the state, and you will be told in a mellow accent that the scale is also for weighing rigs coming in from Alabama, although the scalehouse is on the wrong side of the road for that. A more plausible reason is that an overweight Dallas-to-Atlanta trucker who is stopped as he comes into Mississippi on I-20 from Louisiana at Vicksburg and found to be 8,000 pounds overweight, is fined $62. If he crosses the 155 miles of Mississippi and is caught in Kewanee, the penalty goes up 500%.

Russell and Peggy Legg in April, 1980, claimed they had been waved on at the Vicksburg scales, only to be caught at Kewanee and fined $372 because they had traveled all the way across the state without stopping at a scalehouse. Legg was 8,000 pounds over the then 73,280 pounds maximum weight, and not only did the Kewanee scale tender tell him to pay, he also told him to unload the 8,000 pounds of green Mexican tomatoes the Leggs were hauling from Arizona to Roanoke, Virginia. Russell made no bones about being overweight, but the idea of unloading 8,000 pounds just rubbed him the wrong way. While Peggy tried to restrain him, Russell threatened to dump the 8,000 pounds of green tomatoes right there on the goddamn scale.

For four hours, Legg and the scalemen argued and

strutted. The officers tried to be conciliatory and Peggy tried to control her husband's temper. Officer Edward Knowles, who came on duty after the Leggs had been stopped, suggested they call the motor vehicle comptroller's office in Jackson. That did it. The scalemen were told to let the Leggs pay the fine and proceed with their tomatoes.

The confrontations are not always this benign. A month earlier, Marcus Keel of Los Angeles faced felony and misdemeanor charges for allegedly trying to run down a state trooper in hot pursuit, and a year earlier, Delaware trucker Robert Cramer told of scalemen leaving the lights out late at night and chasing trucks that failed to stop, shooting at both trucker and rig.

Cramer said he was shot at by Inspector J. R. Gregory, who gave chase when Cramer didn't stop at the blacked-out scalehouse. Over the state line they went, with Gregory still firing before he gave up and U-turned back to Mississippi. An Alabama state policeman told Cramer he could file charges in Alabama, since he was sure Gregory had kept shooting after they were over the state line, so the irate Cramer waited six hours at the truckstop in Cuba, the first exit in Alabama, while officials drew up warrants for him to sign. Then a Mississippi trooper drove over to say he would talk to the witnesses, and if he felt the shooting had occurred in Mississippi and not in Alabama, he'd return and have Cramer sign Mississippi warrants. The officer didn't return and Cramer drove home to Delaware, assuming that the Alabama warrants were enough. When he called the Mississippi trooper two days later, he was told he'd have to come back and sign warrants. Cramer dropped the case.

Keel tried to avoid both the Kewanee scales on the interstate and on U.S. 80 by running into Alabama on state highway 19, a rural road that begins east of Meridian and runs southeast into Alabama in Choctaw County. But Mississippi officers had set up portable scales on the back road and, they said, when Keel's rig was driven onto the scales, it was so heavy its weight wouldn't register. The officers directed Keel to follow them back to Kewanee, but when they approached the scalehouse on the interstate, they said Keel turned off his lights and gunned his engine for Alabama. With the help of the Mississippi Highway Patrol, the scalemen were able to stop the truck before the state line, but not before Keel allegedly ran into one of them. When they got Keel's truck to the scales, it weighed in at slightly over 103,000 pounds. Keel was charged with attempted assault with a vehicle, failure to stop at a weigh station, driving without lights on an interstate highway, failure to stop for blue lights and a siren, and operating an overweight truck. He was fined $758 and his overweight fine was $2,808. He was freed on a $10,000 bond.

Sometimes a trucker outwits the Mississippi scalemen. Up on U.S. 61 one February night in 1979, a trucker was heading into Mississippi from Tennessee. He failed to stop at the Mississippi scales and Officer Robert Rosenthal ran out, hopped into his squad car, and careened after the offending rig. Rosenthal's cruiser, unfortunately, collided head-on with an oncoming vehicle on two-laned U.S. 61. The driver of the other car escaped unscathed. Rosenthal was killed. Who the trucker was has remained a mystery.

Near Manchester on I-24, midway between Nashville and Chattanooga, the Tennessee DOT operates another notorious set of scales. Truckers have written angry letters to Governor Lamar Alexander and to trucking magazines about rip-offs at Manchester. When Georgia driver David J. Allen was given a citation saying his load was 2,500 pounds overweight on one axle, he said that was impossible. He had come from Wisconsin and cleared all scales, including the Tennessee port of entry. Besides, the load was palletized so that it couldn't have shifted in transit. At this point, he was threatened with jail, so finally agreed to pay the fine.

Tennessee allows only 73,280 pounds and a 55-foot length, while next-door Georgia goes for the 80,000-lbs.–60-ft. standard. However, Nissan Motors recently looked over both Tennessee and Georgia for a Datsun pickup-truck plant. Nissan would be shipping a lot of pickups on 60-foot truck transporters. And wouldn't you know it, Governor Alexander let it be known that Tennessee might open its highways to larger trucks.

In 1980, Pennsylvania joined the 80,000-lbs.–60-ft. weight

and size limitation, but the country still has its iron curtain, stretching from Illinois and Indiana on the Great Lakes through Missouri and Arkansas to Mississippi on the Gulf Coast. The only way to legally haul 80,000 pounds from Kansas City to New York is to make a 500-mile detour north around Lake Michigan. "So you either drive around the iron curtain, which costs a lot in diesel, or you pay a fine when you drive onto the scales," says Kansas reefer owner-operator Roger Jestice, who pulls produce to New York. "What I end up doing, though, is to wait till the scales close, so I can get by them without getting caught." Another late-night ploy when you know you're overweight is to "go behind the scalehouse" with a $20 bill. In 1978, CBS's "60 Minutes" did an exposé on "bumping," the widespread practice of falsifying weight tickets.

Under duress, the Carter administration made one attempt at ending all this nonsense, which the Transportation Research Board estimates is costing consumers between $1.6 and $2.8 billion a year. The immediate spur was not inconsistencies in weights and sizes, but skyrocketing fuel prices. The year was 1979, and the country was fuming at OPEC, fuming at the oil companies, and frustrated with Jimmy Carter. By June, diesel fuel cost 40% more than in January and angry truckers were ready to just park their rigs and walk away from the whole mess. For a change, they had the four-wheelers' sympathy. Motorists grumbled through week after week of vapor-thin gas supplies and worst-ever lines to the pumps. During most of the spring, the static had been ominous on the CBs. One beefy voice after the other came over the static, telling how much it cost in diesel to drive from Florida to New Jersey, from California to Chicago. If this doesn't stop, someone said, people better get used to paying six dollars for a pound of hamburger. The gripes helped the independents develop a sense of themselves as a beleaguered force, but there was also a sense of vagueness, a feeling that things were unfocused. On top of sky-high prices, diesel supplies were short in many areas and truckstops began to limit purchases. Forceful action, however, seemed impossible. Independent owner-operators, after all, didn't belong to any union and they were never long enough in one spot to organize one. A strike would be messy and ill organized. Besides, what *could* be done and who should do it? And even if it were possible, who should negotiate with whom?

William J. Hill, an independent from Pittsburgh, formed something called the National Independent Truckers Unity Council, and in March and May fired off letters to President Carter, DOT, and ICC urging the government to allow truckers to at least pass along the increased fuel costs. But who did Hill speak for? The consensus up and down the highways was that nothing would really happen until the public got a jolt. Fresh produce was the only area where the ICC had ever allowed independents to work flat out. If people saw the shelves of supermarkets empty, maybe Washington would pay attention. Alex Carlucci, who became president of a hastily formed New Jersey independents' council, put it this way: "Sure the public is going to yell at us, but that's what we want. We want people to yell at the governor and at the president."

The Independent Truckers Association, headed by *Overdrive* editor Mike Parkhurst, called for a national shutdown to begin June 11. Three days before then, owner-operators began parking their rigs before setting out on week-long trips, and in the West and Midwest, some truckers blockaded fuel pumps and one major highway. Drivers forced nine truckstops to close in Utah and in Massachusetts, and other independents planned a 40-truck convoy to the Statehouse in Boston. The next day, the "wildcat protest" had spread to 14 states. In Indiana, drivers parked 300 rigs, four abreast, for a mile on I-90 near Gary, and the shutdown spread to 29 states. But the press statements of the various self-styled leaders began contradicting each other. Hill announced a nationwide shutdown *would* start on June 20.

Alabama Governor Forrest (Fob) James called out the National Guard after LTD Linda Pruett was wounded by bullets from three snipers while traveling with her trucker husband on U.S. 82. The White House and the ICC played down the effect of the shutdown, but by the twentieth, over 75,000 trucks—fully 60% of the long-haul rigs operated by independents—were off the roads. Iowa Governor Ray proclaimed a "disaster emergency" because truckers in his state had virtually shut down pipeline terminals. Next, he ordered a temporary lift of the weight limits "to restore shipment of petroleum products." By midweek, supermarkets in Washington and other areas were reporting scarce supplies of some items—Florida shrimp and Wisconsin cheese—and predicting shortages of meat and other staples if the shutdown continued much longer.

Using their CBs to form almost military formations to seal off terminals and to create traffic tie-ups, independents in New York and New England staged hit-and-run blockades. A 40-truck convoy on New York's Long Island Expressway backed up rush-hour traffic for 30 miles. In Pennsylvania, state troopers called in wreckers to haul away a deliberate bottleneck on I-80. At Levittown, at the eastern end of the Pennsylvania Turnpike, 30 independents seized the Five Points intersection. The party turned ugly and two nights of violence followed (dubbed "the nation's first full-fledged energy riot" by *Newsweek* the following week). In California, farmers plowed under fields of rotting lettuce, and in Florida and Georgia, fruit was spoiling to the tune of $4 million a day. A New York state official announced the cost of feeding a family of four rose 1.07% in one week because of the shutdown. Layoffs in meat-packing houses began—in Iowa, 1,500 workers were laid off in one week—and only a third of the usual herds reached Nebraska feedlots. Washington scurried to give truckers some of the things they wanted, suspending the farmers' first call on diesel, which President Carter had enacted four months earlier, and asking the iron curtain states to raise the weight limits. Almost two years after he first said he would, Carter produced a trucking deregulation proposal. "I consider this legislation to be one of the most important proposals that I have ever made to the Congress," the president said.

The anger was far from spent, however; gunmen in cars without license plates patrolled the Mississippi pinewoods, ordering trucks to turn back. In Illinois, two drivers were injured after the tires of their trucks were blown out by gunfire. On I-59 in Alabama, Robert Tate's truck ran off the road and jackknifed after a bullet went through the cab and hit him in the leg, severing an artery. Tate bled to death before anyone spotted him. Miraculously, he was to be the only fatality of the shutdown. Teamster President Frank Fitzsimmons asked Carter to fire ICC Chairman O'Neal, and fleet owners piously called for more vigorous FBI action "to keep the highways open," while, behind the scenes, rooting for the independents to win their demands. In Washington, Vice-President Mondale pleaded with some of the leaders in revolt "to get the country moving again," but Bill Hill said he could do little to change truckers' plans to stay shut down. A delegation of shirt-sleeved drivers met with a presidential adviser in the elegant Roosevelt Room, and when O'Neal authorized a 7% surcharge on all freight to help truckers meet the soaring fuel costs, the independents' ranks fell apart. Parkhurst and the ITA wanted to hold out for at least a 10% pass-through surcharge, a rollback of the 55-mph speed limit on interstate highways, and complete equality for independent truckers, but Hill, Carlucci, and others pronounced themselves satisfied and ready to go back to work. The pattern of random violence continued for another week, with arson and sniping incidents, and when it was all over, freight rates had doubled—from $2,400 to 5,400 a trailerload on the California-to-Boston run—and the inflation rate had gone up 1.5%.

The shutdown got attention. Hill appeared on the "Today" show and newsmen swarmed around blockaded terminals and truckstops, pens and cameras poised. *Newsweek* quoted reefer driver Ed Carpenter as saying produce haulers were especially under the gun with the 55-mph speed limit, that Congress should allow them to go 65 mph because that would reduce a coast-to-coast run by 12 hours. "If we don't make our destination on time," Carpenter explained, "they don't take the load. It happens every day. That's why them boys got the hammer down. They'd got to get there."

What else? the reporters asked. Well, we want a single national license plate and permission to drive in the fastest left lane on interstates. What else? Carefully, the truckers explained they wanted a uniform 80,000-lbs.–60-ft. limit so as to avoid "loading to meet the lowest iron curtain denominator."

The newsmen wanted to know what the iron curtain was. Sometimes it worked. Iowa's Ray wasn't the only governor who suddenly saw the wisdom of the 80,000-lbs.–60-ft. standard. After 100 independents blocked a truckstop for a weekend in Southington, the Connecticut Transportation Commission agreed there might be some merit to the truckers' beefs. "We're in a crisis situation," Arthur Powers said, "and we're going to do everything we can to alleviate it." What Powers didn't say was that a month earlier, the Connecticut General Assembly had, on his department's recommendation, rejected an increase in the 73,000-pound weight limit.

On weight and size, President Carter jawboned the iron curtain states and managed to extort a lifting of the lower limits "during a declared fuel emergency." Besides Iowa and Connecticut, the states of Missouri, Tennessee, and Maryland approved a temporary 80,000-pound measure, while the House Ways and Means Committee conducted hearings on higher weights. On the House floor, Representative Marty Russo said the government can review road damage, if any, at a "distant date to see how the roads are holding up." A year later, Missouri and Tennessee quietly slipped back to their old 73,000-lbs.–52-ft. maximums, but in 1980, the iron curtain was down to six states—Mississippi, Missouri, Arkansas, Tennessee, Illinois, and Indiana—while a total of 18 states didn't allow 65-foot twin trailer combinations.

Twin trailers, or "doubles," are the most energy-efficient mode of freight haulage. A tractor pulling two 26–28-foot trailers, with an overall length of 65 feet, makes an even better showing in fuel-use tests than "piggyback" trains—trailers on railway flatbeds widely touted as the ideal hybrid of road and rail transportation. A 1975 DOT study found that twin trailers used less fuel than other modes in a test run between Portland, Oregon, and Los Angeles, comparing fuel consumed in loading, transfer, pickup and delivery, as well as that used in making the 950-mile run. As a result, the Federal Highway Administration, the Departments of Energy and Agriculture and the American Association of State Highway and Transportation Officials have endorsed the nationwide use of 65-foot twins. Doubles, however, are either verboten or permitted in a bewildering checkerboard of eastern states: no in Alabama, yes in Georgia, but no again in South Carolina and Tennessee; yes in New York and New Jersey, Maryland, and Delaware, but no in Pennsylvania and all of New England. On the other hand, "triples"—a tractor pulling a semitrailer and two trailers, and carrying a gross weight of as much as 105,000 lbs—can run in Arkansas and 10 western states.

The iron curtain clanged to its death on New Year's Day, 1982, when Indiana's new 80,000-lbs.–60-ft. law went into effect. A month earlier, Mississippi—over the objections of its three elected highway commissioners—had raised its weight limits on the interstates to 80,000, and in September, 1981, Missouri had gone to 80,000. That left Illinois and Arkansas as the last states with maximum gross weight at 73,280 pounds.

Do the two holdouts have a point? While there are 25 states that allow gross weight limits in excess of 80,000 pounds, there are 18 states, mainly in the West, that allow over 100,000 pounds, ranging from 109,000 in Alaska to 101,000 in Wyoming. Also, the 10 Canadian provinces, which have highways and bridges built to essentially the same standards as those in the United States, allow gross weight limits of 110,000 pounds. Eighty thousand pounds translates into 36 metric tons, and in Europe the maximum is generally 38 metric tons, though France, Italy and Denmark allow heavier trucks, and Sweden runs tractor-trailer combinations of up to 52 tons or 114,500 pounds. The Western Highway Institute in the San Francisco suburb of Burlingame has found that larger trucks not only mean greater fuel efficiency, but that tractors pulling multiple units can haul more cargo with less adverse effect on highways and bridges. By distributing weight over more axles, doubles and triples reduce the bending movement on bridges. Also, multi-trailer combinations generally have an excess of brake power because each additional set of axles means an extra set of air brakes. Actually, they can stop on a shorter distance on a wet pavement than conventional trucks and even passenger cars.

The next argument that Illinois and Arkansas come up with is safety. The highway mastodons are simply too dangerous, they argue. Unfortunately, the holdout states don't have lower fatality rates than the rest of the country. In fact, the states allowing gross vehicle weights over 80,000 pounds have better safety records than the former iron curtain sextet.

The last excuse that the Illinois and Arkansas DOTs come up with is that their roads just aren't built for such heavy loads. The real reason, of course, is money. Ticketing overweight truckers helps pay the state DOT salaries. Never mind that loading a coast-to-coast run for the lowest weight limit decreases productivity and fuel efficiency nationwide, and increases transportation costs that are ultimately passed on to the public; the ports-of-entry bureaucrats, with their assorted powers and responsibilities, exert strong influence on state legislatures. In many states these personnel are a branch of the highway patrol.

"Illinois will never go standard," says Chicago-based owner-operator Milton Green. "They may go up to national standards, then back down again to catch truckers and make money. Trucks are where the money is."

This sort of cynicism isn't just widespread, it is the absolute rule on the road. With the exception of the Teamsters, everybody in trucking—carriers, independents, and groups representing shippers—supports the increased uniform weight and length standards. The Brotherhood of Teamsters is against it because larger trucks will mean greater loads and greater loads will mean fewer drivers, but there are other opponents outside of the trucking industry. The American Automobile Associations, representing over 20 million motorists, are constantly attacking trucking, and the Association of American Railroads has always been against *anything* that benefits road haulage.

The only rational solution would be for the federal government to preempt the whole issue. In 1981, Nevada Senator Howard W. Cannon introduced legislation that would take care of at least half of the mess. When the Democrats controlled the Senate, Cannon was the Commerce Committee chairman (and according to a grand jury indictment, the object of an unsuccessful Teamster bribery attempt to sidetrack deregulation). His 1981 bill would set nationwide size and length standards, but *not* weight standards. It would cover all trucks using interstates and designated federal highways. It would make 65 feet the standard and forbid states from banning twin-trailers or denying them reasonable off-highway access to such things as repairs, rest, fuel, and food. The conflicting state regulations, said Cannon in introducing his bill, "are very costly in wasted fuel and place an undue burden on interstate commerce."

It's either that or a lot more trucks. The federal government has calculated that by 1995, the amount of goods needed by the American public will double. This means that trucks will either start carrying larger loads, or there will have to be a lot more of them on the highways.

8
LEARNING HOW

They switched over at 2:00 A.M. Karen wasn't so sure she'd get the hang of this dephasing business. She'd been dropping off for a while, been awake for a while, then dropped off again. The sleeper compartment was hotter than the front. The bunk air vents opened directly to the outside, and to keep the sleeper halfway quiet she had had to close them.

They were halfway across Kansas, at a rest area 80 miles west of Salina, Junior told her.

It was cold when she got down and ran to the rest rooms. She just couldn't get used to peeing in his Port-a-Potty in the back. Besides, she wanted to stretch and to splash water in her face in the ladies' room. Climbing back into the driver's seat five minutes later, she turned up the heat. Junior was sitting in the jump seat smoking one of his slim cigars.

"I thought you told me to hit the bunk immediately, that any drowsiness built up from the driving shift can be put to good use now."

"I said that?" he asked with mock incredulity.

She swallowed a gulp of lukewarm coffee. "You said it's no use running a sleeper team if we're both tired at the same time."

"I know," he said seriously. "I just gotta wind down."

She pulled out. "Anyway, no need to continue to St. Louis?"

"Nope."

She had hoped he might want to run into St. Louis and check one more time with his broker. "So I stay on till Salina, then head south on I-135 to Wichita, than I-35 on straight south through Oklahoma City, Dallas . . ."

"Let's hope I wake up before Dallas," he interrupted.

She had never been this far east, but she had looked up the itinerary on his Rand McNally and memorized the route.

"Two plus six means I wake you up around eight o'clock."

"Executive hours, practically."

She gunned up through five gears. The cab was comfy and she watched the reflections of his cigarillo glow in the windshield and the passing flatland. She felt he didn't want to talk, which was fine with her. She was beginning to like the silence between them. She kicked up to the highest gear and remembered Pat Timmins teaching her to get the vehicle speed to coincide with revolutions-per-minute, or rpm. She remembered the first time she had driven a truck, John egging her on for fun. There was just too much truck to steer! Just knowing *where* the truck was on the road was a feat.

John had borrowed the truck at the garage where he worked on and off, and they had gone up Cowiche Mountain to screw in the cab. It was so nice and quiet up there, and the drizzle and night breeze wafted smells of pine cones into the cab. She liked to place her hands on the steering wheel, her feet on the pedals. One night he let her sit on his lap and steer as he drove down to Yakima, but she wanted to experience the feeling of moving the thing by herself. The next time, she had done it, with him glued next to her and shouting, "Attaboy, girl!" He had shown her how to hold the truck in lane, how to check the big mirrors to estimate where the edges were on both sides. He had taught her the little trick of keeping an eye on the bottom left corner of the windshield to mark the spot where the dividing white line ran away under you. If the truck drifted, the white line moved from its place in the windshield corner. After Melissa was born, after John had left her the first time and she had been fired from the office job, she had plunked down her entire severance pay—minus babysitting money for Marianne Adams—at Mountain Trucking School. A truck, she knew, was something she could handle.

The instructor was Patricia Timmins, a transplanted Texan who talked like Junior and was the mother of four and grandmother of one. "Honey, I've had girls come in here say-ing they're going to drive with their husbands and don't want to learn about shiftin' and holdin' a truck in lane." Karen assured her that she was serious and the instructor ended the interview by saying, "You'll be washed out by next Thursday or you'll stay on and become employable. But in either case we don't refund."

At the front office, Karen became an "enrollee" and was told that at Mountain Trucking School, future drivers of America trained on a variety of diesel equipment in four weeks' days or six weeks' evenings, with free job placement assistance for those who passed the Washington Department of Motor Vehicles Class A test. Karen took days because Mari-anne Adams had a new boyfriend and wanted Karen to baby-sit *her* kids most evenings. There were 10 in her class: herself, 6 guys on unemployment, plus an Exxon mechanic named Ron, a former army MP named Morgan Kessel, and Ray Olson, a minister whose congregation was shrinking, he said, because of fundamentalist inroads in mainline religion. After one week, one of the unemployed dropped out. The rest of them got through the classroom battle with a 13-speed trans-mission and were out driving a 1974 Kenworth around painted oil drums in the vacant lot behind the school. The Kenworth was the only tractor-trailer they ever saw, and when Pat Timmins was called to the phone once, Reverend Olson wondered aloud whether Mountain's claim that its student drivers trained on a variety of equipment wasn't deceptive advertising. Morgan said they shouldn't complain. He'd been ripped off by a trucking school in Newark, Delaware, offering a correspondence course that consisted of 30 home-study lessons but guaranteed a job after graduation. Maybe they were lucky.

To qualify for highway driving, they needed 60 points on Pat Timmins' score sheet. Several of the boys made it easily, but after two days of "doing the barrels," Karen's highest score remained 57 points. Pat spent extra time with her and post-poned night driving until she had caught up. "Hon, what counts is consistency—like with men." Then came a series of backing exercises: backing straight back between the oil drums, alley docking, jackknife parking at 90 degrees from your start-out line, and—horror of horrors—blind jackknife back to your *left*.

"There's more than pride involved here, reverend," Pat Timmins said, flunking him for two days in a row. Backing gave Karen fits at first. She thought she'd never get the Kenworth to get around the barrels backwards.

But two days later, she was in the Kenworth out on the highway for the first time, with Pat in the jump seat and Reverend Olson squeezed in the back. Pat was teaching them downshifting—getting the truck speed to coincide with the engine rpm. When it was Olson's turn, the teacher had him slow down to 10 mph, make a 90-degree turn onto the training field, rev up and skip into third gear. "Like an eel squirmin' through a jar of Vaseline," Pat complimented. Olson beamed. Pat lectured on defensive driving and gave them periodic quizzes, which didn't count for points but did motivate them to study harder.

"A real trucker would rather own his 18-wheeler than a house," Pat said. "You can always buy the house later, when you retire." She had all sorts of stories about students who had made good, guys who had bought gleaming rigs, gorgeous trucks, magic beasts with vertical grilles and steps as high as your shoulder, Freightliners that made your eyes pop wide open and chrome so shining you could shave in front of it, customized Kenworths in full war paint, Peterbilts with cabins so beautiful you want to wash your hands and wipe your feet before climbing aboard. "Independents have the most beautiful trucks, naturally. Who has ever heard of anyone falling in love with the boss's rig?"

Karen studied at night after she put Tim and Melissa and Marianne's two kids to bed. Pat knew how to motivate her students. "If you think of an 18-wheeler as a five-axled truck, a way of moving freight, you just don't understand," she'd say. She had seen all kinds.

"I've comforted mamas who said Junior would turn into a juvenile delinquent if I didn't enroll him, and others who felt I was stealin' their Baby-Boy by admitting him. I've been asked to falsify a DOT certificate, train a friend's son for free, and act as matchmaker for an assortment of both male and female prospectives." She had had prospective students who slammed down the phone when told they wouldn't be paid while they learned, prospectives who proposed marriage to her, and prospectives who worried more about their CB nickname than their backing test scores. "A 'handle' is something very personal, very intimate, but how many Gypsys are out there?" she asked, grimacing. "How many Highway Hobos, Tennessee Travelers and Geargrinders, and among the ladies, Mini Semi and Ramblin' Lady? Karen Long, don't disappoint us. Don't call yourself Evergreen Roadrunner or Washington Hiphugger." When they got to talking about foul language, Pat Timmins said she didn't appreciate truly foulmouthed sickies—and there were some tanker drivers around Brownsville where she came from who were. But she wasn't fond of bleeding hearts, either, "who come off like they never scratch where it itches."

She called her best students "naturals"—both in attitude and aptitude—"like the dog on the Mack truck." Naturals got jobs easily and were a blessing for a hardworking instructor. Anybody who wasn't working after the course was an ex-grad. Ex-grad's weren't much.

The first thing she told us was that trucks are divided into eight classes. Class 1 is small trucks under 6,000 pounds, Class 2 trucks weigh between 6,000 and 10,000 pounds. These two classes include pickups, vans, and light four-wheel vehicles. Classes 3 through 7 are the medium-sized trucks weighing between 10,001 and 30,000 pounds, usually gasoline driven, although diesel engines are muscling in. Pat Timmins only glowed when they came to the top end of the classes, everything above 33,000 pounds. The total weight of a Class 8 is generally around 80,000 pounds. "The DOT deals in numbers, not in beauty, but Class 8 is beauty," Pat lectured.

The DOT suggested that truck-driving courses last six weeks, or 240 hours of instruction, half of which should be spent driving in all road and traffic conditions. Pat was convinced it was only a matter of time before there would be federal training requirements, and people would have to be certified to drive a rig in interstate commerce.

Pat Timmins pronounced Ron, the Exxon mechanic, a natural. She never called Karen a natural, but worked with her a little more than with the boys.

After school one night, Karen, Ron, and the reverend reconnoitered the downtown route they'd take to qualify. Karen and Ron went for a beer at Ballentine's afterwards. It was the last week before graduation and the Washington Department of Motor Vehicles test, and Karen was still practicing the horrible backward serpentine and having to do half a dozen pull-ups from alley docks. Once, in the serpentine, her trailer kicked too far left. She stopped, almost in tears, then turned the wheel left, backed and, in the mirror, saw the trailer head straight back into the docking. "You're getting there, hon." Pat smiled. The next day, Karen handled the serpentine with only one pull-up and one "out-of-position."

John showed up the night before the graduation road test. He brought $100 and played with Tim while whispering to her that he sure was horny. Tim told his father Mom was going to trucking school and John became prying, suspicious. She wanted to throw it in his face that it wasn't 100 bucks every five, six weeks that kept a roof over his children's heads, but she didn't want him to think he'd get off the hook if she started earning good money as a trucker, so she said as little as possible. She let him have her after she put Tim to bed—to get it over with. For some reason, sex after all these weeks drained her of her confidence and lying there in the darkness at nine o'clock, she had her first anxiety attack. Thank God she had at least stayed on the pill. Getting pregnant was all she needed. She wanted to be rested for the crucial day, but finally got up and sat studying for the written test half the night in the kitchen. She concentrated on the taxes, licensing, and permits chapter.

In the morning, John said he was going back to Portland, "to sort out his life." She didn't know what to say, and before he had left, she hurried downtown to meet Pat Timmins and her classmates for a pretest trial before the road test. Pat threw them a curve, saying she didn't want them to be too familiar with the turns and route they'd be testing on. She had had the school staff "plant" 10 deficiencies along an alternate route. As they rode around in the pretest trial, Karen was able to identify five of the deficiencies and her self-assurance began to come back. Then it was on to the huge Department of Motor Vehicles parking lot.

To earn the Class A permit you had to score 200 points. On the test, Karen got a 300-pound examiner, who climbed up in the jump seat of the Kenworth with amazing speed. She raked too many gears and was less than brilliant on coupling and uncoupling the trailer, but she scored 122 on the examiner's sheet, against a class average of 118 points, and Reverend Olson's 112 points. Tomorrow came the final written test of 199 questions. Two hundred minus 122 meant only 78 points separated her from the Class A permit.

John was still there when she got home, and for the first time, she wished he'd just leave. He did, after dinner and after she'd given him back a $20 bill "for gas." Tim cried and Melissa cried because she saw Tim cry. Karen put them to bed and read Tim his favorite Miss Piggy story. "You're my man now," she whispered as he fell asleep with a sniffle and a long, unhappy sigh. She wanted to call her mother in Seattle, but was afraid she'd begin to explain a lot of things, and she couldn't afford the phone as it was. Instead, she locked the doors and took a hot bath, telling herself she was 23 years old and that she'd better rack up those 78 points tomorrow because . . . because there was no other way. She went to bed with the *Truckers Manual*, but fell asleep after five minutes and didn't wake up until Tim hopped on the bed at seven.

She was wrong on 20 questions only, and scored a grand total of 301. To everybody's astonishment, Ron failed the written test. The fat examiner, however, pronounced Ron "still alive" if he'd take the test again the next morning. Morgan was the valedictorian. The graduation party was at Ballentine's. It started out a little subdued because of Ron, but most of the boys brought their wives and girl friends. They had invited Pat Timmins and she showed up in a black vest over a silk shirt, designer jeans, and Tony Lama boots. Karen had a margarita too many and suddenly hit on a handle for herself—Sweet Pickle. They all liked that and Karen sat back feeling good at the satisfaction on their faces. The girls were proud of their guys, who joked about doing the barrels in their present condition. Pat pronounced them "truckers from the word Kenworth," and told them not to become strangers. "Come by in your rigs and tell me about openings in your companies, about what the boss will accept. You too, hon, you come by if you have any problems. If nothing else, you're the prettiest boll weevil in the class."

9
RIGS

Chuck Carlton, Jr., ran a pretty classy power unit. Like other owner-operators with enough moxie, money, and a hefty line of credit, he had "spec'ed" his current tractor with loving care, not bought it off some showroom floor. He had started with a 1980 Peterbilt COE (cab-over-engine), with a nice wide 240-inch wheelbase, and an all-aluminum frame to cut weight and lower cost-per-miles. He had ordered a Cummins KTA engine, boosted to 600 horsepower, a Horton clutch fan, Spicer integral (beltless) power steering, Southwind engine preheat, spin-on primary and secondary fuel filters, Kenworth ether starting system, Kysor automatic engine shutdown for low oil pressure and high water temperatures, RTO transmission with temperature gauge, Rockwell 12,000-pounds front axle, Robertshaw low-coolant and oil-level warning system and a pair of 1,000-liter fuel tanks. If he could justify it to himself, there wasn't any extra goody he wouldn't install, whether it was the sleeper-controlled heat and air conditioner, the Air Glides suspension, the pair of Naugahyde Cush-N-Air high-backs, or—the final touch—pinstriping on the cab by Pacific West Painting in Maywood, California. If you didn't count the 1976 Kenworth W 900 he had sold for a nice price to a bedbug hauler leased to United Van Lines, the bottom line (before financing) was just a shade under 100 grand.

He hated to look like a Christmas tree and had gone easy on running lights, but since he had bought the new Pete, he had added a superheterodyne fuzzbuster, which offered the ultimate in detecting police radar over hills and around bends. Last year, he had been a sucker for one of those ion generators you clip on the sun visor to blow negative ions in your face to overcome fatigue. A hundred and fifty bucks for nothing. But independents were suckers for anything that promised to help them stay awake, drive a little farther, and shave another penny off the cost-per-mile.

Building trucks is a bit like making cars. But only a bit, and the biggest difference is in North America. Here, truck makers work hand-in-glove with their customers, one-truck owner-operators as well as big fleet owners, who all demand the highest engineering and operating standards. The customer dictates how the tractor should be designed and built. He is meddlesome and difficult, but for the manufacturer the payoff is priceless. The operating experience, worth millions of miles of road testing, quickly gets absorbed into the models. The manufacturers actively encourage this feedback. (During most of 1980, the engine division of Caterpillar sponsored a heavy-duty fuel-consumption contest called the Cat Economy Challenge to test out its newest fuel-efficient engine line on drivers and owners.)

Everything starts with the chassis, usually made of steel beams, but what's added, from the engine and gearbox to axles and suspension, can come from the outside suppliers. Practically all American truck makers are "horizontally integrated"—that is, they are assemblers, not manufacturers in the true sense, and the finished product is personalized way beyond the chrome and paint job. An American Class B long-distance rig belongs to a company or a man. European and Japanese truck manufacturers tend to be "vertically integrated," making their own gearboxes, axles, and even engines. You buy a European or Japanese truck off the shelf.

European and Japanese makers such as Daimler-Benz, Volvo, Iveco, and Toyota have found the export road to the United States strewn with punctured egos, as one by one they have failed to appreciate both the pride and demands of 130,000-miles-a-year independents and the punishing extremes of distance and climate in America. They have sold trucks in the Class 6 and 7 categories (9 to 15 metric tons) with their fuel-efficient diesels, but their only entry at the top of the heavy-duty line has been through the back door, by teaming up with, or buying into, American firms: Renault with Mack Trucks, Volvo first with Freightliner and finally buying up the faltering White Motor Company.

The overcapacity in truck making is worldwide, but it is especially acute in Europe, where tradition and national jealousies have prevented mergers, or even the development of standardized components that would mesh into any Fiat, Berliet, Daimler-Benz, or DAF truck. Excess capacity also exists in the United States, although American manufacturers have already gone through the merger and shakedown process. "We estimate that American heavy-duty truck manufacturers have the capacity to build between 250,000 to 260,000 Class 8 trucks annually," says John Hanrahan of International Harvester's heavy-duty marketing and products. "Yet in the best year, we only sell 160,000 heavy-duty units. So we are operating with an excess capacity in North America."

There were nearly 40 truckmakers in North America in 1950. In the mid-1950s, there were 10. Now, there are 3 giants —tottering International Harvester, which also makes farm and construction machinery, Ford, and General Motors (through its GMC subsidiary); three specialists—Paccar (Peterbilt and Kenworth), Mack, and Freightliner; plus tiny Marmon. IH, Ford, GMC, and Mack are traditional "Smokestack America" manufacturers from Toledo, Ohio (IH), Detroit, Michigan (Ford and GMC), and Allentown, Pennsylvania (Mack). Paccar and Freightliner are West Coast upstarts (Freightliner has always been somebody's subsidiary) and pintsized Marmon is a Texas company.

White Motor Corporation threw in the towel in 1980 and filed for Chapter 11 bankruptcy. A year later, it sold its Canadian operations, then finally gave up completely, selling its manufacturing plants in Farmington Hills, Michigan; Dublin, Virginia; Ogden, Utah; and Orville, Ohio, plus its parts and branch distribution networks to AB Volvo. The Swedish automaker (and Scandinavia's biggest trading-industrial group with annual revenue of over $10 billion) plans to continue making White trucks in Class 8.

Peterbilts come into the world at the bottom of San Francisco Bay, in Newark, across from Palo Alto. Kenworths are born in Seattle. Depending on whether you talk to a Peterbilt or a Kenworth owner, a Pete is either the Mercedes-Benz or the Rolls Royce of Class 8 truckdom, or a Ken is both of these things. The two are rivals in horsepower and reputation, and Paccar keeps the Bay Area and the Seattle halves separate and competitive.

There actually was a Mr. Al Peterman. He was a wealthy lumber-mill owner in Tacoma, Washington. Dissatisfied with the logging rigs on the market, he bought the Fageol Truck and Coach Company in Oakland and renamed it Peterbilt. The year was 1939, the same year Freightliner went into business in Salt Lake City. Peterman wanted heavy machinery to haul logs from the Rockies to his sawmills, and he skillfully applied Fageol's know-how in buses and mid-sized trucks to build the brute leviathans he wanted. After World War II, Peterbilt introduced the cabover, and by the 1960s began building them of aluminum. In 1958, the company was bought by Paccar, headquartered in Bellevue, Washington, but the Peterbilt has remained the king of the road—majestic, all-powerful, and just as extravagant, a combination of computer science and battleship engineering. They are built to climb a thousand uphill miles, to cross the Rockies and bake for days in the blistering desert. The beauty of a Pete lies in the simplicity of its lines and its massive body. There is an assembly line at Peterbilt's, but each truck is specifically built to meet the needs of the buyer. A trucker's ultimate wet dream is to order a Peter 362 with all the options, and then fly to San Francisco and pick it up.

Kenworth is its own legend. It is also the most expensive truck. The Kenworth Truck Company was established in 1916. Until 1923, it was called Gersix because of its six-cylinder trucks that could carry loads up to 6,000 pounds, and sold for $4,000—double the price of a Mack. During the 1920s, production expanded as rapidly as the size of the trucks, to 10,000, 20,000, and on the eve of World War II, 35,000 pounds. In the sixties, Kenworth launched the baked-paint-and-chrome era and made innovations in suspension systems that are still state-of-the-art. Peterbilt and Kenworth are lean, nimble, and virtually independent assemblers, each building its own models for its customers, but sharing the combined muscle power of the Paccar management, especially when it comes to negotiating component prices with suppliers and continuing to compete with International Harvester and Ford. Paccar is the opposite of such clumsy, politically motivated European mergers as Iveco—the German-Italian combine of Fiat, Magirus-Deutz, Lancia, and Unic.

Mack has been in business since 1900 when four New York brothers started to build buses. In 1905, the Mack Brothers Motor Car Company moved 80 miles from Manhattan to Allentown and quickly expanded their production. During World War I, they built a four-cylinder truck with a high cab and a snub nose for the U.S. Army. When British troops first saw it behind the Flanders battlefields in 1917, they nicknamed it the Bulldog. The name stuck and eventually became the company emblem. In 1953, Mack was the first American truck maker to build its own diesel engines with an optional turbocharger. The Maxidyne series was met with considerable skepticism, but with the energy crisis and the sudden premium put on fuel savings, other manufacturers followed Mack's lead and introduced engines "governed" at lower rpms for impressive fuel-cost reductions.

Freightliner struggled for 40 years, almost went out of business during World War II, had one hit, and recently ended up as a subsidiary of Daimler-Benz. Like Peterman's Peterbilt, Freightliner grew out of a special need. In the 1930s, Consolidated Freightways of San Francisco was a conglomerate of six western carriers, and it needed a lightweight cabover. It tried to get one of the established manufacturers to build such a truck and when nobody would, CF set up its own factory in Salt Lake City and began assembling an aluminum cabover tractor that it called the Freightliner. The plant was moved to Portland, Oregon, and when CF's capacity for Freightliners had caught up with its needs, it began selling the extra trucks to independents under long-term leases. Eventually, anybody could buy a Freightliner.

An often forgotten fact is that manufacturers don't simply sell trucks; they have to sell a complete service (cars are sold like washing machines, goes the saying, trucks like machine tools). To get marketing organization and dealerships, Freight-liner formed a loose partnership with White Motor in 1951. Over the years, however, Freightliner sales surpassed sales of White tractors and White's long decline began. In 1975, CF terminated the agreement. In 1979, the year of the energy revolt, Freightliner came out with the FLC 1200 series that was one ton lighter than any other Class 8 power unit. Freight-liner dubbed it the Efficient Machine and made 1979 its record year. With the economic downturn, sales in 1980 plunged 25%, however, and Consolidated Freightways tried a merger with White before throwing in the towel and selling out to the big Stuttgart automaker. Daimler-Benz makes Mer-cedes-Benzes, but it is also the world's biggest truck producer. At home, Daimler is strapped with the world's most expensive labor force, and the company has both ruthlessly automated and moved abroad. It makes cars and trucks in Argentina, Brazil, India, Iran, Spain, South Africa, and Turkey and has opened an assembly plant in Virginia to assemble up to 6,000 Class 6 and 7 trucks a year from parts shipped in from its Brazilian works. Experts give Daimler the best chance of any multinational truckmaker to crack the North American market.

There is one more independent assembler of tractors—Marmon. In 1931, Marmon Harrington began building trucks in Indianapolis, and although the company has moved to Dal-las, it still brings out some 300 Marathon and Marauder models a year, big, sturdy, squared-off machines that are often the choice of nostalgic truckers in love with tradition. There is no assembly line at Marmon's; everything is done piecemeal and by hand. The company also earns a living modifying other manufacturers' trucks for off-road use in the construc-tion industry. The Marathon cabover has a flat windshield and is nicknamed the Priest.

If Marmons are a rare sight, International Harvester's Transtar is the most frequently seen rig on the road. The Transtar doesn't have the impressive lines of the Petes and Kens, but behind it is the power of a big truck maker and a network of dealers and service centers so dense it could handle every other brand produced in North America. The

Transtar and the top-of-the-line Eagle have looks that don't exactly make the asphalt melt and, say a lot of owner-operators, if IH trucks often look beat up and poorly maintained, it's because they lack the savage splendor of the western-style rigs. (To this, IH owners answer that company equipment is often driven by several drivers and that it's the companies that don't take pride in their trucks.) Independents are not big fans of IH trucks, but fleet owners love International Harvester, which tells fleet owners its equipment delivers the maximum load for the minimum pay-out. The International LX series, totally new from the ground up, was introduced in 1980. It incorporates all the latest energy-saving advances in truck engineering, from aerodynamic shapes to lightweight all-aluminum cab design.

In recent years, labor problems, plunging markets, and soaring interest rates on International Harvester's mounds of debts have brought the company to the wall. A $4.9-billion restructuring by 225 banks was worked out, but the terms were stiff. Until 1985, IH will essentially work for the banks and forego any capital spending needs—estimated to total $500 million a year if the company is to keep up with the competition. Harvester's lenders were so tough because they were anxious to avoid the problems they ran into with their loans to White Motors; but Wall Street analysts wonder whether the bank noose isn't so tight that IH's leadership in Class 8 trucks might erode, especially since the banks also imposed restriction on Harvester's captive credit subsidiary, which had allowed smaller carriers to finance their IH truck buys with IH. In August 1981, the company laid off 2,000 of its 30,000 North American employees, and announced that its losses that year had exceeded half a billion. The company lurched from crisis to crisis, publicly playing down the seriousness of each setback and forecasting recovery just around the corner. It asked Ohio and Indiana for state assistance to help keep two truck plants open, asked its suppliers to freeze prices and the United Auto Workers for wage concessions. "The odds on their avoiding bankruptcy are pretty slim," Larry Hollis, a Milwaukee analyst said. "It just depends on what the threshold of pain is for the banks."

Henry Ford began making a utility version of the Model T in 1905, but it wasn't until 1960 that the Ford Company plunged into the heavy-duty market. To make a splash, Ford offered a 100,000-mile warranty (the first of its kind among Class 8s) on its H series that year. During the next 20 years, Ford continued its successful attack on the heavy-truck market, bringing out an L series and giving round numbers to its successive editions: the 900, the 8000, and the 9000 series. Its newest is a conventional, or "long nose" model, the LTL 9000, with a hood long enough to accommodate the large diesel engines needed for its 44,000–60,000-pound gross weight ratings. This tractor can haul 154,000 pounds of freight. Behind the success of the 9000 series is a story of top-notch R and D and a revolutionary suspension system. Ford makes more trucks than any other company in the U.S., although in the Class 8 category, it ranks behind IH and Mack.

GMC is fourth (Chrysler dropped out of the Class 8 market in 1979) with its Astro and General series, well-designed trucks that can compete in price and power with any of them. The front of an Astro is unmistakable. Its two characteristics are an enormous windshield and air intakes in, of all places, the bumper. GM was the first truck maker to realize the importance of air drag and to study the phenomenon in a wind tunnel. It was also the first to pour lots of money into fuel-economy research.

General Motors is also Detroit Diesel Allison, and much of the R and D money has been spent here to allow truckers to carry heavier loads, to enjoy longer replacement cycles, and to reduce downtime. The economics of the engine is crucial and IH, Caterpillar, and Cummins have remained fiercely competitive.

A diesel engine, costing $13,000 or more, may be a quarter of a tractor's price. For years, Cummins Engine Company of Columbus, Indiana, has been the leading supplier of Class 8 diesel engines, and half the new heavy-duty rigs sold today are powered by Cummins engines. To stay ahead, Cummins' expansion plans require $500 million in outside financing, and the venture is fraught with risks. Earnings records have been volatile. Caterpillar engines, called Cats, have an unmistakable sound, crude and metallic, and at night Cat owners pulling into a truckstop will sometimes keep their engines idling for a while to let the other guys in their sleepers know a pro has rolled onto the lot. Caterpillar's 3408 engine delivers 450 horsepower and 2,100 revolutions per minute. It can't pass California pollution emission tests, and Golden State honchos have to have it installed out-of-state.

Cummins makes the largest of them all, a 600 hp, 2,100 rpm monster, also verboten in California, that weighs 3,590 pounds and is called the KTA 600. Like most new engines, the KTA series is turbocharged, which means the exhaust gases are compressed with air and forced back into the cylinder heads, increasing engine compression. At certain speeds, a turbocharged engine can deliver 20 to 40% more power for the same amount of fuel. Mack has been in the forefront of shedding weight, dropping 600 pounds from its 350-horsepower turbocharger engine, and since the fantastic run-ups in fuel costs in the late 1970s, the entire industry has been on a weight-loss binge.

Every penny counts. A trucker typically gets 4.5 miles to the gallon on his rig. If he drives 130,000 miles a year, he uses almost 29,000 gallons. At $1.30 a gallon, that's $37,700. At $1.29, it's $37,410. If he always tanks up where diesel is sold one penny cheaper, he will be nearly $300 richer at the end of the year. Changes in his driving habits alone make for dramatic savings. Easy starts that let the engine do its work in its own time, progressive shifting and keeping the engine speed at manufacturers' recommended rpm when cruising, instead of full-bore jackrabbit starts and general hotdogging, can reduce costs by 10%, saving our 130,000-miles-a-year trucker $3,700 annually.

A fully loaded truck, traveling at normal speed, uses half its engine's horsepower to push air out of its way. Moving it at 60 mph is like shoving a 13-by-8-foot brick wall down the road. Add a little head wind and you have a major consumer of horsepower. Air deflectors, fairings and gap sealers, plus nose cones for the trailer, all help carry the airflow away from the flat faces and around the whole rig, achieving a 20% reduction in fuel consumption and saving another $7,400 a year. The newest diesel engines provide an average of 8% better fuel economy, knocking 2,250 gallons off the 29,000 annual gallons, and saving $2,900. Radial tires cost about $138 each, or, for a 10-wheel tractor, $1,380, but they are amortized in less than six months through reduced fuel consumption, adding $1,180 to the yearly savings. Frequent tune-ups that keep the engine crisp and performing properly shave off other pennies. With the exception of the engine, most of the fuel-saving components pay for themselves in one year or less. If our trucker drove the same 130,000 miles a year and paid $1.29 a gallon, his savings would be $12,230, or, over the five-year "life" of his rig, $61,150.

Rockwell International, Eaton, Fuller, and Spicer furnish axles and infinite gear ratios, and make gearboxes of every kind. (Eaton's newest off-on fan clutches alone provide 10% fuel savings.) Idling costs fuel, but few truckers are willing to shut down in the winter and crawl back in the sleeper at 10 below for eight hours. The newest "add on" is therefore auxiliary generators, which allow the engine to be shut down, but still operate cab heaters or air conditioners, heater blocks, TVs, microwaves, refrigerators, stereos, and power tools during layovers. An idling engine guzzles around a half gallon of diesel an hour; an "aux" averages a pint an hour.

Cost-per-mile stress and peer pressure are turning independents into spec experts, and word of mouth is traded thick and fast over the CBs and the coffee cups. "Keep her wound up tight, cruise at 1,900 (rpm), don't let the engine lug down," says one guy. "Listen," says another, "My new Mack is 'governed' at 1,800 and Caterpillar just came out with one governed at 1,600." "Yep, a lot of guys are gonna have mental problems chugging along at 1,600." "Goddamn engine's gonna melt down at those low rpms." "No it ain't. You just need some reeducation, buddy."

Because practically all truck makers in North America are assemblers, component suppliers enjoy steady growth and the benefits of enough high-tech R and D to challenge the world. All European truck makers, even lofty Daimler-Benz, now offer Eaton's range of gearboxes and the economical new Cummins engines, and Rockwell and Eaton are really beginning to bite into the international axle business.

One hundred million people are directly employed in highway passenger and freight transportation throughout the world. The Geneva-based International Road Transport Union estimates the world fleet of trucks at 85 million, and expects the total to exceed the 100-million mark by the end of the 1990s. The United States, Japan, and Western Europe are the three main markets and manufacturing centers for trucks. In a good year, American truck makers produce close to 4 million trucks and vans of all classes, mostly for domestic use. European manufacturers make 1.5 million and export over half the output, many of them to other European countries. Japan makes a sturdy 3.3 million and exports 80%.

But newly industrialized countries like Brazil, Mexico, Egypt, India, and Nigeria are building their own fledgling truck industries, to stem the outflow of hard currency and to act as a stepping-stone to industrialization. The Soviet bloc is making a belated effort to boost its truck output. The latest Russian Class 8 trucks already resemble European vehicles. Many of the components are copies of Western products and the new Kamaz truck plant on the Kama River northeast of Moscow was built with Western help.

In examining total truck traffic, the International Road Transport Union estimates current world ton-miles at 2.12 trillion. A national breakdown shows the U.S. with 28.8% of the entire world, followed by Russia with 12.3%. Next is Japan with 4.3%, West Germany with 3.4%, and Britain with 3.2%. On a continental level, North and South America have nearly half the world's commercial vehicles. Europe, with Russia included, is second at 24%, followed by Asia, where steady growth has resulted in 22% of the global total. Africa has only 3.1% of all trucks, but it now has the highest growth rate.

Tomorrow's trucks will be increasingly international as manufacturers adopt the American way and share components. At its Warren, Michigan, technology center, General Motors has established a "world truck" group. A cab being designed for a British GM truck should be suitable for an

Argentina GM truck with little modification, even if roads, geography, and service sophistication inevitably determine what sort of trucks a country uses.

More exciting than the world truck is the "million-mile truck" suppliers are working on. Today few trucks can travel 500,000 miles without the need for a major overhaul, but Ruan Transport Corporation, a Des Moines carrier leasing to independents and hauling bulk commodities with its own fleet, has managed to persuade Freightliner, IH and 28 component suppliers to jointly develop a "million-mile" rig. The Ruan Mega costs 20% more than any other truck, but it is expected to last at least 50% longer and significantly reduce maintenance costs. Most of the technology used to make the Mega is either off the shelf or only slightly changed, but competitors agree Ruan is on the right track with a longer-life truck. Other fleets are expected to follow Ruan's lead and seek more cooperation and longer warranties from assemblers and component suppliers.

Larry Shinoda, a designer who has influenced hundreds of designs for White, Ford, and GM before founding Shinoda Design Associates in Livonia, Michigan, thinks consumer demands, government regulations, and technological advances will decide what tomorrow's truck actually looks like. Under the relentless pressure of fuel costs, all manufacturers have cleaned up the drag or air resistance of their models, but, predicts Shinoda, aerodynamic research will force radical styling changes soon.

To help cut fuel costs further, computers are crawling under the hood of heavy-duty diesels. American Bosch, a subsidiary of United Technologies, is building state-of-the-art microprocessor fuel injection controls. The critical factor in diesel engine performance is the fuel injection system, the mechanical device whose cam pushes a plunger that squirts the right amount of fuel into the engine. The Bosch system not only controls the volume of fuel to be pumped, but includes sensors measuring cylinder–air temperature and pressure, exhaust pollutants, and engine speed. The microprocessors constantly use this information to adjust timing and fuel injection and insure the most efficient engine performance possible. The saving to the trucker is 7% of his fuel bill.

Also in for improvement is the driver's environment. The cabover (with the cab over the engine instead of behind it as in conventional, or "long nose" tractors) was invented to shorten the overall length and squeeze more payload through state maximum-length regulations. But in a cabover, the driver sits right on top of the front axle, giving him a bumpier ride. Says Shinoda, "Truck makers are going to have to look at cab suspension, better driving comfort, and ease of maintenance, all the things that would make trucking cheaper and more profitable for the operator." The Ford CL 9000 series has a full air-suspended cab with four air bags, and Mack offers a cab suspension that is hinged at the front and has air suspension at the rear, but the increased weights on the front axle makes steering even harder, compounding the problem. Tremendous strides have been made, however, in the area now called "climate control"; as the built-in heater–air conditioners are available on virtually all trucks, visibility has been improved and noise reduced. Closed-circuit TV, allowing the driver to better see the flanks of the trailer and what is behind him, should be coming soon, together with airline-type containerization, allowing break-bulk shipments and a variety of cargoes on the same vehicle.

Truck engineers agree that the biggest single impact on future cab designs will come when, and if, the federal government preempts the states on size and weight laws. The Department of Transportation has floated the idea that size and weight regulations should only fix the dimension of a truck from the back of the cab to the rear of the trailer. This would free designers from the tight space constraints that have forced them to squeeze tractors and lead to true living space–size sleepers. Says W. W. Edwards, director of GMC's truck and coach engineering, "If we had that freedom, we could make a more competitive truck, provide more room for engine installation; it would give more cab room, more driver comfort, and easier maintenance. At best, today's trucks are a compromise."

10
GLORIOUS NONSENSE

What makes a guy risk everything for one brief shining moment of glory before his peers? Bobtail racing, that's what.

It's the damnedest thing to see Petes, Kens, Macks, and Fords thunder away "bobtail" (without trailers), smoke belching from the stacks, hitting a hundred as they go for the pole and the first prize. What's craziest is to see owner-operators stoke engines rated for 600 horsepower to as high as 1,000 horsepower, usually managing to bust up several magnificent machines in one racing weekend.

The season starts in April with the Truck 200 at the North Carolina Motor Speedway in Charlotte. In May, there's *Overdrive*'s National Championship in Englishtown, New Jersey, where Crazy Eddie's U.S. Diesel Truckin' Nationals are held in August. On Father's Day, you've got the Great American Truck Race at the Atlanta National Raceway and a month later the Trucker Jamboree in Norwalk, Ohio, a second run of the Truck 200 in Dover, Delaware, and, on the West Coast, the *American Trucker* Trucker Championship Drag in Irvine, California, where all entries must be working trucks, diesel powered and using "standard rubber," that is, stock over-the-road tires. In August, there is the Diesel Drag Racing and Custom Truck Show at the Capitol Raceway in Crofton, Maryland, which bills itself as the biggest truck race on the East Coast, and at Pocono Lake, Pennsylvania, the Bobtail 250. Over the Labor Day weekend, there are a bunch of races, and in the fall, it's the Mother Truckin' Drags in Woodburn, Oregon, and more gum-ball racing in California and at the Bonneville Salt Flats in Utah, the legendary home of land-speed records situated off I-80 west of Salt Lake City. Truck-pulling contests, where contestants take turns trying to drag a giant, 32-ton sled a distance of 300 feet, have become a big-time summer spectator sport in the Midwest at such places as the Pontiac Silverdome, home of the NFL Detroit Lions. And year-round, Tyrone Malone, the "king" of diesel racing, hauls his circus of souped-up rigs all over the place, burning rubber at county fairs and raceways, and showing off his shining metal at truckstops and the occasional shopping mall in between. "Truck racing is getting bigger every day," says Malone. "The trucking industry is starved to death for entertainment."

Truck racing generates as much industry excitement off the track as on. The federal DOT, and ATA, the Teamsters, vehicle, tire, and component manufacturers and their trade press are against the races, predicting at best a black eye for trucking and at worst a bloodbath one of these days. Big-time bobtail racing began with the Atlanta race in 1979. It was originally called the Gould Bobtail Champion 200, but the DOT pressured Gould, Inc., a major industry supplier, into dropping sponsorship. The Monday before the race that year, Goodyear officials were quoted in the *Wall Street Journal* as saying their tires were not designed for such speeds and that the company would not be responsible for accidents and injuries resulting from a failure of its tires. Firestone bought air time on Atlanta radio stations to warn drivers and spectators alike of the dangers. A spokesman for the American Truck Racing Association (ATRA), which ran the race, replied that the Firestone radio spots represented harassment since none of the trucks in competition was running on Firestones. To counter bobtail racing, the ATA has organized the National Truck Roadeo in Kansas City. Here, fleet drivers who have been accident-free for one year, compete in a "grueling" three-day test of efficiency and care of equipment. At the end, the winners get photographed with their trophies against a huge Pepsi billboard.

So why will a guy risk life, limb, and livelihood to tool around a raceway for 132 laps? Says Ken Farmer of Pisgah, Alabama, who won that 1979 Atlanta race in his Ken, powered by a Cummins KTA 600, averaging 113 mph, "I think this is a big thing for truckers. It gives those guys with outstanding equipment a chance to really turn it on without worrying about the law. But I also like that $15,000 prize money." Runner-up Lester Hawk of Hixson, Tennessee, competing in a '78 Pete powered by a Detroit Diesel V-8, said, "I've waited about 25 years to do something like this. I wonder why they've never done it before."

Malone, who organizes 40-truck events as a warm-up to his own team's shenanigans, says it even better: "I'll never forget one guy who got a check for $150 and a small trophy. He and his wife and two kids waited around while I talked to the newspeople. Then he said to me, 'I have been trucking for 17 years and I really don't care about the money. But to be second in this event of 40 trucks, this trophy is really small. Is there any way I can have a bigger trophy?' We learned something there. It is the only thing in 17 years that the man could bring home and put on his mantel and really be proud of. He came there with his family, brought a picnic, and joined in. This is what makes truck racing."

Malone's rigs don't really look like tractors anymore. The chassis have been lengthened, spoilers or wings have been added, and 1,000-rpm 12-cylinder engines put under the hoods. Bob Motz of Akron, Ohio, has put a jet engine into a Kenworth and bills his rig "the world's fastest truck." And then there are Doyle Montgomery of West Chester, Ohio, who races in a twin turbocharged '71 Ken, and Jim Lemon of Cherokee, Oklahoma, with his '78 Ken with a Cummins engine. But who's the fastest?

Malone, who makes his home in the California desert town of Visalia, set the first record in 1971. The place was the Bonneville Salt Flats in Utah, where all sorts of weird contraptions race. In his Ken, powered by a Detroit Diesel engine, he was off, accelerating slowly in order to save his tires. Once he hit 80 mph, he poured it on. At 100, the plastic hood began to vibrate; at 110 the front spoiler was rattling. The tachometer registered 3,000 rpm and Malone was doing more than 140 mph for a stretch, giving him an average of 114 miles per hour. Five years later, in Super Boss, his new model Ken, he averaged 144 mph, a new world record. For an officially untimed international record, he took Super Boss to Australia (the 16,000-pound rig flew Down Under aboard a Boeing 747) and won the First International World Cup Quarter Mile Drag Race against a jet-powered Ford called Waltzing Matilda. This win was achieved in approximately 14 seconds at an estimated top speed of 100 mph. The Australians couldn't let that one stand and in January 1979, two Aussies drove Waltzing Matilda at 172.76 mph over a quarter mile. No one would recognize their Ford as a truck, however. Instead, they said it was really a high-powered rocket.

No matter—Bob Motz intends to beat that 172.76 record. He has put a General Electric J79 jet engine from a B-58 bomber into his Kenworth and in 1981 got it up to 167 mph in 8.52 seconds in the quarter mile. He expects the 1,750 horsepower to blast him over the 200-mph mark. To slow him down again, he's got nine parachutes rigged to the truck.

Bobtail racing is a little more sedate. Here, it's not a matter of hitting 172 mph in 14 seconds out on the Bonneville Flats, but of keeping it up for 200 or 300 miles. And here, Doyle Montgomery's 90-mph average and 106-mph qualifying speed are impressive. Doing 200 miles in two hours, 23 minutes, and 48 seconds won Montgomery the 1980 Truck 200—a full 34 seconds ahead of second place Mike Adams of Seneca, South Carolina.

The races are often run in conjunction with truck shows, and they are a mixture of conventions, showroom hoopla, country-and-western benefits and family fun. There are cash purses, trophies, exhibitions, and pretty girls—present and past Penthouse Pets, Miss Owner-Operator, etc. You can win the Most Outstanding Wrecker award if you've got a wrecker, the Most Outstanding Garbage Truck, or the Best-Appearing Truck honors. Rodney Derstine, one of Tyrone Malone's drivers, says it's really the owner-operators that make the events worthwhile. "They'll come over and tell us how neat these trucks really are and how much they would like to have something like this," says Derstine, grinning. "Then they pull away in an $80,000 decked-out Pete and I say to myself, 'I would really love to have *that!*' "

If you don't want to enter your Pete in the race and you don't want to enter it in one of the beauty contests, you can drool over the supersharp, special purpose, customized rigs. Beautiful fleets and tractors go to the event just to display themselves, and there are endless booths filled with engines, wheels, air deflectors (the big thing in the cost-per-mile–conscious 1980s), chrome bumpers, stacks, fenders, digital instruments and filters, and new accessory inventions. If you don't own a tractor, but are willing to stand still for the salesperson's spiel, you can have a Polaroid taken of yourself leaning against one of the beauts. The wife can ogle the Most Livable Cab or taste the "truckers' chili." Junior can get a model kit of one of Malone's machines or get lost among the T-shirt and patches booths or down where the action is, the pits.

The race goes on for two days—side-by-side qualifying races on Saturday and the main event on Sunday. The entrants who make up the first four rows are the eight men who qualify at over 100 mph during practice runs. The pit crews work furiously. "My crew can pour on 11 gallons of fuel and check the temperatures of the front tires in 22 seconds," says Montgomery. "That *has* to be a record."

Tires *are* a problem. Drivers fight blowouts left and right after a couple of dozen laps. Montgomery says he rides the same set of Goodyears in two consecutive races because they seem to run cooler than new tires the second time out. Motz runs on AMG FlexCure retreads and Malone on Bandag retreads. In fact, since that DOT-suggested boycott of the 1979 Atlanta Bobtail race, manufacturers have slipped back in, and Malone for one is sponsored by Bandag, Detroit Diesel, Eaton, Diehard and the American Steel Foundation. ("Detroit Diesel says I'm the best salesman they ever had.")

You're in Irvine, on the southern edge of the L.A. megasprawl, and before you even park at the Orange County International Raceway, you hear and smell them warming up. The rabbit starts send black puffs of diesel exhaust over the grandstand and the roar of mufflerless, souped-up engines is deep and deafening, as the aficionados want it. The parking lot stretches forever along the back side of the Santa Ana

Freeway, and you walk toward the noise and the smell with clumps of teenage boys communicating in their own automotive tongue, silent outdoor types with wives tagging along, young families carrying ice chests and toddlers, working-class lovers holding hands. At the gate, teenage security guards check the ice chests for beer and liquor. Sorry, folks, no booze.

The qualifying rounds take all afternoon and are something of a bore. To enliven things, the announcer on the ever-present loudspeaker draws attention to what makes this or that rig special. The crowd is gathered mostly at the starting line, and contestants who resort to such antics as false starts and pretending to line up in the wrong lane get a big hand. The announcer swoons over "Grandpa George Leopard of Oxnard, California, in the less-than-immaculate blue '73 Kenworth on the left going up against Greg Lawson of Lake Ozark, Missouri, in the '78 Ken," and as the two of them take off, the crowd gets a glimpse of the grinning graybeard in the old Ken.

For an additional three dollars, you can buy a pit pass and go around to where the action—and half the crowd—is. Here, between the rows of pairs of working trucks lining up for the qualifying rounds, crews tinker with the machines belonging to the professionals of the truck-racing circuit, the heavyweights the organizers are counting on to increase the gate. One incredible machine is Jerald McBee's roped-off Defiance. It is the weirdest truck dragster anyone has ever seen, a low-slung yellow and red job with the exposed engine mounted *behind* the cab. Twelve tall silver exhaust tubes gleam like organ pipes in the sun, and if you aren't sufficiently impressed, it says right on the side that this is "the world's wildest 10-wheeler." Farther back is Bob Motz's jet-powered Kenworth, which makes the announcer's voice sink to a venerated hush when it rolls onto the course in an awesome crackle of muffler-less impatience. "What do you say to fuel that costs $25 a gallon? Yes, ladies and gentlemen, $25 a gallon. There is 2,000 horsepower under this hood."

All trucks are inspected by mechanics to assure safety conformity. Glass has been removed from side windows. Roll bars, seat belts, window nets, and rear bumpers are mandatory. Some drivers have installed side rails and fuel tank protectors. Many rigs are equipped with double shocks and "cambered" axles that can be tilted to whatever angle is best suited for this particular truck.

Saturday night after the drags, the crowd is treated to a C and W show. On the flatbed rolled onto the raceway, amplified guitars vibrate in the night and lady singers belt out songs like "Truck Drivin' Man," "Girl on the Billboard," and "Passing Zone Blues." One of the musicians switches from a guitar to a harmonica that can cry like a baby. Cutting loose, the band plays honky-tonk gospel, and the lady singer with the husky voice sings "Up Against the Wall, Redneck." Lights burn late in RVs and sleepers.

Sunday arrives bright and hot. Teams make adjustments on their tractors and begin to set up in the pit area. Amateur photographers and girl friends snap pictures of grinning contestants, wearing everything from sombreros to CAT caps, posing in front of aggressive grilles. Grandpa Leonard introduces his perky granddaughter as the best man on his pit crew. Newswriters are there with their notebooks and VIP badges, and small boys listen openmouthed to lengthy technical explanations. Yes, says Mike Adams, dressed all in white, most drivers only wear the outer part of the fireproof driver's suit, but he wears fireproof long johns as well. He used to race in a '64 GMC. He loved it and won a lot of races with an engine so goddamn big he had to weld additional metal on to enclose it. That tractor was never offered commercially with that engine and it was therefore not stock, and it got him disqualified a couple of times. But, Lord, was she a beauty! And what does he drive today? A '75 GMC by the name of Junkyard Dog. Burly and middle-aged and also clad in white, Doyle Montgomery just won the $10,000 Bobtail 250 in Pennsylvania, averaging a blistering 87.99 mph, with Virgil Taylor of Springtown, Texas, nipping at his heels the whole 100 laps in his '81 Kenworth. Greg Lawson is all pro, explaining he's got a rebuilt Cummins in his '78 Pete. "She's also got stock 280 heads with 335 components and injectors."

A little after noon, the pace truck, piloted by a celebrity, rolls out to line up the trucks. Somebody jumps the green flag and is sent to the rear before officials restart the race. The trucks roll around in formation, two, three, four times. The judges still don't like the exact positionings. On the 12th round, the green flag sends them off, stacks belching in a roar.

Montgomery spins out and briefly touches the wall, but it doesn't slow him down. He shoots past Charlie Baker of Hanover, Pennsylvania, who has the inside pole with a qualifying speed of 106.2 mph. On the outside are Richard Craig of Muncie, Indiana, and Jim Bickel, the Liberty Bell driver for the Metzger Racing Team from Silverlake, Indiana. Five behind is Grandpa Leopard from Oxnard, California, in his blue Ken, with Lawson on his mudflaps.

Montgomery is out front and remains in control for the first 32 laps. He goes for the pit and Baker takes the lead. The sweltering heat and the tight curves on the track take their toll. Four trucks sputter out, among them Greg Lawson's. Junior Reed of Franklin, Tennessee, crawls up and takes the number two spot when Baker blows a tire on the front straight amid a shower of rubber. On lap 66, a boom is heard across the track. Craig has blown a tire and hits the wall at the end of the back straight. Though his '77 Kenworth is wrecked, he is able to walk away with only a bumped knee. There are five lead changes between Montgomery and Adams, with Adams leading twice for 12 laps, but Montgomery holds the front spot three times. Grandpa Leopard is the favorite underdog. Baker's right front tire smokes before it blows in the 98th lap. Baker fights for control and manages to roll into the pit with only his rim intact. Instantly, everyone's eyes go for the scoreboard to see who is now in second.

Grandpa blows the engine of the old Ken at the 104th and he limps to the pit to the tune of the crowd's regrets and sympathetic yells. He crawls out, knocking his fist against the side of the hood. His granddaughter kicks the goddamn tires.

Mike Adams is now in the lead and goes on to win under the yellow flag. The order at the finish is Adams, Junior Reed, Montgomery. In the victory circle, Adams explains his tractor was rebuilt with a Caterpillar 400 horsepower, and another bobtail race is history.

11
SUPERSLABS

The forecast called for rain, but nothing could dampen the mood of the motorists and truckers lining up as much as 10 hours in advance at the 10 brand-new tollbooths. Everybody wanted to be the first to drive on the Pennsylvania Turnpike, which the morning edition of the *New York Times* proclaimed the Eighth Wonder of the World.

The highway was laid down on the right-of-way constructed for the never-completed South Penn Railroad (known as "Vanderbilt's Folly" because in 1880, top engineering minds told New York Central's William Vanderbilt it was impossible to cut a railroad through 160 miles of rugged central and western Allegheny Mountains). During its construction, the motorway was nicknamed the "Pipe Dream Highway," reflecting taxpayers' opinion that the project was a Franklin D. Roosevelt scheme to keep the construction industry working, but when it was finished everybody loved it. The two broad ribbons of concrete were divided by a median strip, and every one of its curves was built to keep a runaway going 90 mph firmly on the road. No truck or car had to climb a hill steeper than 3 feet in every 100 (some nearby roads were five times as steep) and, of course, the turnpike bypassed all intermediate towns. At one minute past midnight on October 1, the first limited-access toll road in the United States opened, and by dawn, as the weatherman had forecast, western Pennsylvania was soaked. No matter. Motorists sped along the new superhighway at record speeds. N. W. Denison of the Harrisburg *Patriot* reported he made the 160-mile trip from Irwin (outside Pittsburgh) to where the turnpike ended in two hours and 25 minutes, averaging just over 90 miles an hour, despite slowdowns in not-quite-finished tunnels. "While speed of this nature may sound excessive," he wrote, "it has to be remembered this turnpike has been built for high rates of speed." Newspapers ran daily accounts of new records, and a Harrisburg newspaper photo showed a proud motorist posing beside his 1939 DeSoto sedan. The caption proclaimed him to be the current speed holder on the turnpike at 131 mph. The governor got into the act and told Pennsylvanians that on their maiden trip across the new concrete wonder, his chauffeur and he had achieved a speed of 109 mph.

The year was 1940.

Between 1945 and 1955, the Pennsylvania Turnpike was extended from the Ohio state line to a linkup with the new turnpike that New Jersey built. Other state-built toll roads were constructed across New York, Ohio, Indiana, and Illinois. Fast north-south pay roads were built through Maine, Connecticut, Massachusetts, and southern New Hampshire. California had also opened its first urban freeway, the $5 million Arroyo Parkway (now the Pasadena Freeway) in 1940, and western states imitated the California concept of freeways paid for by gasoline taxes, an essentially cheaper idea than toll roads, since freeways entail no tollbooths to be manned around the clock by state employees.

On April 10, 1956, President Eisenhower signed the Federal Aid Highway Act, the landmark legislation that resulted in establishing the Highway Trust Fund. The Act provided for 90% federal funding of a new, national freeway system, eventually to become 42,000 miles long, and to be paid for, California style, by the highway users themselves in the form of a federal fuel tax and various excise taxes. The cost estimate was a then astronomical $27 billion and the target date for completion was 1969. The plan included the outright purchase of existing toll roads to make the entire network toll free. The first piece of the future interstate system was opened to traffic in November 1956—an eight-mile stretch of what is now I-70 across the rolling farmlands west of Topeka, Kansas. Again, press and politicians searched for hyperbole. It was the world's largest engineering project, they said, as they described

97

how the concrete and steel ribbon would allow motorists to drive at high speed from coast to coast and border to border without so much as one traffic light. "By 1975," a travel editor wrote in the *Holiday Inn* magazine, "it will be possible to speed along at 70 to 80 miles an hour on these superhighways."

Twenty-five years later, traffic crawls along a crumbling interstate system at a snail's pace of 55 miles per hour while the Reagan administration devises ways of making sure the last 3% of the network will never be built.

The Highway Trust Fund was one of the better ideas to emerge from the shores of the Potomac, and the Eisenhower administration's legislation to bankroll the gigantic engineering job was as straightforward as the graders smoothing out the new right-of-way. A federal gasoline tax of 4 cents a gallon was imposed, to which were added a 10-cents-per-pound tax on tires and tubes, and a 6-cent tax on lubricating oil. By expressly forbidding the use of the Highway Trust's money for maintenance and repairs, Congress made sure states with sticky fingers didn't divert money for potholes. To imagine that the states would be able to provide the essential upkeep of the new system was the first mistake.

All went relatively well during the first decade. The new superhighways proved a boon to travel and transportation. Long-distance travel time was cut in half and the highway slaughter was drastically reduced—from over six deaths per 100 million miles traveled to one and one-half fatalities per 100 million miles on the interstate system. Cities large and small were often bypassed; yet they remained far more accessible than they had ever been. By the late 1960s, however, construction began to fall behind schedule. Costs tripled and toll roads were not being absorbed as promised. There was one obvious solution: extend the program, and with it, the taxes and expenditures. This was done in stages, and by 1978, all but 3,436 miles—most of them in urban areas where physical bottlenecks were worst and opposition growing—were finished.

The shift in the political and economic climate began to change perceptions and priorities in the mid-1970s. Urban engineers, civil rights advocates, ecology enthusiasts, "think small" tinkerers and a host of others began questioning the spending of billions on freeways and only millions on mass transit. They began to call road building an evil, accusing freeways of slashing urban cores and promoting ghettos, of bypassing towns and causing their decline, of creating noise and pollution, and even of taking "all the zest out of travel." Increasingly, the Trust Fund came to look like a swollen, reactionary monster, paving over America with unneeded and unwanted highways. After the 1974 oil crisis, the pressure became irresistible, and two years later, Congress rewrote the act, redefining "highway construction" to also mean the three Rs the states were clamoring for—resurfacing, restoration, and rehabilitation—and allowing states to "trade in" as yet unbuilt chunks of the network for mass transit. Over the next two years a dozen urban areas traded in interstate highway allocations totaling $5 billion for other transportation projects. Celebrated trade-ins included Manhattan's Westway, and I-210 outside New Orleans, along with segments in Boston, Philadelphia, and San Francisco. As an omen of things to come, one of the final acts of the Ford administration's Transportation Secretary William Coleman was to authorize a link on I-66 connecting the Virginia suburbs and Washington on the conditions: 1) that the right-of-way include a median strip where Washington's Metro rapid transit system might lay its track; 2) that trucks be banned; and 3) that the use of inbound lanes be restricted during morning rush hours to car pools, buses, and vehicles coming in from Dulles International Airport. In fact, said Coleman, interstates in major cities should not be expanded because such growth put added emphasis on vehicle traffic to the detriment of mass transit.

The plan to incorporate existing toll roads and make the entire system free ran into political roadblocks. For a state, tollbooths are bigger gold mines than gambling casinos, and no state government has managed to kick the habit. Connecticut and Maine have managed to keep tolls on their incorporated stretches of the Florida-to-Maine I-95 artery, and Maryland and Delaware have managed to impose tolls on their *new* sections of the interstate. More mysteriously, New Jersey has managed never to build a 50-mile stretch of I-95. Northbound from Philadelphia, the interstate peters out north of Trenton in the I-295 loop, only to pick up again at Fort Lee and run across the Hudson River into Manhattan as the George Washington Bridge. Not that anyone driving from Washington to New York could get lost. You're barely out of Baltimore before the intertwined NJTP signs of the New Jersey Turnpike point you safely in the right direction, via the world's most heavily traveled toll road.

But inflation, not stubborn tolls in the Northeast (there are no toll roads west of Oklahoma, and with the exception of Florida, none south of Kentucky), has done the greatest harm. Congress has never had the nerve to increase the federal fuel tax. It was four cents in 1958 and it's still four cents in 1982. A similar political paralysis tends to seize state legislatures when it comes to asking highway users to pay the true cost of maintaining roads and bridges. Across the country, governors have requested percentage gasoline levies, to break out of the painful lockstep of penny-per-gallon increases in an era when fuel prices have skyrocketed. Only New Mexico, Indiana, Kentucky, Massachusetts, and Nebraska, however, have imposed some form of gasoline-tax indexing. To pay for the highways, Illinois levies the steepest tax per gallon, 22 cents. Texas is the least expensive, charging 9 cents on the gallon, while the national average is creeping toward 18 cents.

Declines in retail gasoline prices in 1982 and an actual slump since 1974 of the miles traveled have kept states on the rack. The fall in fuel prices was cheered by consumers, but lowered the states' "take" at the pump. At the same time, more fuel-efficient cars and trucks have contributed to a further depression of future projections. State highway departments are literally broke. Maintenance is kept to a minimum, especially in northern states where deterioration is the severest. Sun Belt states, on the other hand, have immense highway mileages to maintain. (New York has just over 100,000 miles of roads and streets; California nearly double that, and Texas over two-and-a-half times as many.) When it was built, the interstate system's life expectancy before total overhaul was 20 years and, says Federal Highway Administrator John Hassel, "many sections of the system are reaching the 20-year design life, that is, they're wearing out pretty much on schedule."

What hasn't been kept up is routine maintenance. As the network has aged, the country is spending less and less on it—in constant dollars, the 1980 outlays for roads were half of what they had been 10 years earlier. Some 15% of the 42,500-mile interstate system requires resurfacing and 3–5% more will need it each year, says Hassel. After 19 years of service, the Woodrow Wilson Bridge connecting Maryland and Virginia on the heavily traveled Maine-to-Florida I-95 corridor has deteriorated so rapidly that it had to be rebuilt at a cost of $60 million. Forty percent of the country's 3.9-million-mile road system is in substandard condition, the American Association of State Highway and Transportation Officials warned in 1980.

And the cost spiral soars on relentlessly. While the federal government still collects four cents on each gallon of fuel sold, the cost of road maintenance is double what it was in 1970 and construction costs are 133% higher. Ecology has dictated new construction procedures that cost big money, but worst of all are the political delays. Politicians stall a project for months, even years, for fear of offending pressure groups, and every day they stall, the cost goes up. And don't think government-related interference stops once the contracts have been let, say highway engineers, who spend half their time catering to officials, government agencies, and pressure groups when they are not answering public queries of why it takes so long to build a road.

New construction costs have also gone through the roof. In 1980, the Carter administration's Transportation Secretary Neil Goldschmidt said he was toying with the idea of adding a couple of pennies to the fuel tax to rebuild the Highway Trust Fund, by now in the red. The interstate system was 96% finished, but the last 4% might never be built, he said. The original estimate for the entire system was 27 billion in 1956 dollars. To finish the remaining *four percent*, he said, would cost 50 billion in 1980 dollars.

The American Association of State Highway and Transportation Officials got out the pocket calculators and estimated that to merely *maintain* highway transportation productivity the United States would have to spend $160 billion by 1990.

The first Reagan administration budget, however, cut back on federal outlays for the nation's highways, which, the DOT said, are ever more pitted, pocked, and potholed. By delaying and slowing down construction of the remaining interstate gaps, the Reagan government will slash $9.1 billion from highway spending between 1982 and 1985. But, said the DOT, only a third of all major roads can be termed "good." One out of five major bridges and half the major spans are said to be in need of repairs.

On the state level, the question of voting for new taxes to maintain the existing infrastructure can no longer be postponed or politically torpedoed, although state legislators still have a hard time recognizing that without money to fix the existing road network, the country will face crippled transportation before the end of the century. Over half of the paved roads, or about a million miles, are cracked, buckling, or otherwise in disrepair, and those bumpy miles cost drivers $20 billion in wasted fuel and another $6 billion in car and tire damage every year, according to the Road Information Program, a research organization funded by the auto industry. Fuel-efficient cars and reduced driving continue to erode the traditional source of maintenance funds, and with South Dakota leading the way in 1981, state legislatures have finally begun to raise fuel taxes, some changing from a set per-gallon levy to a tax based on a percentage of the price at the pump, thus tying the tax rate to the rising price of gasoline instead of the tumbling amount of gasoline purchased. In Florida, Governor Bob Graham proposed to extend the state's 4% sales tax on gasoline—on top of the eight-cent gas tax—after a blue-ribbon panel estimated Florida would need $2 billion by 1985 to maintain and finish its hunks of the interstate system. In California, state DOT Director Adriana Gianturco was called on the carpet and accused of wasting state resources looking for "Mickey Mouse" high-speed rail solutions while letting the magnificent $15 billion freeway system deteriorate.

Ironically, it is pioneer Pennsylvania that has the distinction of being the most bereaved state when it comes to highway funding. The Keystone State's troubles date back to the

1920s, when Governor Clifford Pinchot campaigned to "get the farmer out of the mud." By the time the Pennsylvania Turnpike opened that rainy October midnight in 1940, the state had taken over so many rural roads that today its 45,000-mile state system exceeds all of the state highways in New York, New Jersey, and the five New England states *combined*. When the interstates came along there was little money left even to meet the 10% matching funds the 1956 Federal Highway Aid Act required. So Pennsylvania borrowed the money through bond issues and created a debt of $2.3 billion, which translates into nearly $200 million a year in debt service that must come off the top of the annual road-tax revenues.

Politicians in Harrisburg have aggravated this by compelling the state DOT to divert 10% of its budget to the state police, another 10% to municipalities. In all, nearly half the department's income is siphoned off for other-than-highway uses. As a result, Pennsylvania was forced to halt all new highway construction in 1977, and through the years, it has lost close to $1 billion in matching federal funds.

The deadliest highway in the country is Pennsylvania Route 22. Running parallel to the turnpike some 40 miles to the north, Route 22 begins as a freeway on the Ohio state line west of Pittsburgh and, after Monroeville, winds east as a two-, and sometimes, four-lane road through some of the most rugged and beautiful Allegheny and Laurel mountains into the coalfields of Cambria County to Lewistown. Here it runs down the Blue Mountains alongside the Juniata River as a freeway, becomes I-78 after Harrisburg, and finishes, past Allentown and Bethlehem, on a bridge over the Delaware River to Phillipsburg, New Jersey. Truckers call it the Killer Highway, Graveyard Boulevard, and the Coffin Trail.

The stretch they are talking about is in Cambria County, some 25 miles of mountain road with 8–10% grades that are like a roller coaster in the summer and a slalom run in the winter. Billboards erected by the Ebensburg-area clergy and Cambria County commissioners keep score of the dead. (THIS IS A DANGEROUS HIGHWAY! DON'T CLOSE YOUR EYES TO PRAY.) The Vintondale Borough sponsors a billboard saying LAST CHANCE

TO PRAY! ROUTE 22 FAMOUS CHICKAREE MOUNTAIN 4 MILES AHEAD, and the Youth Groups and St. Charles Immaculate Conception Church's billboard features a freshly dug grave with the current number of killed in it, and a text saying, ROUTE 22 IS A GRAVE SITUATION! At the "killer curve" east of Ebensburg, small white crosses have been planted in memory of some of its victims.

In 1975, the Cambria County girl scouts collected more than 6,000 signatures on a petition to Governor Milton J. Shapp, which resulted in more promises. The winding road with its poorly banked turns has dozens of blind curves to test anyone's nerves, and hundreds of side roads and driveways with obscured vision run into it without warning. And Route 22 is no lightly traveled "scenic" mountain diversion for tourists. Year-round "coal bucket" trucks haul coal from the Cambria mines to the big Bethlehem Steel facility in Johnstown. More than one sermon in Cambria County churches and more than one newspaper editorial in Harrisburg have wondered whether the reason for the neglect of Route 22 might possibly lie in the fact that it runs parallel to the moneymaking Pennsylvania Turnpike.

When it comes to paying for roads and potholes, truckers are as cagey as fat-cat politicians. And they have short memories. Trucking before the interstates was bone-crunching, and before the U.S. highway system it was, well, primitive. A trucker runs from Denver to Los Angeles today in 18 hours and a sleeper team can haul 40 tons of freight from New York to San Francisco in some 56 hours. When it was first tried in 1911, a seven-ton rig made it from Denver to L.A. in 66 days. The following year a Packer truck carried a three-ton load from New York to San Francisco in an earth-shattering time, 46 days. The same summer a 3.5-ton Alco truck (built by the American Locomotive Company of Providence, Rhode Island) set out from Philadelphia with three tons of soap consigned to a silk mill in San Francisco. Ninety-four days later truck and cargo reached their destination intact. Because of the excise tax imposed on larger vehicles in the 1956 Highway Act, the trucking industry was initially opposed to the interstate system, but swung around when it was assured that all funds would be held in trust for highway use only, and when carriers and truckers began to realize the time and effort the new superhighways saved them.

The trucking industry called diverting Highway Trust funds to mass transit a betrayal ("let 'em create their own fund," was the word), but however crazy it may seem, the industry periodically tries to undermine the remaining underpinnings of the fund. In 1981, *Overdrive* launched a lobbying effort to reimpose the excise tax on new cars (dropped in 1971 to stimulate sagging sales) in order to shift part of the tax burden from truckers to car owners. The ATA likes to point out that during the past two decades, the industry paid $33 billion into the Highway Trust Fund. Class 8 trucks represent only 1.3% of the total U.S. vehicle registration, yet heavy-duty trucks pay nearly half the money in the kitty. What the ATA doesn't add is that Class 8 rigs average over 100,000 miles a year, more than 10 times the motorists' average.

What the industry wishes no one would point out is that while cars continue to be down-sized, to become smaller, lighter, and (what Detroit doesn't want to advertise) less powerful, trucks are getting bigger and heavier. Heavy-duty trucks may pay registration fees that are as much as 100 times as high as passenger-car fees, critics of the trucking industry say, but the big rigs still don't pay their way. For one thing, every truck mile is the equivalent in damage of nearly 10,000 cars, the critics maintain, extrapolating figures from a road-test study conducted by the American Association of State Highway Officials. The damage coefficient, this study found, is increased by 5 to 10 times when you double the axle weight on most pavements and for most weights. And there are more and more heavy-duty trucks, compounding the problem.

There is much wringing of hands about where the $160 billion to repave the roads by 1990 is to come from. As state DOT engineers like to say, highways are like babies; they need a full measure of tender loving care. Unfilled potholes get bigger, unsealed seams allow water to seep into foundations, which can then freeze and cause whole sections of concrete to heave. One of the most obvious problems, apparent to any motorist, is bridge approaches. As *Commercial Car Journal* pointed out in a 1979 study of the deteriorating roads, bridges are immovable, whereas approaches are laid on filled ground that tends to settle. Eventually, the approaches need major repairs. "Drive on any interstate and you will notice that what repairs have been made are most often on bridge approaches," the fleet owners' trade magazine said. "But in many instances they are haphazard, temporary fixes."

Trucks get blamed for *all* highway woes. Print and electronic media love to do investigative reports on trucks and highways (*"semi*-safe" is a favorite part of a headline), usually detailing how burly truckers terrorize four-wheelers and how overweight leviathans not only grind the interstate system to pieces prematurely, but pulverize modest farm-to-market roads. Such stories never mention that dollars spent on maintenance make the difference. Interstate 80 through Pennsylvania is one of the heaviest-traveled truck routes in the country, and it is in terrible shape. Parallel to it, but some 50 miles to the south, runs the older Pennsylvania Turnpike. The difference is thorough and continued maintenance, made possible by income from the turnpike's ever-rising tolls. When print journalists and TV crews say overweight monsters "pound" I-80, they usually fail to mention the rough roadways of the New Jersey Garden State Parkway or the Baltimore–Washington Parkway, where no trucks at all are allowed.

"If one accepts the theory that axle weight or vehicle weight is the main cause of pavement deterioration and pavement wear," says John L. Reith of the ATA's Interstate Cooperation Department, "then these parkway surfaces should have lasted 300 to 400 years. But they didn't. The Baltimore–Washington Parkway had to be resurfaced in 22 years despite the fact that the heaviest vehicles it ever carried were a few buses every 24 hours. The Garden State Parkway had a similar history. So the parkways, without heavy truck traffic, lasted about the same time as other roads."

What the critics get wrong when they interpret the American Association of State Highway Officials' damage coefficient, says Reith, is that they totally ignore all other factors in road wear. The study was designed to show the effect of vehicle weight on highways independent of weather, chemicals, proper maintenance, or any other factor. Numerous papers have been written on road deterioration and the great majority conclude that vehicle weight is only one of a number of factors affecting pavement life. Studies of Oregon and New York highways found that weather, water, and chemicals are far more important in determining a road's wear than is vehicle weight.

Still, calls are always sounded "to do something," and proposals range from a downward revision of weight limits and an increase, finally, in that four-cents-a-gallon federal fuel tax, to special high-speed "truckways." Despite a 1975 Federal Highway Cost Allocation Study which found that tractor-trailers were responsible for 18–18.6% of the federal highway costs and were paying 18.9% of the federal fuel taxes, the newest idea is that the whole user-charge structure is distorted and inefficient to begin with and that trucks will have to pay more to use the highways.

12
DOUBLE NICKEL

Watergate, originally a bungled burglary, had become a symbol of the practices and malpractices of the Nixon administration by the fall of 1973. The country was reeling after seven months of unfolding drama that reached ever higher into the White House. Abroad, the Vietnam War wouldn't end, and in the Middle East, American foreign policy was put to a severe test when, on October 6, war broke out between Israel and its Arab neighbors. Secretary of State Henry Kissinger shuttled from Moscow to Cairo to Tel Aviv and, with the United Nations, managed to bring about a truce after six days of war. In retaliation for the United States support of Israel, the Arab oil-producing nations placed an embargo on all petroleum shipments to America, and on November 25, President Nixon announced a variety of actions to reduce oil consumption. The presidential directives ordered a cutback in home heating-oil deliveries and a 15% reduction in gasoline refining. The country's service stations were to close voluntarily on weekends and homeowners were asked to lower their thermostats to 68 degrees F. to cope with the heating-oil cutback. The president also urged a reduction of driving speed limits to 55 miles-per-hour for intercity trucks and buses and to 50 mph for cars, as well as reducing or totally eliminating ornamental lighting for the coming Christmas season. To deal with the "energy crisis," the president asked Congress for legislation giving him broad emergency powers. House and Senate couldn't agree on "windfall profits" for the oil industry, but passed two energy-conservation measures—daylight saving time throughout the country for the next two years and a nationwide 55-mph speed limit. Before adjourning for its holiday recess, Congress authorized the immediate construction of the trans-Alaska oil pipeline and Federal Energy Director William E. Simon announced a standby gasoline rationing system, although he remained optimistic that rationing could be avoided if the public continued to cooperate in the conservation effort.

Nixon's call for a voluntary speed limit of 55 mph for commercial vehicles and 50 mph for cars met with strong objections from truckers, who pointed out that their running times would be longer—and their incomes proportionately lower—and that large trucks would actually burn more fuel at such a low speed. They also complained that fuel prices were rising faster than freight rates, and that illegally high prices were being charged by some truckstops. To dramatize their grievances, some truckers called for a three-day work stoppage in early December. Relief was promised. The new federal fuel allocation program gave high priority to freight haulers, the ICC announced it would streamline its procedures for reviewing freight rates and the Internal Revenue Service confirmed a number of cases of price-gouging by truckstop operators.

The "double nickel," as truckers soon baptized the 55-mph speed limit, was born in a crisis. Within a year, statisticians reported that highway fatalities had gone down to around 50,000—usually without mentioning that the energy crisis had caused a slump in road traffic, indeed in the whole economy. The lower speed limit acquired its own, somewhat hypocritical constituency. To be for a return to the higher limits was to be for more highway slaughter. But zero highway fatalities could be obtained if the speed limit was lowered to 10 mph. Obviously, everybody could live with 50,000 annual highway deaths, but not with the precrisis 52,000.

Speed limits had always been the affair of the states, usually 65 mph on major highways and often 70 mph on rural stretches of the new interstates, but to make the new national conservation effort stick, Congress authorized the Department of Transportation to withhold federal highway funds from states that failed to comply. The result was Orwellian. The DOT began suppressing all its own precrisis evidence on highway fatalities that didn't fit the Newthink.

The first DOT report to become unavailable was also one of its latest reprints, a booklet titled *Accidents on Main Rural Highways Related to Speed, Driver and Vehicle.* Most of the original study was done in 1957 in order to help convince Congress that a high-speed interstate system offered by far the safest form of long-distance motor travel. The report was published in 1964 and reprinted in 1974, and was authored by David Solomon, chief of the environmental design and control division at the DOT office of Research and Development. By 1977, any request for accident statistics resulted in the DOT sending you its blue-covered Fact Book, leading off with a presidential message on the importance of the 55-mph speed limit in saving lives. The Fact Book concentrated almost exclusively on the benefits of the double nickel and no longer mentioned that highway deaths can occur at speeds *under* 50 miles per hour.

Solomon, who was 50 when he reviewed his report in the months preceding the congressional action, was recognized as one of the leading experts on highway safety. Virtually no safety survey or study of any consequence in the world escaped his notice, and *Accidents on Main Rural Highways Related to Speed, Driver and Vehicle* was based on exceptionally massive research. The study included detailed analyses of 290,000 drivers and 10,000 accidents. Now, however, he was a nonperson.

What unspeakable truths did the report contain? Basically, that you are four times as likely to get killed at 40 mph in rural areas on local roads as you are at 65 or 70 mph on an interstate—even taking into consideration that you are more likely to die once you get in an accident at the higher speed.

Nothing here that everybody didn't know already. Since 1925, when New York opened the 15-mile Bronx River Parkway without side roads and cross streets, and with opposing traffic divided into one-way streams by islands of grass and trees, highway engineers had worked to make fast superhighways safer than any other roads. In 1928 in Woodbridge, New Jersey, the first cloverleaf interchange was built, a system of overpasses tied into swooping access lanes allowing traffic on two divided highways to cross and merge without danger of head-on collisions. No curve on the Pennsylvania Turnpike was less than 2,800 feet in radius, or banked at less than half an inch to every foot of pavement width. To hold to a minimum climbing speed of 20 mph for big trucks, no grade was much more than 3%. All these principles were combined and expanded in the interstate system, for which highway users by 1976 had paid $67 billion, or an average of $16.7 million for every mile. For decades the statistics had been this: whether in a truck or car, you are twice as safe on a controlled-access highway, where the fatality rate of 2.7 persons per 100 million vehicle miles is less than the national average.

Accidents on Main Rural Highways Related to Speed, Driver and Vehicle, which Solomon recanted in 1979 when he said he "believes" in the 55-mph speed limit, contained other statistics that any trucker traveling his 100,000 miles a year knows in his guts, and most police statistics confirm in footnotes:

—Young drivers are the worst drivers. "The lowest involvement rate was for 40-year-old drivers, traveling at 65 mph on these main rural highways . . . the highest involvement rate was obtained for 18-year-old drivers traveling at 30 mph."

—I know this road like the back of my hand. "Drivers residing within the county where the study site was located have involvement rates nearly twice as great as drivers residing in other counties or out-of-state. At night, local drivers have involvement rates more than two-and-a-half times those of other drivers."

—the slower the better. "The involvement rates for both two- and four-lane highways were lowest at moderately high speed and highest at the very low speeds."

The summary of the Solomon report stressed that there were more accidents when there was a great difference of speed between vehicles, but that a slight variance of two to eight miles an hour had little or no effect on accident rates. Undeniably, you are more likely to be killed if you get in an accident at high speed, but in almost all conditions, with the exception of nighttime driving, you are much less likely to get into an accident in the first place if you drive fast. For the 1974 reprint, Solomon noted that little had changed in motorists' relationships and driving habits in the 10 years since the original report was issued, a contention reconfirmed in 1980, when a General Motors study reported that three-quarters of all collisions occur less than 25 miles from the driver's home and 80% of all accidents causing injury or death involve cars traveling under 40 mph.

Between 1974 and the election of Ronald Reagan, the Department of Transportation was a veritable Ministry of Propaganda. The "55 we can live with" campaign was massive, and it was echoed by state DOTs and state highway patrols. They had little choice but to follow the party line. The bill Congress had passed not only denied highway funds to states that failed to comply, it included a quota system of traffic citations by enforcement agencies, which meant that a state could also lose its highway funds if its cops didn't give enough speeding tickets. The quota system totally disregarded the other Big Four causes—driving under the influence, which accounts for half the nation's highway deaths, failing to yield, improper turns, and disregarding traffic signals. State troopers supported the double nickel because it sounded respectable and because their bosses, the governors, told them to. No state could afford to lose the federal highway dole.

Rebellion was brewing in the West, however. In 1979, the Wyoming legislature voted to repeal the double nickel, but knuckled under when the federal dragon spat flames and threatened the direst of consequences. Successive DOT secretaries, from the Nixon administration's Claude Brinegar to the Carter government's Joan Claybrook, spearheaded public relations campaigns to make Americans believe "speed kills" to the exclusion of nearly all other causes. Depending on who was talking, the annual number of lives saved because of the double nickel varied from 4,500 to 6,000, but on July 10, 1978, Claybrook claimed government mandates on seat belts, tire standards, and car construction by her department had, since 1968, saved 28,000 lives. What was never said was that between 1942 and the energy crisis, the death rate had continually dropped while the average speed had continually gone up, and that the most dramatic drop came during the five-year period that followed the 1945 lifting of the wartime 35-mph limit. In 1942, the death rate was 11.4 per 100 million vehicle miles. Twenty years later, it was 5.3, and with the exception of slight increases in 1960–65 and 1975–80, the fatalities continued to drop toward 3.3.

The Carter administration's DOT zealots tried a last stand on behalf of the double nickel, setting compliance levels against which to measure each state's enforcement of the speed limit. For the period ending September 30, 1979, no more than 70% of all drivers could exceed the 55 restriction. The permissible percentage exceeding the speed limit would drop every year until 1983, when no more than 30% might go faster than 55. States that were unable to reach that goal risked losing up to 10% of their highway funds. If that wasn't enough, the DOT said it would also consider the "quality of a state's 55-mph legislation." Minimum penalties or no penalties would give a state a black mark. Also, a state was to propagandize the party line. The DOT said that when it came to dishing out federal highway money, it would go so far as to take into account a state's "efforts to gain the support of companies/agencies having control over fleets of vehicles."

With the election of President Reagan the climate changed. For one thing, the 1980 Republican party platform included a plank calling for abolishment of the double nickel. "We believe the federal 55-mile-per-hour speed limit is counterproductive and contributes to higher costs of goods and services to all communities, particularly in rural America," the GOP election message read. "The most effective, no-cost federal assistance program would be for each state to set its own limit." After his election, President Reagan didn't exactly rush to abolish the 55 restrictions, but his transportation secretary, Drew Lewis, went on record as favoring a return to state speed limits. As in previous years, the 1981 Gallop Poll showed a nation of hypocrites. Three out of four Americans favored retaining the 55-mph speed limit, but only 29% said they obeyed the law all the time and 48% admitted they exceeded the double nickel most of the time.

Something else changed—the size of cars. The DOT's National Highway Traffic Safety Administration had to admit that the shift to smaller cars to save fuel was causing more Americans to lose their lives in highway accidents, and that by 1990, highway fatalities might increase by 30% (from the 1980 low of 27,000 a year to about 35,000 a year) principally because small cars will then constitute about 50% of cars on the road.

Following Wyoming, other state legislatures introduced bills skirting the speed law imposed by the Nixon administration, but as long as there was a threat of losing federal highway funds, no one seemed ready to actually *abolish* the double nickel. Nevada found a nifty way to make an end run around the DOT in Washington and the reviled 55 restriction. Governor Robert List signed a bill into law in April, 1981, that called for a whopping five-dollar fine for driving up to 70 miles per hour in the state. Said a governor's aide with considerable understatement, "It's a very popular bill." The primary benefit of the bill was the provision preventing demerit points, used to determine insurance rates, from being attached to speeders' licenses *below 70 mph*. This "decriminalizing" of speeding offenses caught on in Washington and Colorado, and by the fall of 1981, 22 states had some form of legislation pending that would accomplish the feat of decriminalizing speeding while keeping it illegal to speed. In Virginia, long famous as a strict double-nickel state, a bill to repeal the 55 lost by only four votes. Montana was the boldest of them all, with two bills pending in the state senate that would raise the speed limit to 70 mph outright.

Elsewhere the driving public still faced the worst of both worlds—capricious enforcement. Few highway patrols will bother to write a speeding ticket on interstates to anyone going less than 65, or from Texas on west, a little under 70 mph. But you never know, and since 48% of all drivers admit to exceeding the double nickel most of the time, enforcement is no longer a matter of nailing the exceptional offender, but of picking at random.

Road patrols emphasize one of two basic methods of dealing with speeders: they either park prominently marked police cruisers in plain sight, usually at a center median crossover, to give an impression of strong enforcement and to gain a "halo effect" that slows traffic, or they use unmarked cars in the honorable tradition of the American Indian camouflaging himself under a buffalo pelt to move in for a kill. Most highway patrols agree that the halo effect only slows down traffic for some three miles beyond the parked trooper, whereas the sight of some poor soul pulled over by an officer in an unmarked car has a more lasting effect. Yet with tightened budgets and shrinking manpower, the halo effect is the most cost-effective. Interstate truckers, however, are not impressed by anything short of a heavy fine, and police safety campaigns usually single out truckers as the bad guys. ("Every time you look in your rearview mirror these days, it seems to be filled up by the grille of a big Mack diesel.") That truckers are the main culprits and victims of double-nickel enforcement is a matter of sheer mathematics, since they spend most of their waking hours behind the wheel. If you drive 130,000 miles a year, your chances of *anything* on the road is more than 10 times greater than if you do the average motorist's 9,500 annual miles.

With profit margins slimmer than ever and fuel and fixed monthly costs rising, truckers try to make up by driving a little faster and a little longer. If the bears have radar guns, truckers have CBs to warn each other and they have radar detectors. The ultimate in electronic fuzzbusting is superheterodyne detection. These $200 to $400 units are lightweight travel tissue box–sized gadgets that can be snapped onto sun visors or mounted on dashboards, when not concealed behind the front grille or somewhere else aboard an 18-wheeler. These little black boxes beep away when radar is in use down the road. The newest units have no volume, no squelch or sensitivity switches, just a small red light that tells the driver that the unit is on. The better "fuzzbusters" can detect a bear sitting behind a tree 3.5 miles away on an unobstructed four-lane road and can pick up those tiny "handgun" blips the hidden patrolman may be firing down the highway at oncoming traffic. When the trooper turns on his radar gun, its transceiver transmits a signal on one of two federally allocated frequencies. The original frequency was 10.525 gigahertz, commonly known as the x band. Later, the Federal Communications Commission assigned the 24.150 ghz frequency as the second, so-called k band. The newer fuzzbusters can detect both x and k band microwave signals, but to foil detection, police technicians often "detune" their units, in violation of FCC rules. Some states have outlawed fuzzbusters and the FCC has shied away from declaring such laws unconstitutional (the Communications Act allows anyone to receive any radio signal at any time). Police have had little luck in convicting people saying on the CB, "Smokey is taking pictures down here, watch your step." In a celebrated New York case, the court ruled that first of all there has to be evidence that there are people in the area who respond to the warning, and second, that those people are themselves committing crimes. In other words, to flash your lights or to get on your CB to tell people who are not necessarily speeding anyway to watch out for a speed trap is not in itself an offense.

Forming convoys, or in true trucker parlance, "running together," is a way of improving working conditions. "Come on an' join our convoy, ain't nothin' gonna git in our way," sang C. W. McCall in his 1975 hit song "Convoy." The lead trucker in a convoy is the "front door." He's the sacrificial lamb, the one the bears will catch, but he's the one protecting the rest of the convoy. The last truck is the "back door," in charge of checking out anything coming up from behind and the standard query to him is, "What's it look like over your shoulder, good buddy?" The best position is in the middle— the "rocking chair," where you just listen on your CB and follow the leader. When a convoy is bigger than 10 trucks it extends over several miles. This can increase the risk for those in the rocking chair, since a patrol cruiser can come onto a highway in the middle and start hitting there. A long convoy demands increased CB vigilance by everybody.

In principle, the interstates eliminated "roadside justice," since they bypassed all those little localities that used to mine the roads for revenues with hard-to-read speed-limit signs and mayor's courts and justice of the peace courts. Also, *Overdrive* magazine helped take a $50 traffic ticket all the way to the Supreme Court in 1972, thereby disabling 17,000 mayor's courts. The case was *Ward* v. *Monroeville* and it established that you're entitled to go to a court of record where the mayor who derives the revenues from finding you guilty isn't also the judge.

Still, speed traps are a lucrative business. Motorists caught speeding in Connecticut bring the state over $20 million a year. The state's speeding law cuts local municipalities in on the bonanza, as 10% of all revenues generated by the courts are returned to the towns where the speeding arrests took place. On the Fourth of July and other big holidays, Connecticut troopers go all out, nabbing motorists by radar surveillance teams sitting in stalled autos and plainclothes troopers posing as stranded motorists. Connecticut State Police can be positively creative, dressing troopers as hitchhikers sitting off the highways with knapsacks loaded with battery packs and radar guns that are pointed at passing vehicles, while other troopers wait farther along the highway. In Pennsylvania, state troopers ride around in unmarked sports cars, panel trucks, and vans. Most highway patrols and state police routinely deny that their officers have a quota of tickets, but stories do surface of officers dismissed for not writing enough citations. One was M. J. Peterson, who was dismissed from the South Dakota Highway Patrol three years short of his 20-year retirement after not submitting "a minimum of 55 written contacts (arrests and warnings only) during each summary reporting period." His story was detailed in the July-August 1980 issue of *South Dakota Peace Officer*.

Besides the CB grapevine, the truck magazines carry the message. *Overdrive* has its Radarscope column, *Owner-Operator* has its Backhaul and Bullsheet, and *American Trucker* its Road Noise, Field Reports, and most popular, its Buford T. Justice Hall of Fame, a monthly listing of the top 10 ticket-happy bears in the land. Buford T. Justice is the caricature of the self-advertising backwoods peace officer (played by Jackie Gleason in the *Smokey and the Bandit* films), who first appeared in the movie *Walking Tall*, and is actually based on the life of the late Tennessee Sheriff Buford T. Pusser. Truckers nominate their favorite Bufords, and harassing troopers get to stay on the list by popular vote. A typical Buford T. Justice Hall of Fame list reads,

1. Pennsylvania smokey in a white Z-28 Camaro
2. Carl Segretti, Pennsylvania
3. Pennsylvania State Police
4. T. S. Smith, Maryland
5. Tennessee State Police
6. "Biker" Officer Hoxie, California Highway Patrol
7. Massachusetts smokies
8. New York State Police
9. T. Stoner (#424) in Iowa City, Iowa
10. Cale Master, Moline, Illinois

American Trucker also runs a scorecard of the states. "What's going on in Pennsyslvania? They took over the first position as the Most Unfair State in the competition this month. It's still happy trucking in Texas as the State Most Cooperative with professional drivers."

These talk-back columns, where truckers tell of their experiences, are avidly read. They are usually short and to the point: "Virginia: Rookie Cop Kizer of the state police is Buford. He will stop you and have a ticket for 67 already made up. He just fills in your name and address and says his word is the law; signed Carolina Road Runner, Burlington, North Carolina." "Indiana: Beware of the bear, westbound, hiding about 37-mile mark. Monford Laners may cost you $40; signed Broadway Joe, West Los Angeles." Or: "Utah: There's a Buford who hides around Spanish Fork. He'll get ya!, signed Dutch Indian, Clay Center, Kansas."

Then there's the Arizona Highway Patrol officer called Maverick who lives in a trailer overlooking I-40 near the 142-mile marker. Maverick has been known to take pictures from his front porch. "Anyone who runs I-40 has either heard of or met him," says Al Selby of Des Plaines, Illinois. Sometimes, a whole police force is nominated:

> I would like to give this month's Buford Award to the New York State Police. Late one night a small four-wheeler foreign job passed me on the right, raising sod and gravel all over and darn near flipped her greasy side up. On Interstate 84 there's a task force of bears, and this guy passed another rig, then slammed on his brakes, causing a fellow trucker to run into his backseat. When the law got there, I tried to vouch for the trucker, but the knuckleheaded bear threatened to send me to jail if I didn't shut up. He proceeded to give the trucker a citation for several different charges. The semi-intoxicated four-wheeler got off scot-free. What is law enforcement doing these days? The "camera rays" must have infected their noggins; signed Rebel One, Otisville, New York.

Signing his real name, Jim Dugan of Cliffside, New Jersey, told readers of the November 1980 issue of *American Trucker* of an ingenious speed trap operated by Police Chief Paul Arritola on U.S. 95 in Jordan Valley, Oregon. Incensed at being caught in the L-shaped passage through town, Dugan stayed around long enough to learn that Arritola "is shooting down big bucks with his trusty radar gun," taking in $93,000 one year, mostly for himself, since his contract with the 300-population town on the Idaho border allows him to keep the proceeds from all traffic and other fines in return for providing free police protection. An *Overdrive* follow-up in April 1981 to a trucker's write-in anger established that half the budget of the Texas town of Kendleton is raised through fines and penalties assessed from traffic violations and that Mayor Ennis Humphrey gets 10% of all fines he collects as Kendleton's municipal court judge. The *Ward* v. *Monroeville* decision still stands, but the hitch of course is that you have to contest the charge and come back for trial before a judge in the next higher court. Most people prefer to plead guilty, and roadside justice still exists in rural America.

Police commissioners will admit that the 55 mph speed

limit has done little to enhance police reputations and respect for law enforcement, but in the same breath they will usually add that the double nickel saves lives. The original Nixon argument of saving fuel is no longer heard. The National Highway Traffic Safety Administration (NHTSA) and the Bureau of Motor Carrier Safety (BMCS) will generally concede that the price of gasoline and diesel and the economy engines now under most truckers' hoods have more to do with saving fuel than the 55. NHTSA administrator Raymond A. Peck nevertheless maintains his agency has no intention of changing the double nickel, while Federal Highway administrator Raymond Barnhart says he doesn't anticipate taking any action against states reducing the penalty for violating the 55-mph law, but pledged in 1981 to come down hard on any state that enacts a higher speed limit or doesn't show adequate compliance.

Not surprisingly, in states where speed laws have been decriminalized, law enforcement spokesmen will say that troopers are openly discussing their dislike of 55 and in some cases will admit their own patrol cars do not save fuel going slower. Bart Jacka, head of the Nevada Motor Vehicles Department, has gone even further, agreeing that long-distance motorists and truckers can actually cause more accidents if they obey the double nickel because the slower speed tends to induce drowsiness over long hauls. Still, 55 is the party line. "It's a mandate and we're required to enforce it," says Chief Wayne Keith of the Colorado State Police.

Is there any chance the Reagan administration will actually *abolish* the federal double nickel? Presidential adviser Edwin Meese was the keynote speaker at the Independent Truckers' Association 1981 convention in Baltimore and the question was put directly to him. "We are asking the secretary of transportation to come up with a method of eliminating the federal speed limit and getting this matter back to being resolved individually by the states," he said, adding that a federal dictate on highway speed limits was alien to the Reagan philosophy of getting government off people's back, and that in many parts of the country preventing people from driving faster than 55 made no economic sense and was no guarantee of increased safety.

When it comes to trucks and highway accidents, the federal DOT and state police departments know of other, less "sexy" causes than excessive speed. Truckers and carriers don't like to hear it, but too many of them neglect vital parts of their power units. Motorists don't like to hear it either, but roughly 90% of all cars subjected to annual Pennsylvania state inspections are found defective. California, Oregon, and Colorado, not exactly states with reputations for venal highway patrols, have nasty statistics showing that too many trucks have faulty brakes and steerings and wheel problems. In Oregon, 37% of trucks inspected at random were pulled off the road until necessary repairs were made, and California set up a Critical Items Inspection, or CII, program after brake-induced accidents shot up 112% between 1975 and 1978. Since the program's inception, accidents caused by faulty brakes have declined by 8% every year. In Colorado, the state spent $4 million building truck escape ramps at the 10 worst grades in the Rockies.

"We have instituted an inspection program and we're trying to do it at the ports of entry where you are already stopped," Keith told a truckers' convention in Colorado Springs in 1980. "Occasionally we do it on mountainous locations where we have these runaway trucks. We put emphasis on inspecting brakes and steering and we try to do it as quickly as we can. We find that about 50% of the trucks—I'm not talking about just independent truckers because we don't sort them out—have some violation when we stop them. We find about 16% have defective brakes." More than a third of the trucks inspected by the BMCS (Bureau of Motor Carrier Safety) are considered highway hazards and are taken out of service until repairs are made, and the Bureau only inspects less than 1% of the estimated four million commercial trucks and buses operating in interstate commerce.

So frequent inspections are the answer? Not necessarily, said Federal District Judge R. Dixon Herman in 1981 in ruling a year-old Pennsylvania truck inspection regulation unconstitutional. The law had required all trucks over 17,000 pounds registered gross weight to display a valid certificate of inspection and, said Judge Herman in his 27-page decision, the requirement "had only slight, illusory, or problematic safety benefits while it imposed a substantial burden on interstate commerce." The court found that "tractor-trailer combinations from noninspecting states did not have a statistically disproportionate percentage of accidents than tractor-trailers registered in inspecting states," adding that there was no evidence suggesting correlation between mandatory periodical inspections and highway safety.

Traffic engineers know that trucks and cars are an uneasy mix, but their reaction to truck-auto accidents on the interstates has been to impose lane restrictions on trucks, not on cars. In California, trucks are restricted to the right lanes, resulting in much tailgating. If you get two cars driving side by side at 50 mph, a truck has no place to overtake either of them. Even if the next right lane is open, most cars will not get over and let the truck pass. "How many times have you gone around a car and seen the car speed up to get in front of your truck only to slow down again?," says Karen Long. "After four or five times of this, you do some tailgating."

The best example of lack of think-through by highway departments is the practice of sending trucks off on separate feeder lanes ahead of merging interstates. The trucks merge together from the two interstates on a truck bypass and are fed back on the merged continuation after the autos have flowed together. It is an excellent engineering idea. It keeps trucks from having to move over two or three lanes to get back to the right lanes once the two highways have melted into one. If only highway departments would replace the ALL TRUCKS signs with TRUCKS ONLY markers. All too often motorists see those truck bypass lanes have less traffic than the auto lanes and zip up the truck bypass. Says Chuck: "You've wound up that double-breasted Yamaha enough to grab fifth gear and get your 40 tons up and over the hill. You're passing a slower truck in the right-hand lane and all of a sudden there's a pickup pulling a U-Haul blocking your progress! Or imagine the frustration of going downhill, restricted to the far right lane only to come upon Grandpa piloting his 1960 Rambler at 35!"

For truckers the worst four-wheelers are those determined to overtake at exactly the speed limit:

> Here you are, half a day late with 40 tons of frozen salmon from Seattle, hauling down the highway at perhaps 15 mph over the double nickel, and some Freddy Flangemouth in the Corolla puts on his left blinkers. Without so much as a glance in his rearview mirror, he pulls out into the left lane right in front of you. Once he's in passing position he realizes you're there behind him. But he's about to overtake a clapped-out Chevy pickup doing 50. To do this, he allocates an overtaking distance that could comfortably accommodate three Kenworths, two cars with trailers, a VW bus, and a little old lady in a 1969 Ford Fairlane. You end up stranded like a beached whale, flashing headlights, blowing horns and weeping with rage while this Dennis Dimwit in the Corolla calmly proceeds with his maneuver at exactly the speed limit—not one mile more.

13
TEN-FOUR

As Karen told Junior when he took over north of Oklahoma City shortly before dawn Thursday, there were guys in trucking who just shouldn't be.

"What happened?" he asked.

Karen smiled and stretched in the jump seat. "I'm running with a pair of dudes who're just somethin' else. They've been telling me stories on the CB."

"I must have been sleeping."

"Like a baby." She massaged her left shoulder with her right hand and leaned forward to get the thermos. "Care for the dregs?"

"Sure."

She poured what was left of the coffee and asked him if he knew the one about the old guy in a beat-up old car pulling onto a freeway. "He was driving in the minimum speed lane," she said, "but much under the minimum. After a while a highway patrol officer waved the guy to stop and approached. 'I guess you know why I stopped you,' the officer began. 'Sure,' said the old man. 'I was the only one you could catch.' "

Junior gulped down the coffee and winced. Karen asked him if he knew the one about the Texan caught with a stolen car who explained he had found it in front of a cemetery and was certain the owner was dead. Or the one about the Virginia smokey who stopped a driver operating along the highway with his hood up. The guy contended he was lost, and he had heard that when you needed the help of a police officer, you should raise the hood.

"You know about the driver goin' through a blinking

light?" Junior asked, gearing it up. " 'Don't you know what a blinking red light means?' smokey asked when he pulled the guy over. 'Sure, that's why I went through when it wasn't on.' "

"You've gotta tell 'em that one." Karen laughed.

Junior gave her back the mug and suggested they stop for a refill. A glance at the fuel gauge made him add that they could take on a couple of hundred gallons of diesel while they were at it.

"Awhile back I think I saw a sign advertising a 76 truck-stop 40 miles ahead. You want me to ask the guys?"

"Who are they?"

"Supercool and Blue Max. They're both crazy."

Junior grabbed the CB mike and held it close to his mouth. "Breaker southbound. This is Class Act to Supercool and Blue Max. Seems you guys have been keepin' my codriver Sweet Pickle awake and entertained for a while."

"Supercool here," came a voice over the static. "You know the one about the Canadian responding to the pedestrian safety slogan 'Wear White at Night' while walking home one winter evening?"

"What happened?" Chuck asked, turning up the volume.

"Run over by a snowplow."

Blue Max came in and said that was as lame as the South Carolina woman driver who fled a smokey at 95 mph and pleaded she was just recharging a weak battery, or the one about the speeding Vermont motorist who contended he was only cooling off his Saint Bernard dog.

"Class Act here," Junior broke in. "We're runnin' low on brew and number two [diesel fuel]. Do you guys know if we're near a decent truckstop?"

"You're 40 miles north of Oklahoma City and Guthrie's, good buddy." Blue Max spoke in a warm southern drawl. "If you're westbound, there's a 76 stop on I-40 and eastbound there's another 76'er before Tulsa."

"Much obliged," Junior joshed. "We're headin' south, Dallas, Houston."

"Guthrie's then."

Junior couldn't leave it at that. "Now, this is a true one.

And no offense if you're from the Cotton State, but there was this guy applying for an Alabama driver's license, and the examiner asked him when an accident report should be filed. The guy had the answer right there: 'The accident report shouldn't be filed until after the accident,' he said."

There was a silence.

"Blue Max to Class Act. What's your registration?"

Junior smiled. "California, good buddy."

"Then maybe you know that California trucker, who operated under a suspended license, but was quick-witted enough when smokey pulled him over to show his codriver's license."

"No, I guess I don't."

"A sad story."

"What happened?"

"Wouldn't you know it? His codriver's license was also suspended."

Karen swiveled toward Chuck and signaled to him to let her have the mike.

He did and she identified herself as Sweet Pickle, out of Yakima, Washington. She had it on good authority that a South Carolina woman applying for a driver's license said she didn't want to go through the entire test, just enough to permit her to drive the kids back and forth from school.

Supercool got one in about the upstate New York farmer stopped on suspicion of operating while intoxicated. He explained that his car was zigzagging because he had a live sow in the trunk. He did. She weighed 400 pounds.

Karen told about the Oregon trooper who stopped a weaving car driven by a woman. As the cop was interviewing her another car drove up, and the driver staggered over wanting to know why his wife had been stopped. He tested .23 and the wife .26. Blue Max knew one about a New York state trooper who stopped a driver of a swerving car and saw the man quickly switch seats with his passenger. The passenger tested .17—.02 higher than the driver. Supercool had had a personal experience with a drunken four-wheeler. There were six truckers running in a convoy in Indiana, and this guy annoyed them so much shining a powerful mobile light into their mirrors that they all got on their CBs, called the cops, and suddenly on cue squeezed the guy halfway into the ditch. "We just boxed him in right there in the middle of the interstate. When the cops arrived, he was out of his car and hollering, so smokey couldn't get him for being intoxicated behind the wheel, only for being drunk in a public place."

Junior scratched his beard and laughed. Then he gestured to Karen to give him the mike.

"We were runnin' 10 together in Dayton, Ohio, and I was the back door," he began. "We were doing 70, maybe 75, nice and cozy, when I saw an aerial patrol plane clocking us. I tell you, I just saw it over the treetops. So I got on the CB and told the others, 'Time to go have coffee.' "

"And smokey was already waitin' for you on the ground," Blue Max guessed.

Junior took his time. "No, we were coming up on a truckstop, so we all pulled right into the parking lot, and quickly walked into the coffee shop and sat down. Sure enough, a couple of squad cars arrived and the bears walked in, lookin' mad at us sittin' there. But what could they do? They didn't know which driver was drivin' which truck."

Supercool had a grisly drunken driver–smokey bear story. It happened two years ago in Alabama. A state trooper was credited with saving the life of a driver of a wrecked pickup through prompt application of a tourniquet. "Last year while he was writing a ticket, this smokey was knocked down and killed by the same man, driving the same pickup."

Karen got the mike again and asked Supercool how he got his handle.

"Kinda earned it, I guess," came the reply. The explanation was that he had lost air pressure once running downhill in West Virginia. A car in front of him almost came to a complete stop, and he had the choice of ramming the four-wheeler or trying to go around it through a construction site. At 60 mph, there was every chance he'd lay the rig on its side, but he made it through without hitting the car or the construction barrels, and without damaging either his truck or his cargo.

With a wink to Karen, Junior got the mike back and

asked if anyone knew U.S. 70 northeast of Las Cruces, New Mexico.

"Sure do, runs northeast past White Sands up through Roswell and on up to Amarillo," Blue Max said.

Supercool also knew. "Westbound from here to San Diego, you might shortcut down that way."

"Ever run up that way in August?" Junior asked.

Nobody had, but Supercool could imagine it could be as hot as the I-8 stretch east of Yuma. Junior asked if anyone knew about the old F-4 Thermo King refrigeration unit that had no monitor light connected to the cab dashboard. Supercool was running a flatbed, but Blue Max had been codriver on a reefer and vaguely remembered. Next, Junior asked if anyone knew at what temperature rocket fuel exploded. Nobody did, so he told them nitrogen tetroxide exploded at exactly 110 degrees Fahrenheit. Everyone knew that if it was 98 or 102 degrees on a hot afternoon, the temperature inside a nonrefrigerated aluminum trailer would easily be 30 or 40 degrees hotter. Which was why rocket fuel is carried in reefers in the Southwest.

It was getting light over the cornfields on Junior's left, a kind of hazy dawn that Karen thought promised a hot day.

"So there I was runnin' solo with a backload of refrigerated rocket fuel, from San Diego to McDonnell Douglas in St. Louis, tooling up through the pass there and into that 50-mile stretch of desert before Alamogordo and the White Sands National Monument. It was a hot day, as you good people have already guessed."

Junior gave Karen an affectionate wink. "My tractor had a cassette stereo, but no air conditioning, so you have to picture me ridin' across the desert practically naked with all windows open and Streisand wailin' about how you keep fallin' in love until you get it right. After an hour or so, I have to take a leak. I look for a stretch of shoulder that ain't so soft the rig can sink in or keel over, and I stop and climb down. And as I stand there in the shade of the trailer lettin' nature run its course, I realize I ain't hearing that familiar hum."

"We get the picture, buddy," Blue Max came in.

"Then you appreciate that unless I open the trailer doors in the back—thereby letting in hot desert air, incidentally—and read the thermometer I have hanging inside, I have no way of knowing how long the old Thermo King has been out. Maybe the unit conked out five minutes ago, maybe somewhere back in Yuma. The 'reset' button had popped. That's a solder-core circuit breaker, which stops the unit whenever there is low oil pressure or high water temperature."

"But you're still here," Blue Max objected.

"That's because I'm pretty good with my hands."

"Bet your codriver appreciates that." Supercool laughed.

Junior gave Karen a glance and grinned. "I bypassed it by running a jumper wire around the reset."

"In the nick of time?" Blue Max asked.

"I was never foolish enough to open the trailer and find out."

14
SHARECROPPERS

Government should "stand by our side, not ride on our backs," President Reagan said. "We're overregulated," said his Commerce Secretary Malcolm Baldridge. "We should deregulate from top to bottom." Actually, the movement to reduce regulations started to pick up steam under Presidents Ford and Carter, but the Reagan administration seemed to want deeper, more fundamental changes.

The Interstate Commerce Commission is the oldest national regulatory agency. It was created in 1887 to bring some order to the Gilded Age railroading, 22 years after the War Between the States established the primacy of federal authority, a year after the capture of Geronimo ended the Indian Wars, and two years before North and South Dakota became the 39th and 40th states of the Union. When the Reagan administration took office, a spokesman said they would like to abolish the ICC before its hundredth birthday. Said one Reagan cabinet adviser, "The slogan is, '99 Years is Enough!'"

The Carter administration started changing the transportation business in 1978, beginning with the Airline Deregulation Act of that year. That legislation encouraged competition among airlines by reducing federal control over fares and the assignment of new routes and the dropping of old ones. The Motor Carrier Act of 1980 curbed the ICC's control over interstate trucking, and was followed three months later by the Staggers Rail Act of 1980, giving railroads more flexibility in setting rates and more authority to enter into long-term contracts with freight shippers. It also let railroads drop undesirable routes more easily.

By the time debate began in Congress on the Motor Carrier Act, trucking regulation was generally seen as hugely wasteful, insulating a giant industry from the discipline of competition, causing lowered productivity and feeding inflation. As with airlines and railroads, the argument for deregulation was simply, "Increased efficiency means cheaper transportation." In reasonably prosperous times, travelers and shippers will pay billions of dollars less every year—$2 billion less to the airlines, by early estimates, over $5 billion less to the railroads, and as much as $8 billion less to truckers.

The regulated carriers obviously saw "dereg" as a threat to their monopoly privileges, as did the Teamsters, who shared in the monopolists' gravy, and their lobbying in Washington came fast and furious. The American Trucking Association conjured up apocalyptic visions of what would happen if Congress was crazy enough to make the Carter administration's proposals the law of the land. Rate wars on a cataclysmic scale would be followed by lawlessness on the highway, widespread bankruptcies, and collapse of service, especially in remote areas, they warned. Patricia Cully, the owner of System Transport in Spokane, spoke for the smaller carriers when she predicted deregulation would mean ruin for everybody. ICC authorities, she said, were granted only after great expense and effort—she and her late husband worked hard for 15 years to build up System Transport—and eliminating all authority would bring dishonest people into the industry. There would be stolen freight, kickbacks, improper extensions of credit, operations without insurance, high bankruptcy rates among stripped-down carriers, and wiped-out owner-operators. "You will start out with thousands of trucking companies and end up with four or five who will then tell the shipping public what the rules are." Her company held transcontinental authority and its 70 leased truckers grossed $5 million in 1978. For every six drivers on the road, Cully employed one person in the office, "just to handle the paperwork." Her owner-operators paid for their fuel, but System Transport handled just about everything else—fuel bonds, insurance, licensing and permits audits, billing, sales work, and communications. ("We have a $4,000-a-month phone bill.")

The regulated carriers had gained their ICC certificates in one of three ways: One was "grandfather rights." The vast majority of operating rights were held by companies that were operating in 1935 when trucking regulation was enacted. The second way was by application before the ICC. Historically, an applicant had had to prove the service applied for was required "by the public convenience and necessity." Few major applications were granted over the years. The third manner was by buying other people's authorities. Like taxi licenses in New York City, rights were scarce relative to demand, and because the application process was time-consuming, expensive, and often futile, many companies just bought operating authorities. When Associated Transport, Inc., went bankrupt in 1976, its operating rights, carried on its balance sheet at less than $1 million, sold at public auctions for more than $20 million.

To give the debate a dimension, let's invent a carrier and kick around some figures. Cheddar Trucking, Inc., is our trucking company and we're in the pre-deregulation best of times. Cheddar Trucking is in possession of ICC authority to carry cheese from Wisconsin to New York. Let's assume there is no shortage of cheese and cheeselovers. In fact, let's assume there is enough cheese being made in Wisconsin and enough cheese munching going on in New York to keep 300 trucks busy all year round.

Cheddar Trucking has no trucks and no capital with which to buy trucks. At $100,000 each—tractor and refrigerated trailer—the necessary 300 trucks represent a $30 million investment. To accumulate enough profit to finance $30 million worth of equipment would take the better part of the lifetimes of the principals involved. If a lender could be found and the 300 trucks could secure the loan, the cost of borrowing would be steep. Trucks depreciate fast and Cheddar Trucking would need a large down payment, probably 25%. At that rate the debt service would be over $2 million a year.

How does Cheddar Trucking manage to get 300 trucks worth of business? It starts an aggressive recruiting campaign to find 300 owner-operators. Trucking companies using owner-operators have a training department whose full-time function is to find new lessees. So Cheddar puts out the word. Truck dealers are contacted, ads appear in business opportunity sections of daily newspapers and bulletins go up on the closed-circuit TV monitors at truckstops. "Wanted: Owner-Operators. We need 300 well-qualified owner-operator teams to complete our Wisconsin-to-New York reefer division. We offer steady work, fast turnaround, liberal advances, quick settlements. We demand late-model tandem-axle sleeper, good references, clean record. Call our 800-number recruiting office."

In preregulation days, it wasn't uncommon to generate $150,000 worth of business per truck per year on a refrigerated food haul. If Cheddar and the 300 owner-operators it recruits are working on the usual 25–75 split, the owner-operator will get 75% of the $150,000, or $112,000. Cheddar gets the remaining $37,500. With 300 leased trucks that's a gross of $11.2 million a year. Not bad when all Cheddar has is that ICC cheese hauling authority.

To no one's surprise the big trucking companies and their unionized drivers were against proposals to remove most freight-rate and market-entry controls. By contrast, the independents didn't necessarily want deregulation, but did want an expanded list of "exempt products" that anybody can haul (exempt products included processed farm products, fish, newsprint, and curiously, schoolchildren) and to be able to haul *any* "truckload" (more than 10,000 pounds) under a single bill of lading. Congress had given the ICC the power to regulate the fledgling trucking business in 1935, and over the years, as the infant grew into a $110-billion-a-year leviathan, the agency produced some hoary anomalies that the independents thought it was time to get rid of. Why, for example, can farm-product haulers carry milk but not yogurt or ice cream, and why can they move grain from farm to market but not take animal feed back in their empty trucks? (The reason was, of course, that both milk and grain were exempt as unprocessed commodities, whereas yogurt, ice cream, and animal feed were regulated.) They also wanted an end to other so-called nuisance restrictions, such as forbidding the carrying of moneymaking goods on return trips or stops at certain intermediate points. One of the original demands of the previous summer's shutdown had been that the ICC lift all restrictions on regulated goods for 90 days. "We want to be allowed to carry anything," Hill said. "As things stand now, we're nothing but sharecroppers." The metaphor stuck. Some truckers supporting deregulation thought it would help them graduate from tenant farming to homesteading, that they could finally earn enough to own their rig outright. Others had grander expectations. Maybe dereg could make them landlords, allowing them to own several trucks, maybe even hire drivers to work for them and, eventually, make their business into a family-sized mini-carrier.

The energy crisis worked in favor of some form of deregulation. The country could no longer afford regulations that forbade backhauls (and had trucks running halfway across the country empty) or required truckers to take circuitous routes. The big carriers might not like the idea, but major business groups such as the National Association of Manufacturers and the American Retail Federation filed petitions with the ICC demanding immediate lifting of the nuisance backhaul restrictions.

The ATA and the Teamsters were in the opposite corner. They applied their considerable lobbying powers to defeat dereg. The ATA spent more than $1 million on a public relations campaign to convince Congress that deregulation would mean increased prices, wasted gasoline, and slashed service to small-town America. The Teamsters apparently went a bit further. Two years later, as Roy Williams was about to assume the union presidency, a grand jury accused him and four associates of trying to bribe the bill's sponsor, Senator Howard W. Cannon, the Nevada Democrat and Commerce Committee chairman. The 11-count indictment accused Williams and his associates of offering a choice 5.8-acre lot in Las Vegas, owned by the Teamster's Central States' pension fund, at a reduced price in 1979, if Cannon would head off deregulation. The senator refused and in April 1980, the Senate passed Cannon's bill, which proved to have too much free enterprise and competition in it for the ATA and the

Teamsters, who now set to work on the House. By midsummer, the country had the proverbial half a loaf.

The most important reform in the compromise package that finally became the Motor Carrier Act of 1980 made it easier for anyone to get new routes, but independents still couldn't legally approach a shipper of regulated commodities. In other words, a Chuck Carlton, Junior, couldn't phone Dannon Yogurt while in New York and say, "Hey, I'm on a backhaul to L.A. Can I take a load of stuff back West in my reefer?" Only a carrier could do that. The new law contained no exemptions for foodstuffs or by-products and the independent owner-operator was still without a backhaul provision. Nevertheless, the law did eliminate much of the industry's antitrust immunity and gave everybody the right to raise tariffs by 10% without ICC approval. What disappointed backers of true dereg was that the reform bill failed to get the federal government out of truck regulation altogether. "The law nibbles at abuses when it should chop away the waste inherent in trying to run a $50-billion industry by federal fiat," the *New York Times* editorialized on June 6, 1980, shortly before President Carter signed the Motor Carrier Act into law. "Regulatory reform for trucks is no small achievement. It promises considerable consumer savings. It is also the most we are likely to get from Congress in the foreseeable future. The best hope is that partial deregulation will squeeze monopoly profits out of the industry, leaving regulated trucking with nothing to lose from total deregulation."

What happened to the ATA forecast of anarchy and murderous price wars? A recession happened, and none of the booming surges in traffic and volume that greeted the airline deregulation was repeated on the highways. Instead, carriers and independents all faced sagging traffic and falling profits in the face of rising costs. Then the Reagan election victory happened. Within a month of taking office, the new administration said it would seek a fundamental change in government philosophy by appointing more regulators who don't like regulation and who will pay greater heed to business complaints about excessive rules. Even the liberal Democratic House leadership said it wanted to put ice packs on what politicians and business complained was a swollen regulatory burden.

Because Carter was for increased enforcement of the 55-mph speed limit and because he wanted to divert more freight from the highways to the railroads, whatever voices the independents possessed in the 1980 election campaign urged a vote for Reagan. But so did the International Brotherhood of Teamsters—the only labor union to do so. When the Republicans won the White House, the Teamster leaders moved to redeem their IOUs and urged the new administration to pack the ICC with appointees who would stop dereg. This, of course, would be hard for a government committed to reining in the government regulators, but the Teamsters were relentless. When Roy Williams succeeded the late Frank Fitzsimmons, he vowed to continue intensive lobbying aimed at persuading the ICC to move slowly in implementing dereg. Specifically, Williams wanted the head of ICC Chairman Darius W. Gaskin, an economist appointed by Carter who had ardently pursued dereg. But the railroads wanted to keep Gaskin. Dereg had worked for the railroads and the behind-the-scene jousting for influence pitted the ATA and the Teamsters against the railroads and other supporters of dereg.

The ATA and the Teamsters won.

President Reagan's man for the ICC chairmanship was Reese Taylor, a Nevada lawyer and friend of Senator Paul Laxalt (R-Nev.). Taylor's name had been in an envelope Fitzsimmons had handed the president at a breakfast meeting at the White House, but when *Common Cause* magazine called Taylor "handpicked" by the Teamsters, a White House press secretary said the president only agreed to the selection because it had been endorsed by Laxalt. During his Senate confirmation hearing, Taylor denied he was beholden to anybody, but said he'd like to slow dereg. He criticized what he called the ICC's "almost automatic issuance" of new authority, "erosion of the common-carrier obligation" in the agency's licensing policy, and "the last of any meaningful enforcement of truck authority rules."

Emboldened by this coup, the Teamsters moved to actually roll back dereg. During the summer of 1981, union Vice-

President Jackie Presser said he planned to "zero in on Congressmen in whose districts jobs have been lost as a result of deregulation." He conceded the Teamsters wouldn't be able to reverse the course completely, but said the union would work to "bring back a certain segment of the regulatory system."

Dereg and the recession had cost Teamster jobs. A survey of 32 locals showed an average 22% layoff rate in one year. Several financially troubled carriers hadn't paid unionized drivers a 77-cent hourly raise due in April 1981, and Yellow Freight System, Inc., of Shawnee Mission, Kansas, won "flexible work weeks" from Teamster locals at its terminals. Under the new rules, five-day workweeks can begin on Saturday or Sunday, with no overtime for such days. For the Teamsters' 1982–85 contract, Williams agreed that all future wage-and-benefit costs will be paid out of the union's cost-of-living adjustments. In exchange for modest job-security gains, the union also granted work-rule changes raising productivity. Despite the modest contract, union carriers said they were unlikely to reclaim lost business from independents and small, nonunion carriers, because the 30% labor-cost differential between Teamster carriers and nonunion competitors remains.

Although the union organized successfully in other industries in recent years, its overall membership was nearly 400,000 lower in 1981 than two years earlier, and the biggest chunk of that attrition occurred in trucking. Going into the 1982–85 negotiations, the National Master Freight Agreement covered about 300,000 members, a quarter less than 10 years earlier. Williams was convinced dereg was the union's biggest threat and vowed to fight "with every ounce of energy in my body" to halt further erosion of the government rules that had protected the industry and the Teamsters in the past.

Ironically, deregulation didn't do much for the independents. A year after the Motor Carrier Act became law, the ICC had granted more than 36,000 requests to operate along new routes to nearly 3,000 new carriers, but fewer than 10 independents per month applied for the new rights. And those who did soon found that obtaining authority didn't translate into obtaining freight. Asking for authority made you a direct threat to the carrier you were leased to. With a soft economy adding to the woes, too many trucks were suddenly chasing too few loads and too many independents were willing to haul for substandard rates. In addition, a lot of others were hauling regulated freight, as they had done before the Motor Carrier Act, without benefit of hauling authority, or a lease with a carrier holding such authority, a practice loosely referred to as "hot freight."

"There are a lot of guys wildcatting with hot loads, and I don't blame them a bit," said Aero Trucking lessee Ken Young of Eden, Wisconsin. "If you are leased to a trucking company and they find out you have obtained authority, they don't want to talk to you for fear you'll steal their freight."

Most owner-operators were of the opinion that, as usual, they had come out on the short end of the stick. What helped them get that impression was the threatened removal of the 19% fuel surcharge that the beleaguered Carter administration had granted them at the height of the 1979 shutdown. At the time the surcharge was understood to be temporary, although then-Chairman Daniel O'Neal assured the striking truckers the ICC would continue to protect them in their attempts to recover the escalating fuel costs. But ICC chairmen come and go, and in 1981, the now Republican-dominated Senate Appropriations Committee tagged a note to the DOT budget asking about that "temporary" fuel surcharge rule. When was it going to come off?

To an awful lot of independents the surcharge was what kept them above water in the brave new world of dereg. And they knew the carriers knew that and had them where they wanted—begging for loads and for support for continued fuel surcharges. But it would be folly to hope the carriers would ask for substantial rate increases to offset the dropped fuel surcharge, because to do so would mean losing their grip over the owner-operators. Again, there were grumblings over the CBs that it was maybe time for another revolt. But 1981 was not 1979. "Reagonomics" was sweeping the land. Bob Hill, the activist of the 1979 Washington siege, threatened action, but his group, like many others, had lost membership and fervor. Mike Parkhurst and *Overdrive*, which had been stridently pro-Reagan during the election campaign, certainly didn't call anybody to the barricades.

Dereg enabled some carriers to expand their operations into areas that were previously off limits (and much of that expansion came from non-Teamster firms), but competition also drove down rates and, in the first year of dereg, drove 416 companies out of business. Losers included such major operators as Johnson Motor Lines, based in Charlotte, North Carolina, and Wilson Freight Company, a Cincinnati firm that employed 3,400 people at the time it folded. "A lot of good, established carriers are going by the wayside," said Ronald Lindner, vice-president of Advance Transportation in Milwaukee, one area hard hit by trucking layoffs. "There's going to be a real shake-out." Industry and Teamster officials conceded, however, that dereg was not the only villain. Troubles in such related industries as autos, construction, and steel meant less business for truckers. "Traffic is down, it's happened before when we've had recessions," said ATA Vice-President Edward Kylie.

But to the geargrinders and LTDs riding out there on the superslabs, carriers are nothing more than middlemen. "What we had expected from dereg was to be able to compete for both regulated and exempt freight without hassles reported to the ICC," said independent Rick Carpenter of Ashland, Oregon. "What we got looks to me like a bunch of propaganda." Dereg, independents were discovering, cut both ways. Dereg didn't so much mean independents could compete in formerly regulated areas as it meant that carriers could move into the exempt business. The carrier "middlemen" hadn't just managed to keep their regulated freight more or less regulated; they had been allowed to expand into the traditionally wide-open exempt haulage. In this topsy-turvy world, it didn't take long before independents began asking for *more* government regulation. The area was the contract-of-haul hot potato.

For half a century, the industry has been living with the bill of lading as its principal piece of legal paper. In bringing a 20-ton load of oranges from Florida to Chicago, say, three people are involved—the shipper in Florida, the buyer or receiver in Chicago, and the guy who trucks the oranges. The shipper's responsibility ends once he has sold the produce and the trucker picks it up at the warehouse. The shipper doesn't have to be concerned with transit temperatures because the buyer now owns the oranges and has arranged for their transit. Yet the receiver hasn't actually signed any papers since he's in Chicago. The trucker has signed the bill of lading saying he accepted the load in good condition.

But what happens if there's only half a load of oranges and the owner-operator, or more commonly his broker, finds a second shipper's 200 cases of watermelons and yet someone else's lettuce to fill the reefer and make the trip worthwhile? And suppose the receiver of the lettuce wants his consignment redirected to Indianapolis? Does the trucker drop off the lettuce on his way to Indianapolis, or must he run to Chicago first? Over the years, the credit-rating services have sorted all this out and written guidelines that cover every aspect of these trade practices. Considering the billions of tons of food trucked to market every year, it is remarkable how the whole thing works on trust, integrity—and self-interest. The shipper won't keep his client long if he ships rotten oranges, the trucker won't get many repeat orders if he doesn't "protect" the load he has by keeping the reefer cool, and the receiver won't remain in business long if he doesn't accept what he bought on the telephone two days ago.

Unfortunate wording in Section 16 of the Motor Carrier Act of 1980 kicked up a storm. To protect everybody, Congress authorized the ICC to demand written contracts "where appropriate." To the big shippers, brokers, and carriers, "where appropriate" means Congress didn't *mandate* written contracts of haul, only that such written contracts may be imposed if the ICC deems it appropriate. Officials of the regulatory agency don't quite agree. To them, "where appropriate" means the ICC should draw the line somewhere "and not necessarily at the bottom." To find out where it should draw it, the ICC and the U.S. Department of Agriculture held joint hearings in six cities, and to many people's surprise, a lot of independents came out for written contracts. In response to this, dark hints began to be dropped that if written contracts of haul were mandated, produce shippers and receivers would strongly favor fleet owners and regulated carriers over independent truckers.

Why would a third of the truckers who answered an ICC questionnaire want written contracts of haul when they proverbially hate paperwork? Because it would identify all parties and confirm the agreed terms—communications en route, delivery points, and unloading arrangements—and it would spell out prices. When there is an oversupply of one particular vegetable or fruit, receivers will often do everything they can to find something wrong with the produce. They will find fault with time of arrival or temperature of the goods. Written contracts would go a long way to end this practice.

Hauling food has always been a high-risk business and dereg made it even more of a gamble. To widely fluctuating rates, illegal loading and unloading practices, unscrupulous brokers, and the perishable nature of fresh food was added the problem of both regulated and private carriers joining in the now wide-open fray at ridiculously low rates just to cover backhaul expenses.

Seen from the other end of the telescope, dereg has been just wonderful. For shippers it has meant discounted rates, more truckers, improved service, service innovations, and more Teamster Union concessions on work rules. "It's like walking into a candy store," said R. G. Stanley, transportation manager for Union Carbide, which buys about $170 million worth of trucking services annually. He was echoed by the Boston management consulting firm of Harbridge House, Inc., which surveyed 2,200 large manufacturers and found that 55% were getting lower truck rates.

Overnite Transportation Co. of Richmond, Virginia, the largest nonunion carrier, cut its rates 10% and hired 20 more salesmen for its expanded territory. Consolidated Freightways, the biggest West Coast carrier, began offering 6% discounts on certain volume shipments two months after the Motor Carrier Act went into effect. Roadway Express of Akron began test marketing an air-express service and Yellow Freight offered rate discounts of up to 20% on certain types of shipments. William M. Legg, an analyst with the Baltimore securities house of Alex Brown and Sons, calculated trucking rates during the first year of dereg rose about 17%. Several hundred carriers folded, but by the fall of 1981, there were about 18,000 general for-hire truckers, up from 17,000 a year earlier.

The ray of hope for independent trucks was an ICC proposal to allow them to lease directly to private carriers, or private fleets, that is, companies concerned with hauling their own goods only (Sears and J. C. Penney are the Big Two). Before the Motor Carrier Act, the ICC maintained a strict distinction between for-hire carriers (the Big Three are United Parcel Service, Roadway, and Consolidated Freightways) and the private fleets as far as owner-operators were concerned. If an O.O. wished to lease to a private fleet, he had to become an employee of that firm. In 1981, however, the ICC proposed to eliminate the distinction. "We see no regulatory purpose to be served by continuing this distinction of fleet augmentation between private and for-hire carriers and we believe that both classes of carriers can exercise proper control or responsibility over equipment leased with drivers," read the ICC notice of proposed policy change.

The reaction of the independents was cautious. Many feared they would have to run too many empty backhaul miles, that it wouldn't do too much for the little guy, that it would result in low-paying freight. But they also like to applaud anything that means less regulation and less paperwork. J. C. Penney immediately asked truckers to submit proposals on rates they would charge to haul certain tonnages on specific runs.

Those opposing this linkup of owner-operators and private fleets were, as expected, the ATA, plus the Truck Rental and Leasing Association and the National Furniture Warehousemen's Association. The ATA brought up the fuel surcharge bugaboo, saying independents leasing to private fleets would lose this extra income, while conveniently forgetting the ICC was already under political pressure from both the Reagan White House and the increasingly conservative Congress to eliminate the surcharge in any case. Said *Owner-Operator* magazine of the ATA opposition, "they already hold the high cards and, like the regulated carriers, they don't want the little guy to play."

The feeling of smaller truckers was one of bewilderment. Robert Gafford, the president of the small Tennessee carrier Hohenwald Trucking Lines, saw some 20 big carriers expand into his rural area and decided the only way to survive in the new dereg climate was to branch out also. He applied for rights to haul all commodities between eight Tennessee counties and points in all the other states except Alaska. In December 1980, he won temporary authority from the ICC and borrowed $779,000 to expand his fleet and build seven new terminals in the South and Midwest. Seven months later, however, a three-member ICC panel headed by Taylor rejected Gafford's bid for permanent operating authority. He appealed and he was furious.

"I didn't want the rules of the trucking industry changed to begin with, but when Congress changed the rules, the ICC should follow them. Now," he added, "the Commission, under a new chairman, is tightening up everything like it was under regulation again. I was forced to expand to stay in business, and now Taylor has jerked the rig from under me."

A pair of small Maryland and New Jersey truckers trying to stride into the brave new world of dereg also drew media attention. In April 1980, Maryland's D. M. Bowman received authority to haul building materials nationwide, but in August, the ICC said he had never proved there was a market for his services and cut back his authority to hauling building supplies for a single shipper. William Mirrer, a Paterson, New Jersey, trucker who sought authority to carry rubber, plastic, and metal products throughout the country, instead won the right to haul such goods only between Atlantic Can Company plants and other U.S. points.

The ICC got into truck regulating in 1935. Under Taylor, stunned advocates inside the agency now said, the ICC wasn't so much marching forward under the "99 years is enough!" banner as "turning around and marching back to 1935." By the fall of 1981, grants of nationwide all-commodity hauling authority, which had become common, were suddenly a rarity, and Nelson Cooney, general counsel for the ATA, said he was pleased by Taylor's votes in route-authority cases.

The new chairman and his men claimed they were just following the congressional intent, that the previous regime had "far exceeded the boundaries" of the 1980 law. Paul Dempsey, a top Taylor staffer on leave from the law faculty at the University of Denver, wrote that "if the regulatory structure is to be preserved, then . . . 'checks' on aberrant administrative action must be employed." At the White House, however, there were officials who claimed they were disturbed by reports of Taylor's turnaround. The *Wall Street Journal* quoted one Reagan policy planner as saying a number of people at the White House were very concerned, that when Taylor was chosen he knew of President Reagan's fervor for dereg. Trucking company executives tend to think the whole dispute over Taylor's pro- or antideregulation views amounts to something of a red herring. The 1980 Motor Carrier Act mandated reform and under the legislation regulations on entry and competition have been substantially reduced. "The trucking industry has entered an age of entrepreneurism that will reconfigure the industry over several years," said APA's Arthur E. Imperatore in 1982. "There is already a trend toward oligopoly which will continue. Most people won't be able to survive on their own. I can assure you they won't, especially if they behave like they have in the past."

The Teamsters certainly didn't cry victory. Jack Fresser, the number-two man at the union and head of the big Ohio Conference in Cleveland, claimed dereg had cost 22,000 union jobs in his jurisdiction alone. "The steel mills used to ask a trucker the rate," he said. "Now, they tell you what they'll pay." For the first time, the Teamsters were under the same pressure as automobile and steel industry unions to hold down new gains, even to give back old ones. Still, the apparently short-lived era of dereg widened the already ample gap between independents and unionized drivers. Stunned by the effects of the competition in trucking and a poor economy, the Teamsters had a hard time convincing nonunion drivers they would be better off, in the long run, if they voted to be represented in the International Brotherhood. Carriers that were locked into Teamster contracts had a hard time reducing labor costs necessary to absorb the pressures of rate competition, and union spokesmen conceded nonunion companies could cut rates and still stay in a marginal situation. Said R. V. Durham of the North Carolina Conference, "the way things are, voting for the union could mean voting yourself out of a job."

Meanwhile, the owner-operators keep truckin'. They want to remain their own boss. Over the years, everyone agrees, they have served the industry well, often suffering considerable economic hardship. In 1982, over 200,000 owner-operators are still hanging in there, and the economic value of their trucking is approaching $20 billion annually. The independents hope that President Reagan doesn't just *talk* a fine game about getting government off the back of business. The hard-bitten among them say that rather than listening to what the president says, they will watch what he does. The bitter among them say the signs along the road aren't encouraging.

Three days after Valentine's Day 1982, the ICC gave the independents the biggest bouquet of flowers and lollipops they could ever dream of. The February 17 policy statement, based on hundreds of hours of hearings, testimony, and lawyers' work, suddenly and in 38 terse pages gave truckers almost complete freedom to haul *anything*. "Yahoo," cried *Overdrive* in reporting the landmark decision, which could still be challenged in court. "Now, the ICC has made a giant step in the right direction, and if the policy statement holds, the independent trucker will have gotten a new, very strong lease on not just a lot of freight, but on his very life." The ICC abolished the distinction between private and for-hire carriers, meaning that any owner-operator could now go to Sears, Monsanto, Boise Cascade, or any of thousands of manufacturers and haul their goods directly and permanently without having to go through a broker and without having to be leased—and paying a percentage—to a carrier. It meant that the *trucker* would set the hauling rate. Sharecropping was over. The new source of work gave O.O.'s a chance to compensate for the loss of the fuel surcharge that the Reagan budget-cutters replaced with a complicated new scheme. It allowed them to regain their health and viability by competing in all areas of trucking as well as having all areas of trucking compete for their services.

They are depicted as the last American cowboys, a label that holds a certain mystique and nostalgia, but there is no reason to fear they will join the national symbol, the Bald Eagle, on the endangered species' list. Looking toward the end of the decade, their chances look downright promising. According to Data Resources projections, over-the-road freight occupies second place, two decimal points behind airlines, at the top of the big growth areas of the near future.

15
LUMPING

"You know that sitting is the worst of all normal positions for working?" Karen asked, dropping the magazine for a moment. She was lying in the sleeper and reading an old copy of *Fleet Owner* she had found up there.

"You're telling me," Junior said, shifting in the Cush-N-Air seat and coming over one lane for North Freeway before the interchange.

"Standing is the best position and some local delivery trucks are designed for that," Karen continued. "Even lying down is better than sitting as far as body efficiency is concerned."

"Not many people can earn a living in that position."

Karen smiled. "According to this doctor, when a person sits blood gathers in the lower limbs and has a hard time getting up past the 90-degree bend in the seated body and into the central part of the circulatory system. Also, the heart has a harder time getting a full flow of blood to the brain."

"That explains why I ain't too bright."

"You're not taking this seriously."

"I thought we only suffered from hemorrhoids, bad eyes, and premature aging." He remembered a guy telling him a young LTD—she was 24 or 25—had quit and joined the Air Force because her kidneys had gone bad driving.

"Says that among the ailments likely to trouble truckers are nervous stomachs and peptic ulcers, back pain and strain, hemorrhoids and spinal deformities, mainly caused by truck vibration."

"How about your kidneys rattling loose?"

She didn't answer, and he calculated ahead. They'd be

there before five and at least be in line for unloading at seven tomorrow morning. Maybe they could lay over out along La Porte Freeway in Pasadena, where he could take her to Gilley's tonight, or one of the newer cactus cabarets. He might suggest Fool's Gold or San Antone Rose, which catered to the Gucci gauchos. She might get a kick out of that. He had a clean shirt and jeans hanging in the back. "How about truckers as lovers?" he asked.

"Doesn't say."

He liked her throaty voice and listened as she began reading again. She was no Wham-bam-thank-you-ma'am. She liked respect, good manners, even gallantry, and he could think of no better place to begin the evening than a cozy country-and-western hangout. In discos, everybody was pretending, aiming for high-strung competitiveness. In cactus nightclubs, the beat was slower, the bluegrass mellow and people touch-danced.

Her reading interrupted his thoughts. Drivers were compared to air controllers because, with the exception of truck vibrations, they had much in common—long periods of sitting, considerable job stress. "Because the human body can't be redesigned for the current model year, Dr. Glassford recommends that, to reduce fatigue, drivers be taught isometric exercises involving the lower extremities."

He smiled. "Sounds sexy."

"Isometrics means placing stress on muscles without actually being involved in performing a function such as lifting, running or pushing. It's a mind process of straining muscles by just thinking you're doing some work. You can do it driving down the highway."

He had to concentrate on the urban flow surrounding him. "How about coming down and play navigator for a sec?"

"Sure, where are we?"

"Houston."

"Gosh."

"The exit is Telephone Road, on the other side of downtown."

She hopped down and saw they were southbound in the fast lane of a ten-lane swath of city freeway. The opposite traffic was bumper-to-bumper commuters, but on their side they were merely surrounded by cars and going very fast. NORTH MAIN ST., HOUSTON AVE., and QUITMAN ST. were the next three exits. As they hurtled over the small crest, she saw a huge cloverleaf ahead of them, and behind it, the cluster of downtown high-rises against a threatening sky. The black new glass towers and the black sky behind them looked like a strange old painting.

"Telephone Road," she said, opening the McNally on Texas city maps.

"The produce center is off Old Spanish Trail, which is off Telephone Road. I remember that, but there's been a lot of freeway construction."

They were heading right into the thunderclap. EAST I-10 BEAUMONT, WEST I-10 SAN ANTONIO. Junior stayed in the SOUTH I-45 GALVESTON lane and concentrated on the driving.

After the interchange, I-45 curved around the downtown and became Gulf Freeway. With their slanted roofs, a pair of black glass towers looked like stumps sawed off at an angle. Karen had seen pictures of modern architecture like that. On the map, she traced I-45 and found Telephone Road bisecting the freeway.

"I've got it, another three, four miles," she said, looking up from the map. "You should've told me we were running through your hometown awhile back."

"You were sleeping like a princess. Besides, I've only got a pair of distant cousins left in Conroe. And they ain't the kissin' kind."

Big raindrops hit the windshield. Junior turned the wipers to high and slowed down a bit as they headed into the heaviest downpour Karen had ever experienced, a lashing, pelting rain.

"You had showers like this back in Conroe?" she shouted over the drumming on the metal roof.

"Sure. They come right off the Gulf. Gone again in 20 minutes."

The surprisingly compact downtown cluster of skyscrapers was on their left now, and ahead of them the cityscape flattened out and became vaguely industrial on both sides of the elevated freeway. The sky seemed to have fallen in on them and the roadway was white with a zillion rebounding splashes. They were coming down under a bunch of railway bridges. Karen felt they were a moving island in an ocean of water. "There it is," she said, nodding toward the TELEPHONE RD. 1 MILE sign.

Junior slid toward the right exit lane as they sailed below the several underpasses that looked as if they would flood any minute. Time was of the essence, he told himself. It was Friday tomorrow. If he had no lumper problem here, he could be unloaded by midmorning tomorrow, and if he could line up a load this afternoon or first thing in the morning, they'd be safe. Getting empty and reloaded immediately would mean the difference between laying over the whole weekend and making some miles. Drivers made up all kinds of far-out stories as to why they must get loaded or unloaded immediately, and shippers and receivers had heard them all before. As far as he was concerned, phoning ahead and keeping them informed produced the best result. Since Silverthorne, Colorado, he had been on the longhorn twice, the last time at Guthrie's.

They came off the freeway and glided to a halt at the Telephone Road red light. When it turned, Junior made a wide turn and, a block down, turned right again on Old Spanish Trail Road. "From here on, I remember," he said.

They were in a run-down part of Houston and everything was gray and deserted in the rain. But Karen had a sense of accomplishment. They were there. She felt good, almost elated. She'd get to the East Coast the next time. It was all right. Impulsively, she turned toward him. "I want to treat you to dinner tonight, boss," she said with a smile.

She could see she had caught him by surprise.

"How about me treatin' you?"

"This is *my* celebration, my first turnaround city."

"It's my hometown, or almost."

"I said it first."

He gave her a glance. "I'll say, 'Yes, thank you, ma'am,' if I get to take you to a drink at Gilley's or someplace afterwards."

"We're supposed to stay dephased, to maintain the schedule."

"The layover will ruin that."

She sensed what he had in mind. "Let's see how tired we are."

"A deal."

He recognized the faded United Church, the used-car lots, the scrap yard, and tried to remember when he had been at the Houston Produce Center last. As long as they could get unloaded right away, they could look forward to a lovely evening. Maybe a steakhouse. Steak and beer couldn't cost her too much. Or maybe she liked Mexican food. He did, and he'd insist on paying for the margaritas first.

When he saw the underpass, he turned on the right directional blinkers. The access road to the produce center curved left up over the Old Spanish Trail Road, along the railway bridge and the high-tension power lines. He slowed down and noticed the rain had diminished. After a stop sign, the Rector Seal Corporation warehouses were the first buildings. There were parked trailers on both sides. There was B and M's 24-hour Truck Repairs, and on the right, a two-story motel and cinder-block restaurant that just looked too dingy for the evening he had in mind.

"Okay." He sighed, hissing the air brakes and coming to a halt at the gate. From behind the seat he got out the metal record box. He flipped it open, checked the bill of lading and rolled down his window.

"Allen and Company," he announced.

"Second street on your left, halfway down." The guard waved him on.

He left the window open and cut the air conditioning. The air was Texan and familiar, hot and humid. "Sure aren't many lumpers around," he said, swinging down the deserted second street of warehouses. Only one tractor-trailer rig was backed up to a loading dock.

"Maybe they've got a place inside when it rains."

He hated lumpers, or swampers as they called them in Florida. "Last time I was in Tampa I had to pay $50 unloading charge. I asked the guys to give me their names and social security numbers to use for tax purposes because I'm an independent contractor, and they just scattered—after gettin' paid."

He parked in front of Allen and Company and left the engine running. He'd be back in a minute, he told her, and got the record box and hopped down. It had stopped raining. He ran up the stairs to Shipping and Receiving.

"Lumping" is truckers' jargon for abuses of loading and unloading and it is one of the owner-operators' big headaches. Lumping is the coercing of independents and carrier drivers to obtain assistance in loading and unloading of freight. You drive up to the dock at the delivery point, run into the dispatcher's office with your paperwork and want to get unloaded. Sure, but nobody's available right now, says the dispatcher. You go inside, and especially at the huge wholesale produce markets, you see a dozen for-hire helpers leaning on their dollies. You storm back in, but the dispatcher repeats that his men are working another rig. It's Friday. You count how much a weekend layover is going to cost you, and in frustration, you calculate how many hours it'll take how many guys to unload, and end up walking over to the men leaning on their dollies and making a deal with them to help you.

When Congress drafted the Motor Carrier Act of 1980, the lumper section of the bill would have required shippers to load and receivers to unload trucks. Receivers would have been forced to use their present employees or hire additional workers to unload trailers. Page after page of testimony had been supplied by the ICC, but when it came to documenting the problem, lumping disappeared. Several states got investigations going, notably New Jersey. Any trucker who has ever tried to load or unload in the Jersey City area knew exactly what lumping was, but once the investigators arrived, the problem magically disappeared. The only way the ICC and the state officials could get firsthand knowledge was actually assuming the role of truckers and trying to make pickups or deliveries in different areas.

Extensive congressional testimony revealed, in the ICC's words, that "carriers and their drivers were forced to pay loading and unloading fees at docks, produce markets, meat-packing houses, and large grocery stores. If the fees were not paid, the drivers encountered various problems, such as long delays in getting their trucks unloaded, slashed tires, and even violent treatment. Usually, the lumpers required that payment be made in cash, and lumper fees were required even when the driver was ready and willing to do the loading and unloading unaided. The fee was standard and frequently had no relationship to effort or time spent in actual work."

Over and beyond the corruption, Congress was receptive to the truckers' argument that a driver who has spent 10 hours on the road to meet the receiver's time schedule for delivery shouldn't be expected to grab a skiploader and start hauling pallets of produce into warehouses. The receiver has purchased the load and the trucker has now delivered it. Let the receiver pay for and handle his own merchandise.

While denying that lumping even existed, the United Fresh Fruit and Vegetable Association, which has the largest shipper-receiver membership in the fresh produce industry, set to work to water down the proposed legislation. The trade organization was obliged to have the lumper section altered, it said, "because the requirement would be particularly burdensome to small receivers." The defense of small receivers sounded wholesome (although even the smaller receiver must be assumed to be a larger business than a one-man, one-truck operation). Still, the argument must have convinced Congress, because as the Motor Carrier Act reads, the trucker is "permitted" to load and unload the trailer. Additionally, if the shipper or receiver requires the trucker to be assisted in loading or unloading—usually due to a union contract—the trucker must be provided with the assistance, or compensation for having to hire one or several assistants. Perhaps to get away from it all, perhaps to take a well-earned breather after the labors of Capitol Hill, the United Fresh Fruit and Vegetable Association proposed for the Winter 1980–81 season a group tour for its membership that included a cruise up the Nile River from Cairo and a safari in Kenya, starting at $2,999 per person (double occupancy). This led *Overdrive* to wonder how many truckers would be vacationing in Africa that winter.

Junior didn't get to test the Houston Produce Center lumper situation (to monitor enforcement of the lumper section of the Motor Carrier Act the ICC set up an 800-number for truckers). The dispatcher handed him a message from his broker. A fourth of his mixed load was to be dropped at Allen and Company in exchange for a new 24,000-pound consignment, which, together with the remainder of the original cargo, was to proceed to Rahway. Delivery date: Monday, May 27.

The dispatcher, whose shirt patch identified him as Ron, pulled out his own copy of the waybill and the broker's telex. The first words he heard from Junior he had heard from owner-operators a thousand times before.

"Where's the phone?" Junior asked.

Ron's eyes ran over the paperwork. "If you'll pull up to dock 12, I'll get started on you."

"You mean you'll get to me *now*?"

Ron kept reading. "You were supposed to have been here yesterday."

"I had an accident at Silverthorne, Colorado, lost 22 hours."

"I remember now."

"I called you twice."

"Yeah, I see. Pull up at number 12 and you can call your broker while we unload. We'll have you out of here by five."

"Okay." Junior sighed. So much for a cozy layover. He shuffled his papers together and clipped them into the record box and walked outside, checking his watch: 2:25. He crossed to the truck, but Karen was nowhere in sight. Maybe at the ladies' room. He climbed up and two minutes later was doing a perfect blind back jackknife into loading dock 12. Ron was rolling up the steel shutters and a guy was tooling up on a skiploader.

When he was all set, he grabbed the record box and got down. Karen was waiting by the stairs to the dispatcher's office. As he walked toward her, the only thing he could think of was making a joke about staying dephased. If nothing else, they'd be making some money. And she'd get to the East Coast.

16
A WOMAN'S PLACE

In March 1980, a lady truck driver from the Southern California community of Westminster filed a $5-million lawsuit against Chevron, Inc., for dismissing her "for her own good" after she was knocked unconscious by three men and raped when her truck broke down on the Long Beach Freeway one night. Chevron discriminated against her, Barbara Reed alleged, because male truckers who were victims of crimes were not fired "for their own good," while she was ordered to resign her $20,000-a-year job. "I was shocked and hurt when I returned to work four days after the attack and was told by my supervisor that Chevron was letting me go for my own good," said Mrs. Reed, the first LTD at the oil company's El Segundo refinery. "Even though the attack has been the worst experience in my life, I still want to be a truck driver."

This tenacity is a widely shared trait of women in trucking. Like the boys, LTDs hang tough. Most married drivers in independent trucking need and downright depend on their wives as business partners. Wives have always done the bookkeeping, but an increasing number are joining their men on the road. They aren't just tagging along for the adventure, but working to keep together their families and their marriages, to keep the roof over their heads and the truck payments up to date. Taking on a nine-to-five job might be easier, but coming home night after night to feed the kids, put them to bed, pay bills and do housework before crawling into an empty bed while the relationship with the husband remains a series of long-distance calls also wears a woman down. Trucking together avoids the discords sometimes associated with long absences, eliminates "lost weekends," although being on the road often doesn't make a woman escape from household duties and worries over children, but intensifies them. "There are emotional wounds to heal at home between child and parent, food to buy, housework to do and problems to solve, regardless of how hard everyone helps out," Patricia Leigh Dunnbrook of Fort Wayne, Indiana, says. "Regardless of a better sharing relationship with her husband and a sense of pride in her work, a woman cannot overcome the guilt of feeling that she is not totally fulfilling her role as a mother. A phone call home cannot assure her, as she sits behind the wheel miles from home, that her daughter won't come home pregnant, that her son won't become involved with drugs or that a discipline problem at school is being worked on correctly. Yet, there is also a twinge of guilt if she elects to abandon her husband to let him go at it alone when he counts on her."

The Equal Employment Opportunity Commission says women are rapidly gaining employment in trucking, not only as LTDs, but as mechanics and cargo loaders. Surveying 745 carriers, the Commission determined that 10% of all professional and technical jobs in trucking are now held by women and that one out of every four major college graduates holding degrees in transportation are women. The single woman as trucker is still rare, however, and the few there are feel sisterly sympathy toward the female halves of husband-and-wife teams, but that's all they feel.

"Ninety percent of them can't back up, tarp a load or do rugged driving," says Valerie Montana, a Detroit-based owner-operator who says she's on the road 300 days a year. "They're what we call 'fair weather drivers.' They're legal logbooks for their husbands and most of them couldn't *drive* by themselves."

The way Chuck Carlton, Jr., remembers the beginning of lady truck drivers is by remembering the Lee Way Motor Freight uproar. The year was 1977 and the Oklahoma City carrier decided its drivers had to work with female codrivers because the Equal Employment Opportunity Commission in Washington said so. Wives raised hell, formed Trucker Families United, and wrote angry letters to *Overdrive*. "When I

The mighty "Ken"—a Kenworth K100 Aerodyne with sleeper
KENWORTH TRUCK COMPANY

The owner of this Nevada-based Western roadrunner is apportioned in Nebraska and Oregon, pays ton-mile taxes in Wyoming and, per "bingo" plate, has been prorated in Washington, California, and North Dakota   GIL MADSEN

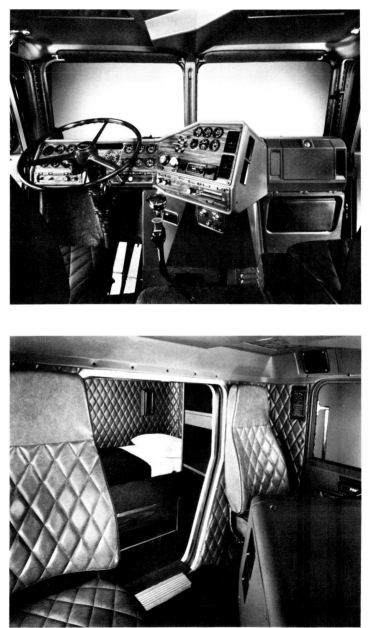

TOP: *Freightliner cockpit and jump seat*
FREIGHTLINER TRUCK COMPANY

BOTTOM: *The sleeper in the Freightliner, all made up*
FREIGHTLINER TRUCK COMPANY

Doing the logbook GIL MADSEN

LEFT: This LTD is using downtime to keep her truck clean GIL MADSEN

Truckstop fuel counter GIL MADSEN

Parking lot of the "Greatest Little City in the World"—Boomtown, in Verdi, Nevada, the last big stop before Shaky Side BOOMTOWN

Water hole in Bordentown, New Jersey GIL MADSEN

ABOVE: Students at a trucking school learning to connect air hoses TEXAS STATE TECHNICAL INSTITUTE

RIGHT: Learning to back into a loading dock COMMERCIAL SAFETY COLLEGE

BELOW: All about horsepower TEXAS STATE TECHNICAL INSTITUTE

TOP: Bobtail racing at the North Carolina Motor Speedway HURLEY SHORT

CENTER: In front of the stands HURLEY SHORT

BOTTOM: Not everybody makes it to the flag HURLEY SHORT

Tyrone Malone above the crowd at a show featuring his rigs
TYRONE MALONE ENTERPRISES

Super Boss, which set the world land speed record at Bonneville Salt Flats at 144.421 mph   TYRONE MALONE ENTERPRISES

Independent truckers protesting rising fuel prices and government regulation in a 15-mph caravan, Las Vegas, 1979 UNITED PRESS INTERNATIONAL

Some of the 80 rigs that blockaded the main gates to the New England Produce Center, Chelsea, Massachusetts, during a truckers' shutdown, which led to the arrest of at least 18 independents UNITED PRESS INTERNATIONAL

"Buford T. Justice" is a familiar figure to readers of American Trucker *magazine* GENE VANDERVOORT

think of another woman enjoying my guy's company for two or three days it makes my blood boil," a Nebraska wife answered Cindy Johnson of Kansas City, who had said she loved life on the road as an LTD "and that includes all of the hassles that are so numerous for independents." Lady truck drivers generally answered the irate wives that if husbands were prone to hanky-panky, they'd do it just as quickly with the women they worked with in the factory and the office as with the lady in the cab. Junior's former codriver Gail Aplin had put a couple of wives on the spot, asking why all of a sudden the wives were protesting lady truckers and overlooking all the greenstampers [prostitutes] working the truckstops. "If you're going to fuss over women being around your husbands, you should start fussing over the ladies of the night knocking on the cab doors at the parking lots and let us gals do our job," Gail had told them. For a while the guys had loved women fighting over them, but an Illinois wife had wiped the grins off the faces, asking, "Why not ask the truckers how they'd like to have a gentleman move in at home with the wife to help with the domestic engineering while they're on the road?"

There was a lot of bad-mouthing of LTDs. Chuck remembered the night Gail and he were running with a husband-and-wife team and the two girls were at the wheels while he and the husband happened both to be in their sleepers. Gail and the woman were just talking on the CB to while away the night, talking about husbands and boyfriends, about LTDs and whatnot, when a male voice broke in and began denigrating women drivers in the foulest language you had ever heard. Junior got so steamed up lying there listening that he got on the CB and learned from another reefer driver that the guy was a bedbug hauler running a little ahead of them. Junior told Gail to step on it and when he saw the United Van Lines rig, got on the CB and told the guy to pull over. Junior got down and walked up toward the United rig, with Gail running after him and shouting that he shouldn't do anything stupid. When he got to the tractor, he saw a shotgun pointed at him. Gail got an arm around him and managed to pull him back to their truck after Junior had told the guy what he thought of him.

In a letter to *Overdrive*, a trucker named William Cartwright wrote that he was tired of hearing women drivers complain about dirty showers and bad food in truckstops. "To me, trucking is for men, and if women drivers don't like the way things are, and have been, they should just stay home and they won't have to worry about the simple things in trucking," wrote Cartwright. "A woman's place is in the home, not in an 18-wheeler." The letter set off a furor, with LTDs answering that clean showers, good food, and friendlier service benefited all truckers. Gail S. Wood of Raleigh, North Carolina got down to basics in answering Cartwright. "My place is anywhere I want to be, whether it is in a truck, office, kitchen or whatever. I am tired of hearing about 'where my place is.' I don't notice a lot of things written about where a man's place is. You don't hear women complaining about men being chefs, hairdressers, clothes designers, etc. If you want to talk about people's places, let's start with married truckers. Isn't the man's place at home, helping his wife raise the children he took the time to father, fixing leaky faucets, mowing the grass and going to church each Sunday as head of the household? No? I agree. If you're happier on the road, then that's where you should be. So why place a restriction on me, as a woman, that I wouldn't place on you?"

Lee Way Motors didn't change its mixed-crew rule, but for a while the question of whether *anybody* had the right to object to driving with any codriver, male or female, was a lively subject on the road. As Junior put it when Karen and he talked LTDs, "With energy costs eating you alive, you see more and more husband-and-wife sleep teams. As far as I know, it isn't so much the wives figuring that if anybody female should spend time with their guy it might as well be they, as it is families trying to stay ahead of the payments." Today, an estimated 5% of all truckers are women. Assuming there are 400,000 long-distance truckers in all, the female population would be 20,000. When the number of husband-and-wife teams is taken into account, the figure is regarded as pretty accurate.

"I have found that if you act like a lady you will be treated like a lady," a 22-year-old Ontario LTD going by the handle Canada Goose wrote to *Road King*'s WIT (Women in Trucking) column in 1981. "Many male drivers have helped me out of countless problems and advised me of tricks of the trade for the future." The term "Lady Truck Driver" has stuck in the highway vocabulary—feminists' egalitarian "woman driver" is as unacceptable as "highway hens" and other epithets—and even LTDs who drive solo agree that most of the guys they meet are really nice. Sexual prejudice exists— dispatchers seem to prefer to believe male codrivers when a male-female team reports an accident—and some lady truck drivers are said to have a different style of driving, some so different they prefer not to team with their trucker husbands. As for sexual harassment on the road, the lady trucker's own attitude is generally considered to be the determining factor. "If you let the guys know from the start you don't party, they treat you decently," says Pat Tierney from Royersford, Penn-sylvania, who has driven solo for four years. Male truckers make a sharp distinction between LTDs and prostitutes soliciting on trucking parking lots, but a number of lady truckers have taken to carrying a piece of pipe on dark nights, a piece of leaded pipe up their sleeve, to be prepared for any situation.

Like Karen Long, an increasing number of LTDs are young women who have decided that being a secretary isn't for them. Bonny Floyd, a former beautician and a codriver of a United Van Lines rig, says anyone who thinks a woman's place is not in an 18-wheeler should have his or her head examined. "The change of company policy that allowed us to go with our boyfriends or husbands has enabled us to get our foot in the door. We're here to stay!"

Dee Atkinson is 26 and single and not the girl friend of anyone she drives with. She doesn't think of herself as a typical woman driver. Most women on the road like new equipment, she comments. She has a fondness for older trucks because she started with one. LTDs, she says, have a tendency to speed, are good at doing paperwork, and their general impact has meant cleaner showers, better food, and friendlier service at truckstops. Dee was 19 and working in a diner in New Hope, Pennsylvania, when a trucker she knew suggested she help him drive to New York. She couldn't resist the challenge and, the first time she tried, didn't find driving a big rig that difficult. It didn't take her long to get the necessary driving experience and obtain a Class I permit. Her friend knew a lot about trucks and Dee formed a partnership with him. They bought a 1965 Diamond T tractor and after much repair work they were in business. Dee, who has nothing of the one-of-the-boys bluster that many LTDs affect, still races the Diamond T at the annual Pocono truck drag race and once placed it first in one class and fourth overall.

If it wasn't for the team driving required, she would like to get into electronic hauling: the transport of computers, telephone switching equipment, and office machines that is part of the household-goods moving industry, but is considered "elite fleet" work. The van used for this work is more like a freight trailer than a furniture van. It has a flat floor so that heavy pieces can be rolled in, and there are no wheel boxes protruding into the load space. Air suspension is a must —the entire rig, tractor and trailer, floats on air. Electronic drivers, she says, have to be prepared "to make some big miles when called on" because the machinery they're rushing cross-country is usually a one-of-a-kind item, and an entire project may be shut down until they arrive. "It's not unusual to have over a million dollars worth of freight on your truck, and delicate stuff at that. It doesn't pay to drop anything."

In the meantime, Dee enjoys driving, even on days when she has to cope with bad weather, poor road conditions, and scalemen who call her in for no other reason than to see if she is alone. "I can truck, see parts of the country I've missed, and earn a living at the same time. I love it!"

Susan Hansen of Camby, Indiana, is 32, divorced, and intent on becoming an owner-operator. She has been driving since 1978 and feels pretty good about being a trucker. She graduated from Massey Business College in Houston with a secretary degree and has training as an OB tech. "When I started driving my first truck, I thought then—as I do now—that it was what I wanted to do with the rest of my life. I haven't any problems working for someone else, but I want to have a rig of my own." To that end, she has saved up $2,000 and could come up with another $2,000, but most people say she needs $10,000 or more for a down payment, plus money to run for six months.

Genie Mack is an LTD who owns her own rig. This Prague, Oklahoma, independent is also something of a celebrity, since she also cuts records. The daughter of an independent, she sang in church as a child, appeared regularly on an Oklahoma City country-and-western TV show as a teenager, and made her breakthrough during the 1979 shutdown when she wrote "We're Independent Truckers," a song dedicated to those truckers shut down at the Truckstops of America in the Dallas area. A couple of albums followed, and her song, "What Will We Do When the Trucks Are Gone?" hit the truckstop jukeboxes. She is leased to Dealers' Transit of Oklahoma and hauls throughout the country.

All-lady teams are rare, but Diane Shaw and Brandy Parkhill are a duo of Tacoma, Washington, truckers delivering Exxon gasoline all over the Northwest. "Because we are women, we must work a little harder to gain respect in our job, but once we showed the men drivers by example that we were here to work, we didn't have any trouble," says Shaw, who at 27 is the junior half of the team. "Physical strength doesn't matter on the job," says Parkhill. What matters, she adds, is a good mental attitude. "You worry about backing into someone when you're at the gasoline station about to unload, and then you worry because someone may drive over your hose while you're unloading. It ruins a hose to drive a car over it."

Parkhill, a single parent with three of her five children still at home, says she always wanted to be a truck driver. Shaw recently gave birth to a daughter, driving the truck until her eighth month of pregnancy. "My stomach was getting big, but it never quite touched the steering wheel," she says, laughing as she remembers the faces of some of the people she saw on her delivery runs.

Husband-and-wife teams are the most popular combination. Bob and Hazel Millage of Ashmore in central Illinois travel to California three times a month together. Then Bob runs to the East Coast once while Hazel remains home catching up on household and farm chores and working on the books. Bob has driven professionally for 21 years; Hazel started last year. They have purchased a Freightliner tractor, a two-tone brown and tan cabover with polished chrome stacks, chrome hubcaps, a double sleeper with a full-sized bed, a tank warmer for the 150-gallon tank to keep the diesel fuel from jelling, eight-track stereo, and mounted in the sleeper, a TV set. Phil and Lynda Hedges are one of two husband-wife teams working for Chesebrough-Ponds, Inc. They travel an average 5,000 miles a week, each driving 50 hours, and have done so for six years, delivering some 800,000 pounds of freight every month in runs all across the country. Lynda has logged 750,000 accident-free miles and is the first woman to receive the company's five-year safe-driving award. Companies like to stress driver safety records and the ATA nominates a driver of the year. (Texan Frank Waldron of C and H Transportation of Dallas is the champion, logging 3.5 million miles over a 43-year period without an accident.)

Michael and Jo Wadleigh of Wilton, New Hampshire, are a young owner-operator duo. Mike had been driving for four years and Jo had just gotten her associate degree in accounting when their respective parents cosigned a lease-purchase on a truck for them. In four years, Mike and Jo had it paid off. "We've seen all 48 states and all sorts of attractions," says Jo. "I want to tell any young couple with a background in tractor-trailer driving (minimum one year) and enough money for the down payment—or loving and trusting parents who will back them up and sign for them—that trucking is one adventure not to be passed up."

The big household goods and electronics carriers—Allied, Atlas, Bekins, Mayflower, North American, and United—actively encourage husband-wife team-ups. Long-haul furniture hauling and the transportation of computers and other electronics is a transcontinental operation in which owner-operators must be prepared to go anywhere and be gone from home base for very long periods of time. Loading and unloading are all-day jobs, which they must supervise themselves, even with hired help. Electronics hauling is usually assigned to experienced owner-operators who have proven themselves to be especially well qualified to handle these delicate, often million-dollar loads. In return, they enjoy the highest rates of pay on the road.

Bonny Floyd, the former beautician, lives with Darryl G. Evans, in their customized Peterbilt leased to United Van Lines, an impeccable tractor with a special, aerodynamic vista-view dome that accommodates a camper table for paperwork as well as a double bed. United has 15 men—it calls them coordinators; the drivers call them dispatchers—responsible for assigning tonnage in geographic regions. "As soon as we empty out in New York, I call the dispatcher for the Greater New York area for the next load," says Bonny. "These days it's not too difficult getting loads to Sun Belt areas. The tough job is to get backhauls to the Frost Belt. We could tell the Census Bureau on a weekly basis where the population drift is going.

LTDs have had a good influence on trucking, everyone agrees. "Most drivers respect us," says Valerie Montana, "even if we get hassled by cops at truckstops at night. An LTD walking from her rig to the coffee shop is liable to get arrested and booked for prostitution, and it's up to her husband to go and get her out of jail. Women driving solo like myself have to carry their Class 8 permit to go to the bathroom at some of the worst truckstops. Whores may *tell* the cops they're LTDs, but they don't have a Class 8 permit to back it up."

A lady behind the wheel is no guarantee of no hassles on the road, either. Kathy Siebert of Toledo usually hauls steel west and fresh produce east with her husband, Mike. Her worst experience occurred in Grand Island, Nebraska, with a load of apples. Mike was lying sick in the sleeper, with 102-degree fever, when the scalemen in Grand Island told her she was overweight on the rear axles by four cartons. Besides paying a $33 fine, she had to find another trucker to help her place the four offending cartons in the sleeper. Maintaining a sense of humor and a tongue firmly in her cheek, Kathy will tell you, "I never overload, never cheat on my logbook, never run over 55—and I never lie."

17
DOWNTIME

Junior swung wide, hand over hand on the steering wheel, and pulled into the fluorescent brightness of the fourth fuel lane, brakes hissing and waking up Karen. He stopped, cut headlights, air conditioning and engine, and heard her stir in the back.

"Gotta get some motion lotion," he explained, rolling down the window.

"God, I really slept, didn't I?" she mumbled.

"Even through the Louisiana scales an hour ago."

"What happened?"

"I had to pay, but I left the engine runnin' so you wouldn't wake up."

"How about a shower?"

"How about somethin' to eat? I'm starved."

"Me, too."

He got down and told the attendant he wanted 400 gallons of number two. The guy nodded and pointed toward the office.

These days, with diesel over a dollar a gallon, you go inside first. Normally, he would have called in his order on the CB, but Karen had really conked out this time, even through the Tooney scales hassle.

The name tag identified the assistant manager as Linda Barrera. She was a tall girl with glasses and a bouffant hairdo. The electronic gadgetry behind the fuel counter looked like a small airport control tower. By the window she had a pair of binoculars. After she had run off his MasterCard, he realized why. She used the field glasses to read his goddamn license plate!

"That's a new one," he said, nodding toward the binoculars when she put them down again.

"Management rule." She wrote the license number in the upper corner before she let him sign.

When he got back to the truck, the diesel was already flowing and the attendant was up on his ladder cleaning the windshield. Karen was getting down, sleepy and disoriented and shielding her face from the harsh light. She had her travel bag with her.

"Why did you have to pay?" she asked and yawned.

"We're almost 5,000 pounds over. I just didn't realize it in the rush back there in Houston."

"Where are we?"

"Lafayette."

"See you in the restaurant."

"Right."

Five minutes later, he pulled away from the fuel islands and found a parking spot behind the main building. The lot was wall to wall with rigs. He checked the flapper valves on the exhaust stacks to be sure the freezer unit was running. It was second nature to him since that hot August his old Thermo King conked out in New Mexico while he was hauling a backload of nitrogen tetroxide from San Diego to St. Louis. He did 20 knee bends and 15 arm and neck exercises and walked around to the main entrance.

Living on the road doesn't mean living out of a garment bag. If today's tractors come with air-ride seats, air-suspension space heaters, and air conditioning along with tape decks and the ubiquitous CB, the truckstops have everything else you will need.

Scattered along the interstates, the 2,000-odd truckstops have grabbed four-fifths of the over-the-road transportation market. It is here that you see acres of parking space, rows of fuel islands, and garage and tire shops equipped to handle maintenance and repairs. Here, you've got laundry rooms, showers, lounges complete with TVs, pool tables and pinball machines, and always, the 100-seat-plus restaurant and the mini-department store that carries everything from 20-inch-neck-size shirts and size-12 cowboy boots to heated rearview mirrors and highway flares, cassettes, and cosmetics. In a section usually marked "For Professional Drivers Only," banks of TV screens run messages of computerized load information, and banks of telephones and panels of direct lines to local brokers similar to hotel directories in airport arrival areas line the walls. The truckstop serves as contact point for both the 1,500-miles-per-24-hour team and the 500-miles-a-day and sleep-at-night company driver. Truckers' credit cards and central billing have become a boon to carriers and owner-operators; and the 800-number telephones, the InstaCom, Com Check and Dial-A-Check allow carriers and drivers, shippers and terminals to keep in contact. Money is telexed to drivers at truckstops; independents find hauls and backhauls on the TV monitors. And truckstops never close.

The newest services are medical and dental centers. Steve Rosenzweig is a doctor who for years commuted on I-95 between his practices in Philadelphia and Washington, and who continually heard truckers on the CB complaining about aches and pains and seeking advice from other geargrinders. Dr. Rosenzweig looked into the idea of opening a truckers' clinic at a busy truckstop somewhere along the heavily traveled I-95 corridor. He asked a lot of truckers what they thought, and a vast majority said it was the most logical thing they had ever heard, that such a clinic would take a lot of worries off any guy's mind. Some even suggested developing a hotline so a trucker hospitalized while on the road could have his wife and family stay at another trucker's home in the area. When Dr. Rosenzweig saw figures showing that the average trucker spends 283 days a year on the road, he was convinced, and in 1981 he opened the first Travelers Medical-Dental Center next to the Union 76 stop in southern New Jersey off I-295. Since then, similar centers have opened at the Truck World Mall in Hubbard, Ohio, and at Toledo Five at exit 5 of the Ohio Turnpike.

Truckers see truckstops as their private preserve and resent tourists, while truckstop owners want all the traffic they can handle. "Goddamn four-wheelers see a lot of trucks parked, so they say, 'Hey, we can eat cheap there,' and pull in," says Mike Carroll, a wiry owner-operator from Detroit. Richard S. Stanley, an economist who has done feasibility studies for truckstop owners, puts it more politely. "Truckers don't want tourists there. They want this to be *their* home away from home."

Truckstops are where the desperate strands of footloose America intersect. It's where teenage runaways hang out, and parents pin up Jane-come-home-we-all-love-you notices on bulletin boards. Old-timers complain that "young cowboys" are giving trucking a bad name by turning its television image of lawlessness into evil swagger. LTDs tend to defend the young cowboys, saying it's 50–50 rotten apples and nice boys trying to make a living.

Here, proud independents who spend the night in their sleepers out on the parking lot scorn company drivers whose rooms at the motel are prepaid by their carriers. Electronics owner-operators scoff at produce haulers, who sniff at hog haulers. Here, you see the crew cuts of the United Van Lines drivers, and husband-and-wife teams wearing almost the same expression under identical Mack caps. You see wiry, angry guys with good-time codrivers, women who have had their knocks in life but know how to grin and bear it. You see a skinny, hunched-over trucker chain-smoking at the restaurant counter while his beefy LTD eats the cream pie. You see rednecks in T-shirts, arms full of tattoos, and you see survivors of the Haight-Ashbury era with pigtails, bad teeth, and kind eyes. At the direct-line panel, a black driver systematically calls the listed brokers, asking, "You got any eastbound load for a flatbed?" You hear no fractured Chicano talk. Midwestern twang and Southern drawl are standard English here. Drivers in overalls swap load tips with potbellied independents while they all wait for the InstaCom okay. You see the rhinestone cowboys with their immaculate sideburns and designer jeans, and the lone Indian trucker with a stone face as richly expressive as Sitting Bull's. The cowboy hats are everywhere, from the rakish utilitarian to the bedabbled, befeathered sagebrush chic. The high-heeled boots and big belt buckle are standard issue.

The best time to talk to any of them is on weekends at

truckstops in the remote outskirts of big cities. Truckers with loads walk briskly to the restaurant and back out. Guys who have to wait until Monday morning stand around in groups, trading gripes and watching who's coming. Downtime away from home is a loss of earning power. On the parking lot, enterprising sign painters set up their vans and, on good Sundays, do a passable business pinstriping tractors and stenciling names on doors.

Inside, when they're tired of talking, the men laying over drift toward the TV monitors and watch the teletexts once more. "Lowboy and liquids. Teams or singles needed for terminals in Houston, Beaumont, Lake Charles, L.A. Qualified operators. One year minimum flatbed and tank experience. Layoffs need not apply." Or, "Westbound loads. Reefers. Call 800-851-0254." The screens also advertise secondhand sales. "'81 Kenworth K100 Aerodyne $67,200." "Oil-field Lowboys. Write or Call." "Truckers, don't get repossessed! Save your credit! Conventional and sleepers, 1977–1980 models. 400 hp or better. We buy your equity." The messages on the bulletin board, between ads for nonlethal automatic pistols for $39.95 and insurance brokers' business cards, contain private dramas: "Don—Sue L. will wait at Big T Motel until Friday noon. Call!"—and maybe cryptic happiness: "Bob Leary, KIZ. Denver 303-883-5674."

Lobster-faced men throw towels into designated bins while an LTD heads for the women's shower. "It seems you only have to walk past a truck and it squirts oil and grease at you," she says. In the restaurant, guys are on their 5th cup and 25th gripe.

Truckstops generate as much as $20 million in sales a year, but they weren't always big business. When construction of the interstates began, most of them were dingy-looking setups: a couple of diesel fuel pumps and a greasy-spoon restaurant. As the network of superslabs expanded, new stops offered a bit more—larger restaurants, rooms with bunks where a dozen drivers slept at once and woke up feeling fortunate if six of them still had their wallets.

Oil companies and conglomerates are the big owners.

Union Oil of California is the leader, with 371 truckstops, followed by Skelly Oil. The newest and biggest of them all is not a Union 76 franchise, but Truckers Inn, a $7-million sprawl of parking lot and five-story 150-unit motel in Jessup, Maryland, off I-95 between Washington and Baltimore. Truckers Inn is resort, social club, eating place, and pit stop for 10,000 members of the semitrailer set every week. It employs 200 people, ranging from a pool man to security guards, who constantly patrol the 300-rig parking area to deter vandals and thieves from what is often a collection of more than $150 million worth of trucks and cargo. Although the owners bristle at the suggestion that prostitutes bang on cab doors at night, desk clerks at the motel are told to be wary of checking in single women from the area, and the security guards are supposed to shunt ladies of the night away from the 13-acre lot.

A warning on the entrance doors says that Maryland Police will ticket rigs parked on the surrounding streets at $50 a shot, and the main lobby is small and unexciting, but there is Mozart on the PA system. Wednesdays and Thursdays are the busiest. Truckers move in and out of the cement-block 12-by-14 rooms of the motel—"nap trap" in road jargon—at a steady pace. Wake-up calls come from a buzzer by the door as many truckers would roll over and ignore the phone by the bed. The one window per room is small and recessed to cut the sound of revving Cats, and a faint "white noise" imitating the sound inside a cab is piped into the rooms. The motel enjoys 130% capacity. The room is $25 a night. Truckers Inn charges $2 for a shower, $30 for an attendant to wash your rig.

The downstairs bar is called the Eighteen Wheeler Lounge and the crowd is pure trucker. Miller Lites and Jack Daniels–and-Coke decorate the counter and the tables. A lighted sign warns on-duty drivers not to drink, but everybody says they're on downtime. Bluegrass music pours from the jukebox and the rap is mellow.

A pair of the west's most famous truckstops—"water holes," in the vernacular—are Boomtown and Sierra Sid's, both off I-80 in western Nevada just before the California state line. Sid Doan's 76 stop in Sparks, in suburban Reno, covers 23 acres and has 400 employees. The showstopper in the huge restaurant-casino is a real live Kenworth tractor-trailer with 31 slot machines. Up front in the cab is a pair of man and wife owner-operator mannequins. The CB monitors channel 17, and when activated, a tape plays the noise of a Detroit Diesel starting up. Each slot machine has a gearshift knob.

Fifteen miles westbound is Boomtown, a hotel-casino truckstop that proclaims itself the "Greatest Little City in the World." Boomtown is immense and computerized, with every service a driver would want, including a hot sauna. Coffee is free, even a thermosful, and every August, owner Bob Cashell lays on a big truckers-only barbecue. For three days, Cashell and staff offer all drivers and their families free steak-and-rib dinners plus limitless amounts of beer and soda, prizes and live music. Says general manager Ed Allison, "Heck, if someone wants to eat 20 steaks, he can." Cashell is even more hyperbolic. "If a driver wants cow turds over easy, you go out and find them and cook 'em the way he likes 'em."

To match Cashell, Sierra Sid holds a four-day "truckarama" every spring. Under a huge tent on the parking lot, Peterbilt, Detroit Diesel, and truck suppliers show their products, and Tyrone Malone and his souped-up racing machines are usually the star attraction. One year, Sid's truckarama featured a boxing match between midget poker dealer David Burnham and a kangaroo.

There are three beefy ladies who run the 42 truckstop at exit 40 on I-80 in eastern Pennsylvania and who feed and mother any trucker who pulls in on Christmas Eve. The rest of the year, Marirose Hileman runs the fuel operations, Diane Brenner takes care of the cash register, and Esther Tatrault runs the kitchen, but on Christmas Eve, Diane puts on that red suit and whiskers and drives everybody up the chimney, as she says.

"When you bang on a trucker's door late at night, the last thing he expects to see is Santa Claus," she says, laughing. "We throw a big party for the guys who are a long way from home. The walls are filled with pictures of last year's party. For a lot of truckers, the Christmas party has become an annual event; it certainly has for us."

Petro Truck Stop on I-10, 12 miles east of El Paso, is the biggest in Texas—and the most automated. Truckers pump their own diesel at a price that's discounted about a nickel a gallon. The showers are free and the ALL YOU CAN EAT sign in the Iron Skillet means what it says, top sirloin steak included. Holding's Little America in Cheyenne, Wyoming, offers a golf course, Louisiana Truckstop in Nashville is famous for its "people," and the 49er Truck Plaza outside Sacramento, California, has computerized weather reports for anywhere a driver may want to go.

From Shakey Side (the West Coast, with L.A. as Shakey City) to Dirty Side (East Coast), from Chi Town (Chicago) to the Big D (Dallas), every geargrinder has his favorite water hole. Necessity, however, draws them all to truckstops. Few other places let them park their 65-foot rigs, and only truckstops guarantee that they can get fuel, repairs, food, and an around-the-clock parking place if they need to sleep. It's the extras, of course, that make a guy truck another hundred miles to get to his favorite place. Overbuilding in the early 1970s left truckstops something of a buyer's market. After Union Oil of California and Skelly Oil Company set the trend with huge, full-service plazas, such nonpetroleum *Fortune* 500 companies as Ryder System, Greyhound, and Holiday Inns jumped in, sometimes just buying Union 76 franchises to get their feet wet. Many 76 lessees found it difficult to survive their first couple of years because they had to pay rents one-third above average and accept margins on fuel sales 40% below average. Greyhound and Holiday Inn quietly dropped out, but the Truckstops of America chain, owned by Ryder, is expanding, and to win customers has created its own FASTRAK credit card for owner-operators.

In CB lingo, a truckstop restaurant is, at best, an "eat 'em up," and, at worst, a "chew 'n choke." But the food is always lousy; everybody knows that. There aren't many mom-and-pop truckstops anymore, and it's a matter of opinion whether the few that are left serve better food than the industrial cuisine

171

the huge plazas dish up. In defense of their prefab grub, the big boys argue that it just can't be otherwise, because truckers want big portions for a price they can handle and they want it fast. Ask any waitress.

Sheryl Obreck, voted the most popular waitress by over 7,000 truckers in midwestern states, dishes it out at Boondocks U.S.A. in Williams, Iowa, on I-35, 60 miles north of Des Moines. "They're grumbling and grouchy when they come in here," she says. "Some of them wait for a big kiss or a big hug, some of them ask you if you want to go around the world with them or whatever, but they all want their food right now."

A good water-hole waitress is a gem and the Union 76 chain runs annual contests, polling 40,000 truckers to find the queen among 800 candidates every year. The winner receives an all-expense paid Caribbean cruise for two. The consensus is that a good waitress has a sixth sense that seems to tell her whether a trucker wants to talk or be let alone. She's ready, Johnny-on-the-spot, with that second cup of coffee, she quickly spots four-wheelers sitting down in the truckers' section and gets them to leave. No hard feelings. She can tell a lady trucker at a glance and serves all truckers *fast*.

The $2.95 spaghetti plate and the $3.95 fried chicken dinner are fast because they stand and simmer all day, and the burgers in all their variations are minced meat thrown on a grill. Since every trucker lives on his own schedule there are no rush hours—breakfast is served around the clock—and the whole menu has to be ready at all times. Being overweight is the occupational hazard of trucking, but especially for long-haul drivers. Sitting immobile behind the wheel 10 to 12 hours or more doesn't help and, say Washington DOT statistics, truckers are careless about where, when, what, and how they eat. Women truckers and the general awareness of nutritional values have begun to change the menus, especially at bigger plazas. Serve-yourself salad bars are spreading East from Texas and many menus feature "lean and low" choices.

Eugene Wittington, the restaurant and motel manager at Truckers Inn, concedes the fare could be tastier, but that speed and simplicity are more important considerations in serving 1,300 meals a day to truckers on the run. "For those whose waistlines are growing faster than the national debt," says Petro Truck Stop's Tom Jordan, he has added a low-calorie section to the usual stack-of-pancakes–steak–fried-chicken–spaghetti driver's delight. Besides eating too much of the wrong foods, and eating too fast and too irregularly, Juanita Myers at the 76 stop at Hebron, Ohio, adds a psychological observation. "Most guys are on their own. The wife isn't sitting across from you and giving you one of those knowing looks when you take another cream pie."

18
REPUTATIONS

The girls head home in their Hondas and Fairlanes before Sunday dawns, often in pairs, counting the night's money and adjusting their lipstick. When the sun, the color of an unripe peach, rises and reveals the rows of rigs, a white tractor-trailer with a cross on its wind deflector rolls onto a lot, ready to service other needs of the downtime crowd. "Praise the Lord for 155 souls saved on this location so far this year," begins the evangelist. "Last Sunday, over 70 people came to this chapel and 3 were saved. During the week, Fred and Melba Wright took the mobile chapel up through Iowa. One was saved and a lot of seed was planted." The chapel trailer has room for 40, but few seats are taken. After the sermon, there's a highway safety movie.

Bunny Gregory is Virginia's number-one double-clutchin'-trailer preacher lady, truckin' for Jesus heaven-bound and movin' on. She hauls in a Ken with her husband Orville and she gives loud thanks to the Lord before the digs into her food—tacos and Spanish rice in Shakey Side truckstops, steak and tossed salad on Dirty Side. The Road Map of Life is the theme of her sermons. Paul Phillips is a highway preacher from Oklahoma City. "Luke 14:23 commands us to go into the highways and hedges and compel them to come into God's House so that it will be filled," he says. "Won't you join us in reaching the lost in the trucking industry?" To reach, Phillips goes to truck races and organizes truckers' rallies at churches that have grounds big enough to accommodate 18-wheelers. Bud Crusenberry bears witness in Tennessee. A driver for 20 years for Smith Transfer, Crusenberry drank and "ran with the wrong crowd, no worse than any lost trucker, but certainly no better." One night he saw the light and began to spend evenings and weekends preaching. He was called on the carpet by the union, but the terminal manager came to his defense and many of his trucker friends came to Christ through his testimony.

In Lakeland, Florida, TWIGS—Truckers' Wives in God's Service—meet every Monday night to share and pray for each other's needs and family problems and for the men out on the road. Up in Toronto, Ken Gerber, George Holz, and Elmer and Vera Margin got a new mobile chapel on the road, christening it Pathfinder. In Oak Grove, Missouri, Rich and Joyce Thebo have established a hotline for day or night counseling and prayer. One night the word is out for Big Red. "We hear you've been a fine trucker and a fine man. You've taken time to help others up and down the road. Now you need to get back to God yourself. Your wife and those teenagers love you very much, and are praying for you. It's time to make a change, Big Red, and get back to God." Bill Payne in Omaha pioneered "Just for Jammers," a radio gospel program for truckers. He produced weekly broadcasts for nine radio stations prior to his death in a truck accident in 1980.

"Yes, you see that stuff now," says Mike Carroll, laying over at the huge Ontario "500" 76 truckstop east of Los Angeles one weekend. "But they're nice. There's no grabbin' you and Hallelujah."

His wife agrees the preachers are not born-again hardliners. "It's the young they're tryin' to help."

"It's like an even keel," Mike feels. "It's the young ones who holler for dope and girls on the CBs, who think that's a great life. Get a load, deliver it, get paid and have fun until the money runs out and you look for another load."

Jerry Brown is a leader in the "highway outreach." He is the owner of Trucker's Village No. 2 in Oklahoma City and director of the big south-central region of Transport for Christ International, which is responsible for sending those 18-wheeler mobile chapels to loading docks, truckstops, rodeos, trucking events, and wherever else owners will allow them to set up. The pitch to management is its highway safety video programs.

"We present the whole man behind the wheel, or on the dock, in the mechanics' shop," says the jovial Brown. "Most folks sometimes forget that man is made up of three integral parts—body, soul, spirit. The average safety program puts its emphasis on the body and soul; body meaning fitness, soul the intellect. Our program adds the other—spirit."

Transport for Christ is interdenominational and not affiliated with anyone. Its half-dozen rigs are highly visible white tractor-trailers with illuminated crosses above the cab and a place for worship in the trailer. Each unit is staffed by a chaplain-driver, usually with his wife. "Many great spiritual battles are fought and many great victories are won here," says Brown, who traces the origins of Transport for Christ to a young Toronto trucker who found God and became aware of the vast spititual needs of people around him. The idea trickled south and the first U.S. chapters were formed in the mid-1960s, to become something of a tidal wave in recent years. "Our mission remains unchanged as we reach out to some of the 20 million people we estimate are in our field of responsibility. We hear from an average of more than one person a week who has turned to the Lord."

The Mormon Church is on the road with its JOCruiser and the JOC Radio for the Man and Woman Who Make Their Living in a Truck show, originating on KOB in Albuquerque. The JOC has established a Road Report Hot Line for truckers to report exactly what *they* find on the highways. The JOC 18-wheeler roams the Midwest and the West in the winter and many drivers report saving hours, even days, by regularly tuning in to the every-hour-on-the-half-hour road alerts.

Allycia and J. C. Taapken are a husband-and-wife team who "trucks with God" and J. C. is Mr. Supertrucker. He won that title in a nationwide contest conducted by *Road King*. Truckers nominated each other, and the thread running through the responses was gentleness and understanding of a family man ready to help others. "They are the virtues most Mr. Trucker contestants rated highly," said *Road King.* Winner Taapken has been a driver 23 years. His father was a trucker and two of his eight children might follow the family tradition. As a Mr. Supertrucker winner, he got a Stetson hat full of dollar bills ($504 to be exact).

Truckers' readiness to help each other and the occasional four-wheeler is praised with words that sometimes make a geargrinder blush:

> I am indebted to long-haul truckers and sure like to reach as many as I can with my thanks [Betty Gable of Pine Island, New York, wrote *Overdrive* in 1981]. For nine years while living in Coral Gables, Florida, I used to pack my four children, pets, and loads of luggage into my car. Each June after school ended, we headed north to visit grandparents. At the start, truckers adopted us and convoyed us on the routes with the fewest tolls, construction, detours, and other obstructions. The same thing took place on our return trip in September. . . . When my daughter at 17 decided to hitchhike from New York to California, she used trucks. She went all those miles with only one ungentlemanly experience. As a mother, a traveling woman, and a fellow citizen, I wish to pass the word—to all you good truckers, you are appreciated.

Not every geargrinder would want his daughter to thumb her way to California with other truckers, but the knights-of-the-road reputation persists. Motorists who do a lot of long-distance driving come to trust the boys in the big rigs, to know that they *know,* if not this particular stretch of highway, the gut feeling of the road, its deepest dangers and meanings, what you can and cannot do. A lot of four-wheelers have adopted the CB, its lingo and ethics, but even before radio communications, the truckers' hand signals were respected by those who understood them. A driver clasping his hands briskly meant a wreck was down the road. A horizontal palm in a downward motion meant you should slow down, for whatever reason. Two fingers held up in a V, whether vertical or horizontal, meant "the law" was nearby, and a fast corkscrew circle with the hand clenched and a finger extended meant the road was clear, that you could step on it. The amount of information passed along up and down the highway was uncanny and many old-timers think the hand signals were superior to radio contact because nobody could listen in. The old system has been rendered obsolete not only by the CB revolution, however. Hand signals can no longer be seen from cab to cab across the wide, landscaped medians of many stretches of the interstates.

Most truckers find the four-wheelers they have to share the road with loathsome, to put it politely. From up in the cab, cars are the enemy, whether the family Cowboy Cadillac (station wagon) or the pregnant roller skate (VW Bug). Motorists refuse the most elementary courtesy when it comes to trucks. They cut in front of them without warning, hog the fast lane at minimal speed, scoot out from on-ramps, and in general endanger their own and other people's lives with a nonchalant stupidity that makes truckers cry or, on the CB, appeal to police for help. "Are drivers specially trained to frustrate and annoy not only their fellow drivers of gasoline-powered shopping carts, but particularly those who pilot the big rigs?" Bob Dunham asks. "More than one fine, long-haul trucker has ended up in the rubber room at the local asylum due to the unyielding efforts of those dingdongs."

"CB clowns" are a new menace. A CB clown isn't just any motorist who has bought himself a 40-channel set at Radio Shack and is now taking the long way driving home so he can try it out on the local stretch of interstate. A CB clown is a person who just has to establish the front door and the back door, introduce himself to everyone in between, ask for a smokey report, a weather update, and an accident report for at least 100 miles in both directions, before exiting seven miles later. The clown is the Detroit paterfamilias taking the wife and kiddies to Disney World, who, by the time he reaches Toledo, is convinced "them poor old truckers" in the southbound lane won't make it to Florida without his undivided attention. He earns his stripes alerting truckers about the Kentucky scales just south of Louisville. He goes past the scales a couple of miles, gets off on a side road, puts up the nine-foot whip antenna (Big Mama) and gets on the air. "This is Life Saver, to all southbound 18-wheelers. There's a funny-looking vehicle parked behind the scalehouse and lots of guys in uniform hanging around." A trucker comes back and asks if the scales are open and is told, "No, but it sure looks suspicious."

Now, all rigs southbound on I-65 and a good number of northbound trucks will hear the message relayed. They begin to figure how much they can scale in at. Some of them begin to pull off and look for alternate routes around the Louisville area. Somebody says the Louisville scales have been closed for nearly two years. An hour later, a Georgia flatbed hauler, running back empty, volunteers to become the front door. He drives past the scalehouse and reports the suspicious-looking vehicle is a 10-year-old school bus with a big sign on the side, Troop 4, Louisville, Boy Scouts of America, that all the 26 guys in uniform are in short pants. They are having their picnic and don't realize the mid-country north-south corridor is in disarray from Indianapolis to Nashville.

By Georgia, the CB clown has pretty well gotten the hang of it. "Breaker, breaker. This is the number-one Life Saver, there's a plain wrapper sitting in the peach grove at mile marker 84." The plain wrapper is no unmarked state cruiser, but a van with New Jersey plates and two guys helping themselves to a few peaches. By the Florida scales, he has informed smokey that the red and white flatbed hauling a big wide machine has lost its overwidth sign, but not to worry, he'll stay with the 18-wheeler all the way. It will take the driver of the red and white flatbed half an hour to clear the scales. When a trucker doesn't answer the CB clown, he flags him down and tells him his CB must be out of order.

Two state troopers parked at a Howard Johnson keep the clown busy for the next 50 miles. So does the fact that he sees two smokies tooling north. He is sure they look like they're going to do a flip-flop and cross over to the southbound. In the absence of a CB clown, truckers sometimes do it to themselves. Miles before reaching a speed trap or a logbook check, you'll hear everybody chatting about it. In fact, you'll sometimes hear about it a day's drive out and by the time you get there, the police or DOT authorities will long since be gone.

The crime wave has not spared trucking, but the increase is mostly of the organized kind, that takes place out of sight of the public.

Over 80% of the dollar losses sustained by the industry stems from cargo stealing. The thefts range from the pilfering of merchandise, stolen one carton at a time and repeated a thousand times a year, to the hijacking of entire trailers. The thieves are people with easy access to shipments. Carton theft can mean a terminal employee knocking two boxes of transistor radios off the dock during the midnight shift and at the next break putting them into his car, or it can mean collusion between driver and dispatcher in dropping off cartons at unauthorized points and destroying all pertinent paperwork.

In 1980, *Truck Tracks* reported on a predawn hijacking that took place along a deserted stretch of interstate in Nevada. The hijackers first asked a trucker whether he had his "ears on." A conversation ensued, revealing the trucker was bound for Denver with a load of shrimp. Farther down the road, a dark, official-looking car with a flashing red light pulled alongside. The driver eased onto the shoulder and stopped. As he stepped down from his tractor a uniformed man stuck a gun in his stomach and ordered him into the shrubbery. "In this case the driver was lucky," the magazine said. "After being threatened and tied to a tree, he was left unharmed and freed himself within eight hours. His tractor was recovered three days later in a city 200 miles west. The trailer and a $200,000 load of frozen shrimp were never recovered."

Those splashy paint jobs that transform company-owned "fruitliners"—vernacular for plain white trailers—into multicolored ads aren't just done to turn fleets into moving billboards, but to discourage hijackings. Levi Strauss and Company of San Francisco is one corporation that found anonymous road equipment created difficulties for law enforcement trying to locate stolen or missing fruitliners and cargo. As a result, it had 3M's Transportation and Commercial Graphics Division design 45-foot-long decals for all its equipment.

Another type of theft that is becoming more and more a problem for owner-operators is the theft of equipment, purely for the equipment and not for the cargo. In many instances, a stolen tractor is taken to a "chop shop," where the Freightliner or the Ford CL 9000 is dismantled and its Cat engine, its Eaton transmission, and other components sold as spare parts at a below-market price. The tremendous escalation in the cost of parts has created a ready and willing market for "hot" parts with no questions asked. Stolen trailers are repainted and fake new identification numbers are stamped on the frames. The Washington DOT estimates the direct cost of stolen cargo to hover around $1 billion, with the trucking industry accounting for $870 million of that amount. The indirect costs in lost business, claims administration, and boosted insurance premiums to shippers, receivers, and carriers are thought to be two to five times that amount. FBI special agents Andrew Palumbo and Robert McCartin advise truckers to be careful of parking in motels and truckstops, especially outside high-crime areas, to keep the fuel supply low when parking overnight at motels or over weekends at terminals so thieves can't get very far during the critical first 15 or 20 minutes, and not to back up to a loading platform until the truck is ready to be loaded or unloaded.

Still less visible forms of crime are buried in the depths of fleet-terminal maintenance and repair shops. The issue is explosive, because at its core is the accusation that the industry is the chief contributor to the highway accidents that either cause truckers to kill themselves and others, or merely cause huge casualty losses.

Safety doesn't make money, and for that reason expenses to keep the rolling stock safe are not very high on any carrier's priority lists. Safety directors are the first to be laid off in a slump, or more frequently, if they protest too much or run too strict a safety check. "Get the load delivered and worry about the condition of the unit later," is the standard overriding order by operations vice-presidents. Instead of being the foundation of any safety program, the Bureau of Motor Carrier Safety regulations are usually the sum total and substance of it. For the record, any carrier executive will proudly say his company complies with all the BMCS rules to the letter, and he will maintain that in the face of accident records suggesting exactly the opposite.

Norman Scott was safety director for Superior Trucking Company of Atlanta until he went public with accusations that targeted neglect *and* organized crime as the root causes of increased trucking accidents. A former army pilot and safety manager for the Hertz Corporation truck-leasing division, Scott claimed not only minimal compliance with minimum safety standards, but collusion between carriers and their insurance brokers for kickbacks on insurance policies, and for keeping relatives with high accident rates or physical disabilities on the payroll. Hiring high-risk drivers at substandard wages and farming out company haulage to sleazy subcontractors who know how to get around union pay scales and seniority benefits—in collusion with local union bosses if necessary—are what labor racketeering is all about.

In reporting Scott's allegations in 1980, the *Commercial Car Journal* said such complaints were by no means isolated incidents. The fleet owners' trade publication discovered that one carrier with an exceptionally poor safety record had hired part-time drivers from a labor exchange working out of a supermarket warehouse in New Jersey. The company was Decana Labor Supply, and the magazine found it was controlled by individuals associated with the Genovese-Catena organized crime family. Another company hiring out drivers to such *Fortune* 500 corporations as Continental Can and Crown Zellerbach was Universal Coordinators, owned by the family of Eugene R. Boffa of Hackensack, New Jersey.

In 1980, the Justice Department had worked over five years to nail Boffa and Teamster Local 326 President Frank Sheeran of Wilmington, Delaware, for racketeering. The drivers leased to Crown Zellerbach and to Inland Container Corporation of Newark, Delaware, by Universal Coordinators, had been members of Sheeran's local. In 1973, they had threatened to strike in a wage dispute. Rather than give in to their demands, Universal Coordinators canceled its contract with Crown Zellerbach and fired the drivers. Within a week, another labor leasing firm, Countrywide Personnel of California, picked up the contract and hired some of the fired truckers at lower wages. What the drivers never knew, the government was to contend in court, was that Boffa controlled Countrywide and that Sheeran received favors from the company. By making it appear that the new company was in charge, Boffa was able to hire union truckers at nonunion salaries, cut back on the number of truckers, and save on seniority-based benefits. Federal prosecutors also alleged that a similar "switch" was pulled at Inland, only this time the corporate name of the firm picking up the contract was Preferred Personnel, Inc.

In Philadelphia, the FBI set up a 12-man Organized Crime and Racketeering Strike Force and a long, tortuous investigation began. Special agent John Tamm was in charge, responding to allegations, tracking down rumors, cajoling and persuading insiders to turn government witness. The son of an FBI agent, Tamm was 28 when he started the case, a very tall, 210-pound guy who resembled a cleaner-cut version of the labor leaders he was investigating. When it was all over six years later, wrote Philadelphia *Inquirer* reporter William K. Marimow, "Watching Tamm, wearing a gold and blue Teamster Local 830 jacket, arrive at work after meeting an informant, one can almost imagine him barreling down the highway in a diesel-powered rig, his intent brown eyes fixed on the traffic below."

Tamm called his probe a Lone Ranger investigation, the "go look for" kind of case. In June 1981, however, Boffa was convicted of labor racketeering. The day Boffa was sentenced to 20 years in prison, Tamm telephoned the Wilmington Teamsters headquarters and, without identifying himself, said he had to talk to Sheeran, that he had some confidential information he could only tell the boss. After a few minutes, the Irishman was on the line. "Sheeran," the FBI agent began, "this is John Tamm of the FBI, and I want you to know you're next. . . ." The Irishman's three-word answer is unprintable. Together with six others, whose names read like an excerpt from a Who's Who of Philadephia-area labor luminaries, Sheeran was indicted on 11 counts of labor racketeering. The charges were that Sheeran and Boffa conspired to defraud members of Sheeran's union, and that the two carried out a plan that resulted in truckers losing wages, benefits, and in some cases their jobs. Sheeran's lawyer managed to get a separate trial for Sheeran, but four months after Boffa's conviction a federal district court jury in Wilmington found Sheeran guilty of all the charges against him. If all counts of the conviction stand up, he could be sentenced to 77 years in prison. His lawyers said they would appeal, and the now 61-year-old Sheeran emerged from the court smiling broadly and outlining his position in mixed metaphors. "They [federal prosecutors] only scored a field goal. We're going to win the second round when we go to the appeals court." The prosecutor told reporters he was gratified by the outcome and that the jury "did a courageous thing in rendering the verdict." The trial was highlighted by testimony from Charles Allen, a confessed "hit man" who was once on the Local 326 payroll. Allen became a government informer, was "wired up" by Tamm and his colleagues, and in 1978 secretly recorded conversations with Sheeran, Boffa, and other defendants concerning their truckers-for-hire business.

Money and safety are closely connected in trucking, and safety directors point an accusing finger at motor freight companies. If top managers would get out of their offices and behind the wheel of a long-haul tractor now and then to experience for themselves the pressures under which their drivers work, the result would be an instant improvement in employee relations, not to say safety. "The guys who are the quickest to put drivers in an unsafe environment have always been the first to buy the biggest car they could find with every possible option," snaps Scott. "They send a driver 500 miles in 90-degree temperature without air conditioning, but they wouldn't think of driving 10 miles to their country club without it. And these same guys can't understand why drivers have accidents or suffer from the 'anticompany' syndrome."

Safety directors say drivers should be thoroughly tested, checked out both mentally and physically. They should be completely retrained periodically. There should be a national commercial driver's license so that truckers with repeated citations can be tracked down and hauled off the road. According to Scott, too many drivers give the appearance of having a "death wish" in their performance and may be psychologically unfit to operate a rig. "Truckers must be raised to a higher level of concern for who they are and what they do if America is to have a safe trucking industry."

Tough laws are on the books, and behind their enactment are spectacular wrecks and frightening accidents. The federal DOT rules tell carriers which driving offenses make a driver unfit and ineligible for hire. Even though a driver may be qualified in all other respects, if he is found guilty of driving while under the influence of alcohol or drugs, he is automatically off the road for at least six months. Weight violations or operating without the right authority don't count against a trucker's record, but moving violations for speeding and other improper traffic maneuvers can lay him up and, as we have seen, make him a prey for shady labor exchanges finding cut-rate work for him.

A 1978 survey of thousands of truckers by Daryl Wyckoff of the Harvard Graduate School of Business found that half of both for-hire drivers and owner-operators "regularly" drive beyond the 10-hour-a-day limit, and one-third admitted they used several logbooks to circumvent the hours-of-service rules. Independents drive faster, the survey found (cruising at 63 mph as against 59 mph for hired hands) and get more tickets (1.33 moving violations vs. 0.41 for common carrier drivers per 100,000 miles). But the survey findings clashed with BMCS statistics on accidents. Wyckoff claimed independents had higher accident rates than regulated drivers; BMCS data says the reverse is true. Wyckoff claims the reason the BMCS data is wrong is that independents don't report all their accidents, whereas private and regulated carriers do. The BMCS, however, says the number of accidents *not* reported by independents is less than for carriers.

That truckers use amphetamines to stay awake and barbituates to come down from "rough roads" is common knowledge, and drugs remain the highway menace that won't go away. Lieutenant Norris Deville of the Louisiana State Police is an expert on the subject and the author of drug manuals for police and highway patrols. He cannot make up his mind which is worse, amphetamines ("uppers") that may cause hallucinations and make drivers see phantom vehicles and traffic that isn't there, or depressants ("downers") that make drivers delay reacting so long they literally slide to their own death—when it is not others that they kill. Deville has seen both. Behind the wheel, stimulants produce an inability to measure time and make behavior erratic and confused, while tranquilizers slow down reaction time. Some truckers have started using the worst of both worlds, Tuinal, a habit-forming drug containing both stimulants and depressants. "One is trying to pick 'em up, the other is trying to lay 'em down," says Deville.

Clues that fleet safety men must watch for in suspected pill addicts, he counsels, are a sudden increase in fuel use, indicating a driver is buying pills at truckstops that put the purchase on the bill, the disappearance of spare tires sold to pay for the drugs, an increase in minor repairs, and the misuse of issued credit.

Alcohol abuse is by far a bigger factor in highway accidents and deaths, however. The California Highway Patrol lists driving under the influence of alcohol and drugs separately in its annual statistics on accidents and fatalities involving trucks. For every highway injury where drugs are the primary collision factor, 18 are attributed to driving under the influence of alcohol. For each fatality caused by drugs, five are alcohol related.

Infinitely less harmful to self and others, if no less sinful in the eyes of the highway evangelists, is the prostitution at truckstops. The evolution that has put LTDs, wives, and girl friends on the road with the men has put a dent in the always nocturnal trade, but the girls who park their Corvettes on the fringe of the lots and make their arrangements by CB are still there, and they still find plenty of playmates. "Just blink your lights when you come in, honey," says the lady of the night in the joke. A second later, every truck on the lot starts flashing headlights. Truckstop owners try to discourage prostitution, but they have learned that if you run an all-inclusive rest-and-recreation emporium, it's hard to exclude certain forms of recreation. And in any case, the subject makes for lively arguing.

"Prostitutes are one thing, but the single and divorced waitresses are another more serious problem for us wives," says one married woman. "They have affairs, not one-night stands, and they don't charge. In fact, they provide transportation and free meals." When a trucking magazine runs out of ideas, it can always do another story on the subject, follow up with a request for readers' views on the proposition, Should Prostitution Be Legalized at Truckstops?—and sit back and watch the mail come in. The responses are good for still another issue.

Spokesmen for police departments with big truckstops in their jurisdiction say prostitution is merely part of water-hole crime, which includes assault, dope, runaway teens, and theft of loads, trailers, and cars. Truckers who want to ban the girls from the lots argue that the activity leaves drivers open to ever-wider checks and searches for drugs and for theft, which in turn leads to increased insurance rates. Searches and seizures at ports of entry have increased truckers' resentment against state DOT officials and scalemen. Truckers like to feel their truck is their home. "I'm in this truck more than I am in my own house," says Arthur Prosser of Monongahela, Pennsylvania. "What I keep in my truck is nobody's business. . . . The Constitution of the United States allows us to bear arms for the protection of ourselves and our families. But the cops enter our trucks and steal from us. I had a buddy shot in Houston while he rested in his sleeper. They shot right through the windshield."

Truckers think searches and seizures are unconstitutional, that they are a form of prying into your personal life. "They don't stop campers and tourists and go through their clothes hamper and toothpaste and shaving kit," snaps Roger Ledbetter of Houston. "It's like somebody going through your dresser drawers at home."

Cleveland attorney Bernard Berkman is something of a fixture at Independent Truckers Association conventions and his annual seminars, with follow-up question-and-answer periods, are standing-room-only affairs. Berkman, who has argued truckers' rights all the way to the Supreme Court, says the law is inconsistent. The Supreme Court ruled in 1979 in a case called *Arkansas* v. *Sanders* that if the cops determine there is "probable cause" to suspect a crime has been committed, no search warrant is needed to stop and search any vehicle, but that while the officers are rummaging through the truck or the car they have no business searching a locked suitcase, sealed cartons, or a satchel with a lock. Since the Sanders case the legality of searching a locked glove compartment has been a matter of contention. According to Berkman, a New York State court recently declared it illegal to search the zippered pocket of a jacket found in an automobile, and a Texas court of appeals ruled that if the trunk of a car is locked it can't be searched, even though the rest of the vehicle can. Both decisions are valid if police stop you on the spur of the moment. If they have obtained a search warrant, however, anything goes.

Long-haul trucking is a high-stress job.

A trucker traveling anywhere from 80,000 to 200,000 miles a year has a great deal more exposure than most people to the constant jarring pressures and occasional moments of stark terror on the superslabs. Truckers have been compared to air-traffic controllers when it comes to job aggravation. They are likely to have psychological problems and to lose their tempers easily. Long-distance trucking entails long, irregular hours behind the wheel, extended periods away from home and family, the need to drive in all types of weather, tight delivery schedules, keeping away from smokey and, for owner-operators, keeping up with the payments on the Big Mack or the Freightliner. Frustration, anger, resentment, and self-pity build up. Still, most insist they love it.

19
GRIPES

"How about the counter?" Karen asked, all pink and pretty after the shower. With the exception of the two seats just vacated, the U-shaped counter was full of talking and eating drivers, and she had an urge for a little company.

"Sure." Junior had splashed water on his face to look halfway decent and was counting on a full stomach and maybe a beer with dinner to lull him to sleep once they got started again.

As they sat down, the waitress cleaned off remnants of french fries and put down fresh paper mats and silverware. As she poured them coffee, Karen leaned toward Junior and whispered, "Aren't you supposed to stay off that stuff before hitting the sack?"

He measured himself one spoonful of sugar and wrinkled his nose. "Theoretically, yes, mama."

Across from them, a black driver with a Clark Gable moustache squashed out his cigarette, pushed the empty plate away from him, and said people in other businesses could work overtime, so why couldn't they?

The driver next to him had both his elbows on the counter and a gold chain practically dangling in his coffee. "They're afraid we'd make a living."

The black trucker blew smoke skyward in a blast of contempt for the Department of Transportation in Washington. "The logbook change is supposed to *expand* our driving time," he hissed. "You tell me why them DOT idiots want new regulations saying we can drive no more than 12 hours in any 24-hour period, when we can run 16 hours in any 24 now."

"We'll end up goddamn losing *hours*," said a Bekins-uniformed driver sitting next to an LTD who looked like she might be his wife.

The husky feller next to Karen asked if the present 10-hour rule didn't let you drive 16 hours the first day, 14 hours the second, and 10 on the third for a total of 40 hours over any three days.

"That's it," said the Bekins man. "Now, they wanna count your hours in 70-hour spreads."

But the subject was exhausted, as no one felt he could fathom the bureaucratic mind of the DOT in Washington. The black driver picked up his check but didn't get up. Karen ordered a steak, rare, french fries, and salad with thousand island. Junior decided on the roast beef, rare also, and a baked potato. He'd take his salad with Italian and a Budweiser. The waitress put Saltines in front of them, and the driver next to Karen asked the black guy where he was headin' anyway.

"Chicago, exempt."

That turned the conversation to "topping." The young cowboy on the other side of the LTD said he hated getting off the expressways anywhere in Chicago. It was virtually impossible to get inside the Loop because of the low clearance obstructions, and the Bekins driver, who needed a shave, said local drivers in Chicago got around because their trucks were built to below-standard 14-feet specs.

Junior nibbled on a Saltine and asked if they'd ever heard the old one about the guy who was topped off on La-Salle Street.

"His trailer was a total wreck," the driver with the gold chain hazarded.

Junior told the story. The guy was southbound through the Loop and thought the elevated train overhang on LaSalle looked awfully low. He hit the brakes hard and slowed almost to a dead stop, but not fast enough to prevent the front of his trailer from running under the girders and getting hopelessly stuck. The cops arrived and traffic was rerouted around the beached whale. They got a wrecker, but nothing could wrest the trailer out. Question: How did he dislodge the rig?

An older man who was busy eating on the other side of

the driver with the gold chain smiled, as if he knew that one.

"Beats me," the cowboy said with a sigh.

The black driver got up. "Hell, he let air out of the tires."

"You got it," Junior acknowledged.

The cowboy slapped his temple, like the people in the V-8 juice commercials. The black driver passed two fingers over his upper lip to be sure he had no food in his mustache and winked across at Junior. "See you guys," he said and left.

But the driver with the gold chain on his hairy chest had another version of the trucker getting topped off on his way to South Water Market in Chicago. The guy was still approaching this bridge that looked awfully low, but he was quicker hitting the brakes, and his trailer didn't slide under and get stuck. Still, he wasn't quick enough to prevent just nudging the overhang and pushing the front edge of the trailer up one inch. He backed out and took another road, a detour, but a route he knew like the back of his hand. There was another low overpass here, but he had always squeezed through before, so he didn't hesitate to highball through now.

At this point, the storyteller left his narrative dangling, but nobody understood it. "That day he was one inch higher," he finally explained.

Karen and Junior got their salads. The cowboy was running a flatbed for C and H Transportation, Dallas, and low underpasses weren't exactly his hang-up. Weight was. Not long ago he had hauled a nuclear reactor for a submarine, Pennsylvania to California. "We used a five-axle low-bed plus a dolly under the gooseneck to carry it," he explained. "The reactor was insured for one and one-half million dollars and the thing weighed 80,000 by itself.

Nobody challenged him and he tried not to sound too important as he described a soda-ash dryer he had delivered for a chemical plant. "It weighed 274,000 pounds and was 105 feet long."

Karen wanted to know if that didn't require special routing, police escort and all that.

"Oh, sure."

She wanted to ask why truckers were fined for being 4,000 pounds overweight, like Junior was tonight, when loads weighing over a quarter of a million pounds could be transported by highway, but the big man on her left and the driver with the gold chain were talking exempt loads and Junior was paying attention. Right now there was a big demand for loads out of Texas, Arizona, and Florida. There were backhauls from the Virginia and Maryland potato and tomato fields as far west as Milwaukee. The Texas rates were over $1,200 to Chicago, $1,300 to Atlanta. West Coast to New York rates were hovering around $4,400, a lot better than the measly $3,400 for the same 3,000-mile run in March and April. In fact, California exempt rates were $400 better than last year.

"What's moving westbound?" Junior asked. "Out of Jersey, for example."

The burly driver next to Karen said he couldn't tell. "You headin' up that way?"—looking from Junior to Karen.

"Rahway," she said.

"They're using portable scales on the turnpike now," he warned.

"The New Jersey DOT are getting to be a pain." The driver with the gold chain didn't elaborate as the waitress served Karen and Junior.

"How about my beer?" he asked.

"Comin'."

The driver with the gold chain put out his cup for another refill. The New Jersey Buford, he said, was Officer Boyle, otherwise known as Kojak. "He's bald-headed, fat, sloppy, and nasty. When he talks he slobbers and foams at the mouth. He patrols the back roads of Delaware County."

The cowboy was of the opinion that the Pennsylvania State Police were still the pits. Now, municipal cops were beginning to use electronic tapes laid across roadways to clock speeds despite a state law prohibiting anyone but state police from using electronics. A judge up in Cambria County had ruled the tapes were okay as long as signs were posted to warn drivers that the devices were in use. The LTD had something good to report about Cambria County despite Graveyard Boulevard Route 22, and the good news was Elias Auto Repair. "You have trouble with your equipment, you call for 'React' on the CB and Elias will get results for you immediately," she said. "They're the only people we've received help from when we've broken down on the road. They're very kind people in that area."

Talking about the Northeast, her husband said tolls on the Connecticut Turnpike had gone up. Now the toll was $1.50 at each of the eight tollbooths on I-95, which meant a five-axle running the entire length paid $12 instead of $5.05, an increase of well over 100%. Car tolls had gone up from 25 to 35 cents, an increase of only 40%. And the entire scale crew at the New London weigh stations were Bufords. "I recently received a ticket for having one blue cab light on my tractor. I realized I was in violation, but what gets my goat is that while I was being written up, no less than three cars drove by the station with one of their headlights out. I received unpleasant comments when questioning the officer about this."

The burly driver was pulling for Ryder Ranger, Yellow Thermo Division, out of Stewardson, Illinois. He was northbound also and told Karen to watch out for the Georgia DOT; they would check her logbook.

"We turned around in Houston in two hours this afternoon," she said. "We're way over."

"Better start doctoring some figures there."

Junior nodded, his mouth full. The cowboy had just come from Georgia and recommended running that way up I-85 instead of I-59 through Mississippi and Alabama.

The Bekins man and his wife were heading west, to San Diego, and the older man who so far hadn't said anything told them to watch out for smokey on I-8 after Casa Grande. "I used to drive 18-wheelers and now I cover 40,000 miles a year in a Honda, selling to drivers and truckstops," he explained. "I personally passed smokey's gun at 68 and watched him stop the 18 I was runnin' with. It is unfortunate that most of the smokies in Arizona harass truckers. Here's a quote from a bear to me: 'We don't stop a company truck, usually owner-operators. They cause all the problems.'"

They chewed on that for a while and the former trucker said he quit driving 18s 10 years ago. "I've pulled a bit of reefer and flatbed and dry box in my time, runnin' between Texas and the East Coast, but I stayed out of New York and Boston."

"You live in Arizona?" the cowboy asked.

The old guy was visibly ashamed of the bears in his home state. "Sun City. Early retirement, but I can't make ends meet, on account of the wife's medical."

Junior liked his roast beef and wondered if he'd end up a traveling salesman in a Honda when he got too old to truck. The waitress poured refills all around, and Karen told herself to remember to run out and get the thermos so she'd have coffee for the night. She thought of Tim and Melissa at the other end of the country, as she saw how the old guy carefully folded his paper napkin, as if it were linen. She missed her kids, but it couldn't be otherwise. They had to have somebody they could rely on while they were growing up. She was sure their father would never change, that it would have to be *her* bringing home the groceries. She wouldn't be back until next week, but she'd be there; they could count on that. She was glad she could work, that she had a job. She watched the LTD, who was drinking her coffee and barely listening to the men's conversation. The lady driver was older, probably had half-grown children of her own somewhere.

The woman became conscious of her glance and responded with a little smile. "We just loaded up in Jersey," she said.

Karen nodded.

"In the moving business, there are enough westbound loads. It's the Sun Belt to Frost Belt loads that are hard to come by."

"I bet." Karen wondered who the New Jersey family was whose belongings the Bekins team were hauling to San Diego, a young family moving up and on, as in all van-line advertising, or a couple retiring?

The woman looked from Karen to Junior talking with the gold-chained driver and back again. "It's hard for a single woman to find a decent man to run with," she said.

Karen felt the woman was seeing right through her, but the LTD went on to say she liked trucking herself. "I like to go, I like to travel, and I like meeting other people."

The men were flaying away at the Teamsters. The former trucker was a retired member-in-good-standing, and the driver next to Karen said it was always the same thing when he was a member. "When elections were held, most of us drivers were dispatched to the Midwest, and those who were around to vote, mainly company people, reelected the same crooked officials."

The cowboy was dogmatic. "The reason the union still exists is because of mandatory dues payments. If the Teamsters was completely voluntary, the trucking end of it would die tomorrow."

"To contest the election, we tried a wildcat strike once," Karen's hefty neighbor said. "But we were told by the union to go back to work or be fired."

Karen had her last bite of steak and a soggy french fry while the woman told her household freight was still slow. "We're making a living out of it though, and I enjoy it," she said. "That's all a person can ask for. That, and to be able to take care of your family." Her name was Frances, she said, and she and Larry here had two sons in high school, living with her parents when the two of them were on the road. "Last year, Larry couldn't see any relief in sight. 'I don't know,' he said. 'I guess we'll have to sell the truck and just blow away.'"

Karen nodded and was about to ask if she missed her boys, when Frances told her that the pickup in loads put Larry and her in a new quandary. If they continued, they'd need a new tractor next year. "The company wants owner-operators with new equipment."

The guys were being entertained by the driver with the gold chain, who was telling them about the trend among women four-wheelers to buy CBs for protection on long-distance travels. Some of them had heard about convoys and how it was safer to run with the big guys in the big rigs. "They usually have handles like Sexy Lady or Witchy Woman. So, after driving all night with this nice person tailgating you with bright lights on, you ask her if she would like to stop for a cup of mud, right?"

Larry was grinning.

"You imagine this lovely maiden with curves more daring than any you find on the Pennsylvania Turnpike. You pull into the parking lot with her Omni-Horizon following you. You have a look at yourself in the rearview mirror, comb your hair, and hop down, right?"

"And?" The cowboy couldn't wait.

"And the Witchy Woman turns out to look more like a defensive tackle for the Dallas Cowboys."

Karen had a laugh with them. Stories like that were usually raunchier. Anybody female was "beaver"—things male were "buffalo"—and there were stories about beaver hitchhikers, beaver troopers, and beaver customs inspectors at the border. The only cute one she'd ever heard was about a down-home trucker named Elmer who picked up a Las Vegas showgirl somewhere south of Jackpot, Nevada—alone, buffaloless, and, she explained, stranded after having been told to get out of a guy's car. Her name was Deirdre. She sat pretty in the jump seat and Elmer drove all afternoon on nothing more than hope. She saw how desperate he was to make an impression, and she listened to him talk about the war being waged in Washington for the passage of a few small, but revolutionary, bills. Long before they got to Vegas they both knew they were in tarnished professions. Elmer rolled his rig right down the Strip to deposit her in front of Caesar's Palace, and the story goes, when he's runnin' that way, he and Deirdre go truckin' occasionally, still two people with strained images and nobody to look to in Washington.

The waitress came around with coffee again, but the hefty trucker and the old guy begged off. The cowboy seemed to want things to go on awhile longer, but Frances nudged her Larry, who rubbed his chin and said he could use a shave.

"No Witchy Woman's gonna see you drivin' tonight," Frances said.

"But suppose she wants to have coffee with me in the morning?"

Frances got up and affectionately jabbed her husband in the ribs.

Karen remembered she wanted to fill the thermos and asked Junior for the keys.

20
"ROLAIDS, DOAN'S PILLS, AND PREPARATION H."

There is something deeply stirring about asphalt and the broken line running toward the horizon. Nearly every American hungers to move on, to get underway, anyplace, away from here. From lore to literature, music to movies, the open road is popular myth and national metaphor. The road tells us about romance and renewal. The road is a challenge and it has vaguely disturbing resonances—freedom that in many ways is unsettling, promises that harbor uncertainty and engagement, new beginnings and mutant adventure. Without a certain risk, travel can seem to be pointless.

It is no surprise that the pop culture has mined truckers for box office and TV ratings, that the media have found gold in them thar horizons and in exaggerated sketches of the men and women who live out there—not to mention the glamorous rigs they drive.

The guy in the horsepower operas is the new cowboy—all guts and prime rib manhood, ready to spill emotions that are vibrant, raw, and unrehearsed. A trucker is a guy who can down a fifth of bourbon without batting an eye, a lanky stranger with muscles like whipcord who can take on three ordinary men in a bar brawl, appeals to the animal instincts of a woman, has nerves of steel, and trucks across the Sun Belt in a gorgeous rig with chrome stacks and wheels, shag carpeted interior, and a blazing hood six feet high. He also has a quirky sense of humor and a wry perspective on himself. "Breaker, breaker, this is Rubber Duck," says a grinning Kris Kristofferson in *Convoy*. "They're all following you," gushes Ali MacGraw in the jump seat, to which he responds in his best sourmash laconic style, "No, they're not, I'm just in front."

After *Convoy,* there was *Thunder and Lightning,* in which an honorable Everglades bootlegger and his girl friend spend most of their time running after a truck loaded with poisoned moonshine while they, in turn, are pursued by a pair of bungling mafia types. Before that, Steve Spielberg, of *Jaws* and *Raiders of the Lost Ark* fame, did a TV movie called *Duel,* in which an ordinary four-wheeler is terrorized by a psychotic semi on speed.

Smokey and the Bandit belongs to the country movies—southern, rural, bigoted, and fun. No muddled messages here, though. Burt Reynolds is a legendary trucker going by the handle Bandit. He and his buddy Snowman (Jerry Reed) have accepted an $80,000 bet that they can drive from Georgia to Texas and back in 28 hours to fetch 400 cases of Coors that can't legally be distributed east of Texas. Bandit drives a sports car to divert the bears should they come around, while Snowman chugs along with the precious cargo and the two of them stay in CB contact. The America they find is a bellyful of laughs, from the Frog (Sally Field), a kinky bride-to-be fleeing from the church in all her veils, to Jackie Gleason as Texarkana Sheriff Buford T. Justice, forever destined to be outwitted and outdriven and to have his police cruiser mangled and destroyed from under him. *Smokey and the Bandit* grossed more than $60 million in the U.S. and Canada in 1977 and has remained Burt Reynolds' most popular movie. *Smokey and the Bandit II* in 1980 was a predictable crash-bang sequel, in which the Bandit, the Snowman, and the Frog transport a pregnant elephant from Miami to a convention of Republicans in Dallas to collect $200,000. Apoplectic Buford is again in hot pursuit.

For their third road movie, director Hal Needham and Reynolds concocted *Cannonball Run,* a film full of pickups crashing through walls, chesty ladies, beer, bikers, and a bully-boy meanness. The picture was a less than perfect transposition of the very real and highly illegal Connecticut-to-California Cannonball sea-to-shining-sea Memorial Trophy Dash, where playboys in souped-up cars cross the country in under 35 hours, averaging 85 mph. Nevertheless, the movie literally *made* the summer of 1981 for Twentieth Century–Fox, grossing $60 million in what *Newsweek* called "redneck drive-ins."

The star of TV's "BJ and the Bear" was a Kenworth Aerodyne 108 because, as the show's producers said, "the truck was as much a consideration in the casting as were the characters. We wanted it to draw attention, to be noticed. The Aerodyne is the kind of vehicle that makes people perk up, even if they're not interested in trucks."

The lettering on the door of the starring Kenworth spelled BILLY JOE MCKAY, OWNER-OPERATOR, MILWAUKEE, WISCONSIN, but BJ, played by Greg Evigan, looked more like a cross between a fleet owner and cat-house proprietor, particularly since he had a bevy of shapely LTDs working for him. In one episode, sabotage is suspected in accidents involving movie stuntmen. In another, the lady truckers are kidnapped to Mexico where they are forced to harvest marijuana.

The small-screen adventures of BJ were pure fantasy. The main beef from real-life geargrinders was that nobody ever seemed to *work*. Also, the NBC show made truckers look like perverted sex maniacs who don't care for human beings or for their $100,000 rigs. Said Todd Stephenson of Butler, Pennsylvania, "The trucker is always shown plowing his rig through herds of police cars with nary a scratch on the truck when he is done." When NBC canceled the series, the producers and Paccar tried to buy back the goodwill of the trucking industry by raffling off the Kenworth Aerodyne tractor in a national sweepstakes open to all Class 8 drivers (a Vermont trucker won it). But the idea of a quartet of lively LTDs had the potential of another "Charlie's Angels" to the Hollywood imagination and for the 1983–84 season the networks were preparing "truckerette" series.

Road movies and truckerette shows aren't made for working highway haulers. The all-night diesel country radio shows are. Between midnight and dawn, when most long-distance haulers are behind the wheel, a number of clear-channel 50,000-watt stations become "the trucker's friend on the other end," filling the lonely hours with music, humor, and words of encouragement interspersed with weather and road condition reports. You've got such household names as Big John Trimble of WRVA in Richmond, Virginia, catering to the I-95 corridor, and in the Northwest, Dan Williams on KEED in Eugene, Oregon, and Don Hinson on KLAC Los Angeles sending truckers across the Mojave Desert. A huge territory from Missouri to the Gulf Coast is covered by Vernon Kay of KWKH in Shreveport, Louisiana, in competition with Charlie Douglas of WWL, New Orleans.

The disk jockeys monitor channel 17 on the citizens' band, and then rebroadcast. "It's a truckers' show," says John Trimble, who broadcasts from the Jarrell Truck Plaza in Doswell, Virginia. "I play country music, and other people can listen if they want to. But the show's for the truckers." In the strict format of AM radio, the diesel country shows can be surprisingly mellow. Big John plays only what his listeners ask for. He never looks at the record charts, he doesn't talk fast, and he doesn't tell a lot of jokes. Twice a week, Trimble hosts "Talkin' with Truckers," a late-night show carried on a network of 10 stations. Sponsored by Cummins, the program features interviews with drivers speaking their minds and focuses on brokers, on the availability of seasonal loads, and on cutting cost-per-mile expenses. All the stations carrying the show have 50,000-watt transmitters, enabling truckers on most cross-country routes to listen in.

Every summer Charlie Douglas takes his show on the road, usually for a five-week tour sponsored by a truck manufacturer and a truckstop chain. One place where you can catch up with Charlie and his "road gang" is the parking lot of the Truckstops of America water-hole off I-75 in Valdosta, Georgia, just over the Florida state line. The center of attention is a stage mounted on a specially built 40-foot trailer. And there, during a recent tour, is none other than Dave Dudley singing under the lights, accompanied by a band called the Freightliners. "Well, we pulled out of Gallup. Rollin' toward that Eastern Seaboard," he sings from his greatest hit, "Six Days on the Road." A bearded sound engineer walks around the stage turning microphones in the right directions. The Charlie Douglas Road Gang is broadcasting live.

Dudley is no spring chicken under his 10-gallon straw Stetson, and sweat pours down his portly jowls as he twangs his guitar and segues into "A Trucker's Last Prayer" and that crowd pleaser of his, "Rolaids, Doan's Pills, and Preparation H." He gives an open throttle performance and the audience loves him. His set is followed by Delilah McLane, a blond songstress of hard country and easy ballads.

A thundershower sends everybody inside and a trucker from Duluth, Minnesota, offers the Freightliners drinks (the stars' drinks apparently are on the house). Twenty minutes later, the show is on again. David Rogers arrives on stage in a blaze of rhinestone and tears into a medley of favorites. In "The Only Shoulder a Trucker Can Cry On," you learn that the only shoulder a trucker *can* cry on is the shoulder of the road. In "Truckstop Café," you hear about the girl that was the "only one," and in hard-stompin' "New York City, New York," that there are plenty of girls in San Anton', Georgia, and Tennessee, but that "I've got mine" in "En-Why-See." Then Beck Hobbs bounces onstage, capturing the crowd with her rhythms and renditions of "Guitar Pickin' Man" and "Honky Tonk Saturday Night." The grand finale belongs to Dudley, belting out "Truck Drivin' Man" to the accompaniment of the Freightliners and approaching thunder and lightning. The crowd demands an encore and Dudley obliges, singing "Six Days on the Road" once more. Four Missouri truckers gathered around one of their rigs play the air horn. The crowd has grown to some 400 spectators and the entire parking lot is stomping with Beck wailing "I'm Movin' On."

As the rain hits again the stars stand in the restaurant entrance signing autographs and selling cassettes to those who want to hear them in their cabs. Douglas goes on the air right there in the entrance, signing autographs and giving away cowboy hats, key chains, and cigars, telling everybody to tune in to Radio 87 WWL, New Orleans, when they leave.

21
SHOOTING SCALES

The traffic was mild and, Karen thought, the night probably was too. She turned off the air conditioning and pivoted the ventilating window open until she felt the breeze and smelled the night air. The interstate was lined with pines, low thick groves that didn't look like the pine stands in the Northwest. Across the grassy divider, a southbound rig blinked his running lights at her. She winked back with hers, but didn't get on the CB. Junior was sleeping so peacefully.

She thought of Colby and the Bay, where she used to go walking with her grandfather before their bedtime. If you walked toward Southworth in the evening you saw Queen Anne's lace and goldenrod and gossamer webs of dew in the grass and bushes. You also saw the lights across the Sound and planes taking off, veering out over the water. Seattle was only an hour away. Every summer her mother took her over for all of August and just came visiting on weekends with her boyfriend.

JCT I-204, MERIDIAN 7.

There wasn't much to say or do in a cab in the middle of the night, but she had never found a cab or a road confining, even when she ran solo San Francisco–Vancouver. If anything, she felt free. There was nothing else to *do*. There were no bills you could pay, no people you had to deal with, no house chores. There were no phones, yet if you wanted to, the next person was as close as the squawk box. You trucked for money, not for romantic reasons like the call of the open road. But when you were behind the wheel for hours, you had all the time in the world, and things came to you. You could think back or forward, but there was no point in memorizing the present.

She was getting used to the Pete, the way it rode, the fingertip control you had on the steering, how tractor, coupling, and trailer responded as if they were one solid unit. She had learned the new Cummins to the point where she was no longer aware of its lower-rpm engine speed. She anticipated bends now, steering and accelerating till the truck drove itself around the curve, and she worked patiently at shifting on difficult upgrades instead of using brute force. It was amazing how smooth you could run 84,000 pounds.

I-20 WEST JACKSON. I-20 I-59 EAST MERIDIAN, TUSCALOOSA.

She turned on the reading light a second. It was almost three o'clock. And Junior's turn. It occurred to her that since entering Mississippi she hadn't seen any rest areas—what was it some truckers called them, lollipop parks? She didn't like the shoulder. Pines grew in sandy soil, and with her weight, one wheel off the pavement in the darkness could mean disaster. She'd wait until the town coming up. She wouldn't mind letting him sleep another hour, but he'd probably not like it if she didn't stick to the six-on, six-off schedule. He liked things to be just right. He hadn't told her much about himself, but when it came right down to it, neither had she. He had picked her up at home because he had wanted to. He had met Tim and Melissa, and the next morning, Marianne and her boyfriend. It had been her own idea that her friends see the guy she was going sleeper teaming with, and Marianne told her in the kitchen she had taken down the license plate and the California PUC [Public Utilities Commission] number on the Peterbilt. And she had given Marianne her mom's number in Seattle.

She was coming up on a fruitliner. She moved out in the hammer lane and pulled abreast. The guy had to be pretty heavy too, going slow like that. Or he knew something she didn't. She saw his nine-foot big-mama CB whip antenna, but couldn't see inside the cab. She put the hammer down and moved ahead. The fruitliner blinked and she came in. Pat

Timmins had told her that in the old days before CB, two flashes of headlights or, in daylight, two fingers displayed in a V, meant smokey was nearby.

Eastbound, I-59 merged with I-20 in gentle curves. There weren't many grades in Mississippi, just gentle hills, long stretches of chalky rock formations with those low pines. If she remembered the map, the two interstates stayed merged until Birmingham, where I-20 continued east to Atlanta and I-59 ran northeast to Chattanooga. There was still no four-wheeler traffic; tourists and rural Mississippians were in their beds at this time of night. After the merge, however, the westbound truck traffic was a little heavier. She returned the friendly blinks of running lights.

MERIDIAN 3, TUSCALOOSA 80.

He had told her he had been married once, that he had a son who was nine. She liked that. A guy in his mid-thirties was weird if he had no past, no bruises, no mistakes. She didn't trust bachelors when they were Junior's age. There was something wrong with a man who had never given in to the temptation, who hadn't lost himself once. A woman, too.

She turned on the radio, low, and dialed for something soft to wake him up. Truckers cruised over the surface of the country without being part of it, but everybody had a wife, an ex, a kid somewhere. That made them human. Truckers were special enough as it was, leading special lives, associating only with their own kind. She got an announcer saying he'd have the weather after this word from White's Home and Auto Center.

"Okay." Junior yawned in the back.

She listened to him stretch and grunt pleasantly. The weather would be cloudy with a high of 81; thundershowers this afternoon.

MERIDIAN NEXT 3 EXITS.

Rueful bluegrass followed station identification. She hadn't seen any signs advertising an upcoming truckstop. In fact, she hadn't seen any billboards anywhere along Mississippi's pine groves.

"What time is it?" he asked.

"Ten past three."

He yawned and began to move.

"Listen, if you want to snooze another hour . . ." she suggested.

"No, no, I'm fine. Did you turn off the air conditioning?"

"I did. You want it back on?"

"Arctic air helps keep me chaste."

Her thoughts drifted, formed ideas. "Tell me, how far is Manhattan from Rahway, New Jersey?"

"What?"

"The dinner is my treat, remember?"

He sighed. "How are we going to get in there though?"

"Running bobtail and park somewhere, then maybe take a taxi."

"Running bobtail through the Holland Tunnel?"

"Why, is that illegal?"

"Guess not." He came down into the jump seat, flashing her a sexy grin and peering into the night. He looked like Tim getting up too early, she thought.

FRONTAGE RD. NEXT RIGHT. A Rodeway Inn sign turned in the sky. Beyond the off-ramp a neon sign offered discount diesel. On the other side of the freeway, a huge parking lot stretched toward Sears and a shopping center.

"Any coffee left?" he asked.

"Sure."

On the radio, Herb Alpert played "Angelina." Junior got the thermos and poured himself half a mug. Karen turned up the volume and let the music invade them. People said self-doubt peaked at night, but she felt exhilarated, ridin' into tomorrow. The wheels sang under her, the trumpet soared. She passed the last Meridian exit and put down the hammer while keeping the beat with her left foot.

Junior downed the coffee in one big swallow, grinned to her and leaned back. "Where are we anyway?"

"Passing through Meridian," she yelled over the music.

"Meridian?"

"Meridian, Mississippi."

"Mississippi!" he shouted.

She saw his face and turned down the volume. He grabbed the Rand McNally and flicked on the reading light.

She felt a wave of panic. "Sure, I-59 up to Chattanooga, then I-75 to Knoxville."

"I thought you'd run up through Georgia." His fingers ran down the small-print index in the back.

"Don't you remember the chunky feller back in Lafayette saying Georgia troopers were checking logbooks. I thought . . ."

She watched him track the coordinates on the state map and found Meridian. "We're almost at the border! How did you get into Mississippi?"

RUSSELL 3, TUSCALOOSA 77.

His alarm was contagious. "The scales were closed," she said. "I passed just after midnight and the scales were closed. I wasn't the only load, by the way. We were five or six running together."

"Goddamn!"

"What?"

"Kewanee. How do we get *out* of Mississippi?" He put down the map and looked at her. He explained what he knew about the most infamous set of scales in the country, about the scalemen's practice of pursuing trucks that failed to stop at the scales when the lights in the scalehouse were out, chasing and shooting at both trucks and drivers clear to the state line. He told her about the Mississippi trick of waving overweight trucks through at the ports of entry and catching them on their way out and tripling the fine.

RUSSELL 2, KEWANEE 5.

"You better let me take over," he said.

What could she say? "If only you'd told me."

"Yeah, we just ran out of luck." His smile was crooked, but it was still a smile.

She remembered it was just a minute past midnight when she passed the Mississippi port of entry from Louisiana. "Maybe the explanation is that they were changing shifts."

"Why should they turn out the lights to change shifts?"

"Doesn't make sense, does it?" she admitted.

"The damned thing is I can't get on the box and ask about the back roads into Alabama. They'll hear me down there, or smokey will."

"How much will the fine be?" She felt she had to ask.

"Everything we've worked for since we left Washington. More than both our weekly salaries, I'd say."

RUSSELL NEXT RIGHT.

She eased off the pedal and thought they were suddenly in luck—two truckstops at the Russell exit. On their side, the black and white sign of an independent advertised discount diesel, and across the overpass on the westbound side, the familiar red-white-and-blue 76 sign turned in the sky. "Maybe we can *ask* somebody," she said.

He grinned. "And sneak out on a back road?"

She hissed the brakes, coming up the ramp to the stop sign. "Maybe there are more of our kind at the 76."

"And more of the local kind on this side."

"You mean you're gonna ask an off-duty scaleman on his last beer?"

"That would be my luck, wouldn't it? Okay, the 76."

She pulled left up on the overpass. "Now that you say so, she *is* pretty heavy."

"Just over 86,000, girl."

"I thought you said just over 84,000 pounds."

"Gross. We filled up—what?—less than 300 miles ago, remember."

She lumbered onto the lot, half-filled with rigs. She imagined the restaurant would be just about empty and most of the drivers here in their sleepers. She swung around, smartly and completely, parked within view of the restaurant entrance, next to the four-wheeler parking area, and shut down.

Junior grabbed the road atlas. "You can hit the sack now."

"And miss all the fun?"

He smiled. "Who was lecturing whom six hours ago?"

"I can always have a glass of warm milk."

When they left 20 minutes and two coffees later, Junior had had a good look at the map and they had met the law. There was only one customer in the place, a trucker from Oklahoma trying to stay awake, as he said when they sat down next to him. He appreciated their problem. "Ports of entry are nothin' but harassment. They've gotta collect to keep their jobs." Unfortunately, he didn't know the territory. Junior took a hard look at the waitress, a lady with short hair and tired gestures, and decided that if he asked, she wasn't the type who'd run out to the pay phone and call the highway patrol the moment the two of them were out the door. She looked troubled when he told her, but she warned them not to try and shoot the scales on the interstate, because the highway was uphill from the scalehouse to the state line. They'd never be able to outrun a Tax Commission vehicle.

As she told them the Tax Commission also maintained a scalehouse on the old highway, but that the road was straight and less than two miles to the line, Karen nudged Junior's arm hard. When he turned, there was the law himself, a trooper crossing to the counter and sitting down five seats from Karen.

The waitress greeted him. "Mornin', Walt."

"Cheryl."

Junior folded the road atlas and, while Cheryl served the sheriff his brew, craned to have a look. Walt was in his forties, a strong compact type. His uniform was crisp and fresh, not as if he had worked all night in it, but just slipped into it. He drank his coffee black and asked Cheryl for the usual. The huge shoulder badge featured the state crest and Confederate flag. The words Lauderdale County were woven in on top.

"Maybe this is the best time to get goin'," the Okie said with a broad wink.

Karen got it. Walt couldn't be having breakfast and chase a rig into Alabama at the same time. And she couldn't imagine that Lauderdale County had any other cruiser on the road at 4:00 A.M. "Let me just go to the ladies' room," she said and got up.

When they were back in the cab, Junior didn't start up, but sat watching the two-toned brown and copper sheriff's cruiser. Karen guessed why. But no Walt stormed out wiping egg off his face.

"Okay," he said.

Karen grabbed his hand and pressed it. They looked at each other. He squeezed back, freed his hand, and started.

He took his time coasting down to the overpass and

across. As he veered left onto the on-ramp he stopped. He had a clear view of the truckstop. The cruiser was still there.

He gunned the engine, rolled down on the freeway, and smoothly went up through a dozen gears until he was cruising at 75. He kept an eye on the rearview mirror, but no flashing red light was in pursuit. In the jump seat, Karen turned on the reading light and bent over the atlas, flipping between Alabama in the front and Mississippi in the middle. The Kewanee pinprick was to the south of the interchange, and U.S. 80 ran straight east into Alabama. On the Mississippi page, the distance between Kewanee and Cuba, Alabama, was four miles; on the Alabama map, it was three miles.

KEWANEE 1.

Karen sat up and felt her head throb, her chest tighten.

"You notice there are no signs saying Weigh Station Ahead!" Junior shouted, easing off the throttle.

"Why's that?"

"The sign probably comes *after*, when it's too late to exit." He geared down, came up on the clutch, and let the engine do the slowing.

KEWANEE RIGHT LANE.

"If only we had moonlight," he said. "I gotta turn off the lights so he can't get the license when we run past."

Karen was a knot of nerves. The landscape was flat enough, pretty open, with no lights anywhere. Junior had to brake to make the curved off-ramp, but he ran through the stop sign as soon as he saw the U.S. 80 arrow pointing left. The thing was to get up speed. She *was* awfully heavy.

"Two lanes," Karen said as they hit U.S. 80. Kewanee was maybe five dark houses on both sides.

Junior geared up furiously.

She saw it first, on her side. The WEIGH STATION 200 FT. sign, then the lights. "It's open!"

Junior gave it all it had. The road broadened on both sides and the scalehouse was set back from the road a little. He saw the black unmarked car that had to be the cruiser and calculated that the road was straight until the top of the little hill ahead. He was doing 60 and the last two digits on the speedometer were 1.8. At 100 feet from the scalehouse, he turned off the lights and thundered into total blackness. Involuntarily, Karen braced herself, as if to prevent being slammed into a black wall, halfway out of her seat, her fingers clawing at the console and the door grip. She saw a figure peer out of the scalehouse window and she saw the huge antenna on top of the little building as they flew by.

Junior felt the road rise under him and told himself he could get them killed this way. He kept the steering wheel aligned by keeping both his arms rigidly parallel to his legs. He counted the seconds, checked the right side rearview mirror, and saw the scalehouse lights recede in a perfect straight line.

The high beam blinded them both when he turned the lights back on. The area was heavily wooded on the left side. On the right, beyond clumps of trees and bushes, railway tracks ran parallel to the road. He kept the hammer down.

"God." Karen heaved, falling back into her seat.

The road curved. Junior squinted to see the instrument panel and read 2.2. "How long again?" he shouted and rolled down his window, fearing to hear a wailing siren behind them.

"She said less than two miles."

"Sonofagun." He checked the mirrors, but the curves limited his rear vision. The decimal counter on the speedometer was coming up on seven. "We haven't done a mile yet!"

They passed the remnants of a shack half off its brick stilts. A crossroad, too, more dark shacks, but absolutely no traffic. The railway tracks were still there.

The speedometer read 3.2 and they were doing 68, too fast for this curved, two-laned road. Junior strained his ears. "You hear anything?"

She rolled down the window on her side, but the wind and the full-throttle engine obliterated any chance of hearing anything from behind. With a quick glance at each other, they both rolled up their windows again. He checked the mirrors again.

"Look!" she cried.

The highway beam caught a small tilting sign in the curve. SUMTER CO.

"Why doesn't it say Welcome to Alabama?" he asked.

Why not? The idea of a trap flashed through Karen's mind. The ruins of a prehistoric gas-and-food place loomed on the left. STATELINE TRUCKSTOP. The sign looked new. She didn't dare believe they were safe. Maybe they were fake signs to lure illegal truckers into slowing down. "Keep going!" she said.

But he eased off, suddenly afraid the Mississippi scalemen could radio the Alabama State Police and get them nailed for speeding. A dirt road joined them from the left and the highway straightened out with a few dark houses on both sides. "We gotta be in Alabama." He checked the speedometer. "We're almost two miles from the scalehouse."

He slowed down as they passed a big schoolhouse that didn't seem to be in use anymore. "This has gotta be Cuba, Alabama."

"Why doesn't it *say* so?"

They were coming up on an intersection, with a pair of closed gas stations, a stop sign, and a blue and yellow county road marker. York was four miles straight. U.S. 80 continued right. Junior decided the interstate had to be left. "Another has-been place," he said, braking and turning left without stopping. "Maybe 20 people live here."

Karen got out the Alabama page and told him the freeway should be two miles up this divided highway.

"I wanna get back on the interstate right away," he said. It was a long upgrade back to the freeway. Anybody could catch him here. "I mean I don't wanna be caught overweight on a county road."

"How about the Alabama port of entry?"

"We'll just slide up on the scales as good boys and pay our excess weight ticket. Forty dollars maybe."

"But can't the Mississippi officer radio ahead!"

"Radio ahead saying what? We're not the only Pete with Great Dane reefer trailer. We may be the only such combination running around here at this hour with California license plates, but the guy never saw the plates. Besides, we may have been in Alabama for hours, maybe pulled over and sleeping since last night."

"The engine's too hot."

"We were chilly, we kept it running for a while getting up."

"Why don't we agree on that then, if they ask?"

"Okay, we took a nap right here. Let's see what the exit is called up there."

"Cuba, obviously."

He gave her a look. "Hey."

"I'm sorry."

"We made it, didn't we?"

She saw the interchange and overpass coming up, the familiar red-white-blue interstate shield, the east Tuscaloosa, west Meridian directional arrows. She kept their two salaries firmly in her mind, all they had worked for since Yakima. It was the justification. She still didn't like it, the idea that a bear could pull them over and make them start lying. Having to lie was humiliating; it made you small and she hated that.

He swung east and down the ramp, picking up speed. He checked the mirrors, geared up and came into lane. He grabbed the CB and, with a wink to Karen, asked if anybody had their ears on, because this was Class Act, with his co, Sweet Pickle, northbound and wondering where the Alabama POE might be located.

The static crackled, but somebody called Blue Mule finally said that as far as he knew the Alabama port of entry didn't open until six.

22
TURNAROUND

Junior Carlton and Karen Long got there on schedule Monday. They got unloaded and Junior's broker had a backhaul to Butte, Montana, loading the next morning at Port Elizabeth, four miles up the New Jersey Turnpike. That evening Junior and Karen bobtailed into Manhattan. They parked on Canal Street and had to walk up West Broadway before they found a taxi. When they said they wanted a steak house, the cabdriver suggested Smith and Wollensky on Third Avenue. Karen insisted on paying. Absolutely. After dinner, they walked across town, holding hands because of what everybody knew about after-dark big-city crime and because they felt good about each other. Times Square was, well Times Square, and Junior didn't much care for the crowd around there. Besides, it began to rain. At the motel on Baywater Avenue in Elizabeth, they became lovers. Afterwards they lay in each other's arms. Karen whispered she was content, the two of them and so on, that it would have been just as nice in the sleeper. He smiled in the darkness and thanked her for saying that. They listened to the rain and the planes taking off from Newark. She said she was also content because they had the backload, but he had fallen asleep. She retrieved her arm from under his neck and before she drifted off she decided she wouldn't call Tim and Melissa in the morning. She wanted to. But it was an expensive habit she couldn't afford, and to hear her faraway voice probably didn't do much more than confuse their little minds. She was a trucker. When she was gone she was gone, but she'd come home. They could rely on that.

To be a trucker was to try and ease into high gear all by

yourself. During good times, you almost made it. In one sense your life was severely controlled, the mere size of your rig dictated where you could travel and where you could stop. You were confined to a society of your own kind, but you were also virtually unharnessed; you belonged to a group of people who hated anything that smacked of regulation—a union, load limits, and speed limits. If you were an owner-operator you prided yourself on providing the most efficient and dependable means of transportation anybody could think of. You enjoyed the independence of looking to no one but yourself for the size of your paycheck. When the economy went sour, you tried to hang tough. You weren't trying to make a million dollars. You just liked to make ends meet, make the payments on the truck. You couldn't afford any personal items right now. Everything you made went back into the truck, and at this rate you didn't know how much longer you can keep truckin'.

The big boys weren't so sure either.

Less regulation, a slumping economy, and penny pinching by everybody in the business was gradually making over the trucking industry. Despite the Reagan administration's limited implementation of the Motor Carrier Act in 1980, dereg upset established patterns. Less than two years after the Act became law, several old-line carriers had gone out of business, several of the top 20 companies were losing money, and over 3,000 newcomers—most of them short-haul outfits—had taken to their highways.

The Big Three—Roadway Express, Consolidated Freightways, and Yellow Freight System—fought their way into less-than-truckload traffic (anything less than 10,000 pounds or an average of 28 shipments to a trailer) that they had previously spurned because of its variety of pickups and destinations and need for complex billing and bookkeeping. But they went at it with determination and money, setting up satellite centers within their service areas, automated terminal technology to get the right shipment into the right trailer every time, computerized paperwork, and guaranteed coast-to-coast deliveries in 78 hours. Less-than-truckload hauling was turning into the most profitable sector of trucking, and Roadway was taking advantage of dereg to expand into the Northwest. Consolidated spent $80 million adding terminals and upgrading old ones to build up a nationwide airline-type hub-and-spoke system, while Yellow Freight fell behind and began offering steep discounts to try to attract less-than-truckload traffic.

If you were a trucker-employee you were either huffing along with the independents or you were out of work. Over 50,000 of the 300,000 trucker-members of the Teamsters were laid off a year and a half into dereg, and the National Master Freight Agreement, once the Teamsters' pride and source of its clout—it covered 1,600 companies—was falling apart under an avalanche of union "give-backs," concessions ranging from incentive programs and work rules to outright wage reductions. The Teamsters approached its 1982 contract talks with apprehension, as carriers served notice that they planned to leave or divide the national employer bargaining group. Company-by-company bargaining favored hard-pressed firms by allowing them flexibility with salaries and work rules, and even industry leaders like Roadway wrangled labor concessions on their own. The ultimate impact of the Teamsters' trouble reached beyond the transportation sector. President Carter's wage guidelines, analysts said, had glorified Teamsters' bargaining and given it a political importance it hadn't had before, and while wage restraint was inevitable under the economic regime of President Reagan, a return to regulation was not only the Teamsters' avowed goal, but a distinct possibility.

As the static along the highways amplified this possibility, the independents told each other they were being screwed—again. But economics and government have always been the twin rulers of the business, and truckers have never really had any say in what they pay for the fuel they burn or in how much they can charge for hauling a shipment from here to there. Again, voices were heard demanding an end to rebel posturing and disunity. The gripes echoed each other: We have no real voice in Washington. Why? Because there is no real trust among truckers. We're just big machinery operators with cowboy hats. We play with big toys with pedals and levers, yet we carry the economy of this nation on our backs.

The bit about no representation in Washington wasn't

totally true. The Independent Truckers Association and others had staged letter-writing and telephone campaigns, sponsored rallies and marched on Congress and the White House. Still, the sense of isolation remained. So did the closed-circuit self-dramatization, and the rumblings of devastating shutdowns to come, actions that might be suicidal, but would still happen.

Few of the carriers, however, were so stupid as to consider owner-operators leased to them as tools to be exploited and discarded when worn out. Most companies realized that maintaining the viability of independents was in their own best interest. The competitive tug-of-war might have companies and independents at opposite ends, but even the big boys understood that if they wished to have the services of owner-operators available to them, they would have to look to the O.O.'s financial stability as an asset to their own business. Actually, some of the carriers, feeling the grim reaper breathing down their necks, switched from union drivers to owner-operators as one way of hedging their bets. A lot of truckers were laughing. For years, the carriers had called independent truckers a bunch of naïve cowboys who didn't know what their own operating costs were, who tried to stay ahead of all the real questions. And who was walking around with egg on their faces two years after dereg? Old-line companies like Johnson Motor Lines and Wilson Freight used owner-operators almost exclusively, and in less than a year had managed to go out of business after their management allowed sales representatives and rate personnel to enter agreements with shippers that were in fact below costs. In other cases there was strong suspicion that management simply didn't know what its own break-even costs were. Other carriers were a little smarter, but still managed to cut their rates so badly their leased truckers left them in droves. How did it feel to realize that the one-truck dumb cowboy might have more sense than big carrier managements when it came to running a business since he was still hanging in there while some of the big outfits had filed for bankruptcy? The carriers didn't say.

And the independents had a couple of other things going for them. Unless Congress decided to repeal the Motor Carrier

Act of 1980, it was hard to see how the Teamsters and/or the American Trucking Associations could totally gut the law. Under the law, owner-operators had options other than hauling exempt or leasing to a regulated carrier. Old mistrust of the ICC kept most independents from seeking the new authorities for foodstuffs and certain regulated goods on backhaul when the agency handed them its 1982 Valentine. Besides the choice of being a private fleet owner or using regulated carriers, corporate America suddenly had a third choice: turning independent truckers into its transportation division. The National Association of Manufacturers, representing 75% of all manufacturing companies, had wanted the owner-operator to compete for the business. Suddenly, it was up to the independent trucker to take his rig to Amoco Oil or TRW Inc., to J. C. Penney, Monsanto, Pillsbury, or Oscar Mayer (all companies who had testified in favor of the new arrangement) and haul their product on his truck and at his hauling rate.

If, finally, imitation is the sincerest form of flattery, the dumb cowboys could look overseas for a confirmation that maybe they were doing a thing or two right. Truckers in Australia and Europe were trying to become more like truckers in North America. (The distinction between American and Canadian geargrinders has never been great since both run in each other's jurisdiction, as they say.) In Europe, the industry and, more important, the attitudes and atmosphere among truckers resembled trucking U.S.A.-style more and more every year. The ITA set up an Australian chapter and *Overdrive* began publishing a monthly column called "Trucking Under the Southern Cross." The highway evangelists also expanded to Down Under. British truckers pointed to their American cousins' masterly use of citizen-band radio in their own fight for freer usage of CB than their government had wanted to grant them. On the Continent, rigs were being polished and equipped with chrome all over, and American-style spec'ing was going hand in hand with the penetration of the component makers—Rockwell, Eaton, Dana, and Cummins. Truckers were starting clubs to fight for their own CB channel, and they got their own magazine. Throughout Europe all these things created more communications among *les routiers,* often in imitation U.S. highway lingo. A Swedish trucker could write *Overdrive* that Europeans might not have the length and weight hassles, but they did have jammed border crossings requiring hours of waiting, and especially in eastern Europe, lousy roads and no detours around ancient towns.

English and French journalists and photographers traveled U.S. superslabs, enthusiastically reporting on a strange and wondrous world and getting bemused cowboys and LTDs to pose before magnificent Petes and Macks. Breathtaking text and pictures were published in coffee-table volumes. In France, Jean-Loup Nory wrote, "These trucks are cult objects, shaped by man to the image of his metallic dreams." "We have trucks in Britain, obviously, but not as flashy or as massive or as exciting as yours," said photographer David Jacobs. "We also don't have the country or desert, which you have. It is the whole mystique of the thing."

The mystique of the thing was not apparent, however, Tuesday morning when Junior rolled out of bed and told Karen to sleep on while he tooled over to get loaded.

"You mean dephasing," she mumbled.

"I mean enjoy it."

For late May it was a blustery kind of day, with plenty of sunshine and white puffy clouds racing across the sky together with a snappy northwesterly wind. They'd run west on I-80 to Chicago, then I-90 the rest of the way, Junior told himself, and they could still hit snow in Wyoming and Montana. He skipped coffee, but let the engine idle a good two minutes before he backed up, keeping the same amount of trailer at the edge of both mirrors until he heard the hinge pin slip in and the steel plate jaws snap closed. He started the reefer unit so he'd get to the dock precooled, but he had been right shutting down last night. If nothing else, cool weather helped with the fuel bill.

The shipper was at the end of McLester Street. Junior could smell the ocean, or at least Newark Bay, behind the unending stretch of terminals, warehouses, waterfront blight, and high-tech container booms. The dispatcher said the loading would be two hours. Tops. Junior asked where he could have breakfast. He walked back seven busy rows of sheds. Planes were taking off from Newark Airport, and between the terminals on the north side he could see the unending traffic on the turnpike. He took his time eating and talked to a flatbed operator from Madison, Wisconsin, who had been laying over since Friday with a busted transmission.

It was ten-thirty when Junior got back to the motel. Karen asked who it was before she opened the door. She was wearing a fresh pair of jeans, a top he hadn't seen before, and her hair was swept up in a cute knot. She had been up an hour and had had an English muffin and coffee, she told him as he just stood there and watched her.

"I'm ready," she said, conscious of his persistent look.

"I just think I'm the luckiest sonofagun, finding you." He grinned.

She blushed and turned to get her stuff. Twenty minutes later they crawled up on the turnpike, northbound on the extension because Junior wanted to show her the view from the skyway before they turned west and north again and caught I-80 up there in the meadowlands between Fort Lee and Hackensack.

"Didn't we come this way last night?" she asked, sitting up in the jump seat.

"Sure did."

The signs said HOLLAND TUNNEL. The left lane of the elevated roadway was closed to repairs and the traffic was heavy—other rigs, four-wheelers, a couple of taxis from Newark Airport. What you saw below on both sides was acres of abandoned railway track, and on the right, clumps of abandoned housing and piers. On the left Jersey City was more substantial.

"Look!" he said, nodding toward the right.

Beyond the dilapidated wharf and dock area, Karen saw the Statue of Liberty. But the lady with the torch was standing all wrong, in three-quarter profile, turned away with a more distant waterfront behind her. Then she saw Manhattan.

The perspective was also unusual, but the view was stunning. The twin towers of the World Trade Center gleamed in the sun, surrounded by sparkling glass walls and other high-risers. A second later the vista was obscured by piers on the Jersey side of the Hudson River. But she caught another glance, and one more through high-tension wires before the road curved left.

"Funny angle, you gotta admit." She smiled.

"What do we care." He grinned. "We got a truck to love, a load to haul, and a clean stretch of superslab up ahead."